Mackinac Island

Historic Frontier
Vacation Resort
Timeless Wonderland

Pamela A. Piljac
Thomas M. Piljac

Bryce-Waterton Publications
6411 Mulberry Avenue
Portage, In 46368

Cover photo:
Fort Mackinac above Marquette Park, by Thomas M. Piljac

Mackinac Island: Historic Frontier, Vacation Resort, Timeless Wonderland. Copyright © 1988, 1989 by Pamela A. Piljac and Thomas M. Piljac. All rights reserved. No part of this book may be reproduced in any form or by any electronic or mechanical means including information storage or retrieval systems without permission in writing from the publisher, except for small excerpts for review purposes. Published by Bryce-Waterton Publications, 6411 Mulberry Ave., Portage, In 46368.

10 9 8 7 6 5 4 3

Library of Congress Cataloging in Publication Data

Piljac, Pamela A., 1954-
Piljac, Thomas M. 1952-

Bibliography   Includes index

1. Mackinac Island (Mich.: Island)—History. 2. Mackinac Island (Mich.)—History. 3. Mackinac Island (Mich.: Island)—Description and travel. 4. Mackinac Island (Mich.)—Guide-books.

F572.M16P55   1988   977.4'923—dc19   88-4962 CIP

ISBN 0-913339-07-5

Printed in the United States of America

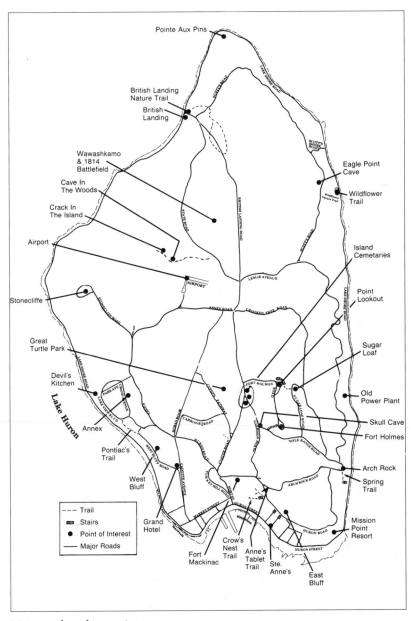

Major roads and attractions.

Acknowledgements

This book has benefited greatly from the generous assistance and insights of Dr. David Armour, Deputy Director; Phil Porter, Curator of Interpretation; and Keith R. Widder, Curator of History; for the Mackinac Island State Park Commission. We would like to offer our additional appreciation and gratitude to the M.I.S.P.C. for generously allowing the use of their archive photographs in this book. We couldn't have hoped for more friendly and co-operative assistance.

We would also like to offer a special thank you to Lorna Straus, both for her help in obtaining background information, and for reading through the manuscript on very short notice. Her assistance was invaluable, and any errors of data or perception that remain are entirely our own.

We are deeply grateful to all those who took the time to answer our many questions, whose contributions reflected both directly and indirectly in the book including (alphabetically): Robert E. Benjamin, George Bodwin Sr., Paul Brown, Jack Dehring, Margaret Doud, Barb Fisher, Roger Fleury, Hope Goodwin, Armand (Smi) Horn, Lawrence Jones, Aileen P. Koehler, Rob Linn, Ann Mater, Mary Kate McGreevy, Paul Miller, Mary Milton, Robert Milton, Melinda Porter, W.T. Rabe, Harry Ryba, Rhonda Schmidt, Anne Steenbarger, and Wayne Zwolinski. There is no other way to acknowledge our appreciation to the many others who spoke with us briefly or anonymously about the island, except to say: Thank You!

A special thank you is also in order to the Grand Hotel and their staff members, both for promptly answering our questions, and graciously allowing the use of an extract from the book *Grand Hotel, Mackinac Island* by John McCabe. The reprint is with special permission from Unicorn Press, publisher, and Grand Hotel, Mackinac Island, Michigan 49757, which commissioned the book published June, 1987.

TABLE OF CONTENTS

Introduction

In today's fast-paced world, all too often we are unwilling participants in a never ending race. Society in general has become enamored with physical objects and monetary goals. The pursuit of success has replaced the pursuit of happiness as our number one goal in life. It is for this reason that we have come to love Mackinac Island. The moment you arrive, you will realize that this is a special place. At first glance, its quiet, unhurried tempo seems quaint but meaningless. But as you become more familiar with the island, an unusual feeling overwhelms you. The stresses of home and job dissipate, tensions release, and you find yourself being gently eased into the friendly world of our forefathers. Time almost appears to stop, and the problems and cares of yesterday disappear.

Mackinac is always an adventure. If this is your first visit, you may have only planned to stop for a short time, assuming it was a place to spend a few hours—or perhaps a day of your vacation. After all, how much can there be to enjoy on an island less than four square miles in size? You'll soon discover that there is a great deal more to the island than you originally thought. In fact, there is so much here to see and do, that it is impossible to absorb it all in one visit—or even in ten. Most of all, its fascinating charm will captivate you. The island weaves a magical spell, and once you experience Mackinac, it is a part of you forever.

When you leave the island, the rest of the world seems
out of kilter. Pollution and car exhaust are more oppressive.
Everything seems to be moving at a faster pace. But the notion
doesn't last very long. All too quickly reality pulls you back,
and the spell of Mackinac becomes a half-remembered dream.

It was once a sacred spot to the Indians of the region,
the home of their Great Spirit, and a summer gathering place
among the tribes. While exploring the region in search for a
route to China, the French quickly realized its great potential. The pelts of furred animals were the most important commodity in the eighteenth and nineteenth centuries. Soon
trappers and traders were busily working in the area called
Michilimackinac, and French Jesuits had established a mission on the island's shores. Mackinac's location made it a
vital part of the northern territory's watery highway used
to transport the pelts and other supplies. After the British
pushed the French out of the region, they moved to protect
their hold on the fur industry from rebellious Americans by
transferring their fort to the island. Two wars and twenty years
saw Fort Mackinac change hands three times, as both countries struggled for control of the northern frontier. They would
fight a bloody battle on the island's heights before it was over.
Later, the American Fur Company (owned by John Jacob Astor)
was headquartered here, and the island became a great commercial center in the trade. As pleasure travel became popular in the 1800's, Mackinac quickly became a favorite vacation
destination.

As you leaf through these pages you'll learn about the
region, its people, culture, history, legends, geography, sights,
and recreational facilities. We try to take you step by step
through all the things you may wonder about—from what
residents do in the winter—to the story behind each historic
site. There are detailed descriptions of every attraction. For
simplicity we have divided them into three geographic touring areas. Perhaps you are intrigued by how the island is
governed. . . Who makes the laws? What are the problems they
face? Is there crime here? What do they do about fire? Almost
every visitor is curious about the inhabitants. . . How do they

cope with the isolation? What is it like to go to school here? You'll find the answer to all of these questions. The information in this book is meant to make your visit as pleasant as possible. You can use it over and over again, and each reading will give you a deeper understanding of all that is here.

So many visitors flow off the ferries every day, stumble through town, quickly load up with boxes of fudge and souvenirs and dash back to the boat. Although some might take a carriage tour or wander up to the fort, most never discover the real island. People who live and work on Mackinac call these tourists *fudgies*. The first step in advancing past the *fudgie* stage is to learn how to say the island's name.

The word is pronounced *MACK-I-NAW*, not *MACK-IN-ACK*. No matter how it is spelled, the *NAC* sounds like *GNAW*. It might take practice, but every time you see that mackina'c', turn it into mackina'w'. Soon it will be second nature!

On your way here, you may have passed through Mackinaw City, and stopped to tour Colonial Fort Michilimackinac. Why the confusion of similar names? Henry R. Schoolcraft, who spent many years on the island and recorded most of what we know about Indian life, language, and legends, concluded that the Indian name for the island was *Mishi-minauk-in-ong*. When the French came, their way of speaking and spelling corrupted it into *Michilimackinac*. Originally, the name referred to the entire straits area, and the French who built the fort in Mackinaw City identified it with that name. When the British moved the fort to the island, they eventually shortened the name to Fort Mackinac. Years later, when Mackinaw City grew into a town, the name was spelled with a 'w' in order to distinguish it from the island.

What does the name mean? Many early Europeans believed that the Indian name meant *place of the Great Turtle*. The shape of the island, rising slowly up to a rounded, humped center, does resemble a turtle. But after years of study, Schoolcraft concluded that the name *Mishi-minauk-in-ong* actually translated to *place of great dancing spirits*. The Indians believed that the island was a sacred place, the home of their Great Spirit and the lesser spirits that influenced their lives. They would meet here to make peace during wars, and to bury their dead to keep them under the spirits' protection.

Our main goal is to provide you with interesting information, presented in a direct, easy-reading style. We studied numerous sources about the island, some over one-hundred years old. We interviewed many people—island residents, visitors, businessmen, workers, former residents, and tourists. In some instances, the various sources disagreed about certain details. In those situations we tried to select the most commonly used or most logical data.

The one thing that we don't do in this book is make recommendations on where to eat, sleep, or buy a souvenir. To us, there is very little on the island that isn't good—it's primarily a matter of individual preference. We'll let you make your own choices and discoveries. To ensure that your next visit to Mackinac is as enjoyable as possible, here are ten tips for having a memorable stay:

1. Make your reservations early, the best rooms at almost every hotel go to the first reservations.

2. Allow plenty of time for your visit.

3. Have a general plan so that you can make the most of your time.

4. Get into the spirit of the island, slow down and appreciate its quaint, old-fashioned charm.

5. Tour all of the island. The downtown is delightful, but there is much, much more to see and do.

6. Bring clothing for warm days and cool nights, and don't forget a raincoat or umbrella in case of sudden showers.

7. Be friendly—almost everyone here is. Say hello to hikers and bicyclists as they pass. Informal, chance conversations with strangers are common here, and you meet some very interesting people that way!

8. Many visitors have false illusions of safety because there are no cars on the Island. Take care when crossing the street. A collision with a speeding bicycle or a team of horses is never pleasant.

9. When the weather is nice, have lunch one day at the Fort Tea Room. The food is good *and* inexpensive, and the view is incredible. This is the only recommendation we will offer!

10. Use this book to make every visit a wonderful, unforgettable experience.

When you come to this fairy island, with its endless sky, tall white cliffs, majestic buildings, and dense woods; it seems so untouched by the modern world that it makes you feel as if you've gone back in time. This feeling has warmed the untold millions who have explored the island's treasures in years past. From the ancient Indian to Samuel Clemens (Mark Twain), from the boisterous fur traders to Senator John F. Kennedy, from the elegant Victorian aristocrats to President Gerald R. Ford—you will join their ranks as privileged visitors to this land of enchantment.

Historic Frontier

Hiawatha's People

Indian Lore

According to Indian legend, the island of Mishi-minauk-in-ong quietly appeared after a deep fog had shrouded the straits for three suns. When the silvery veil burned away, the Indians saw an island floating on the waters. For many days they were afraid to approach this new land, but one day a group of young braves steered their canoe to its shore. They eyed the tall, white cliffs, the dense forests, and gentle sloping hills. A closer look at the magnificent rocks, deep caves, and tranquil springs—and they knew that this was a place of many manitous. This island was different from any they had seen, and the powerful spirits who dwelled in all objects were clearly at home here.

In the morning, they saw the Great Spirit (Gitchi-Manitou) arrive with the rising sun. He stepped through an arched rock near their beach camp, and quickly climbed the hill and disappeared into his tall limestone wigwam. With deep reverence they left special offerings, and hurried back to their canoe. They paddled swiftly across the deep blue water, eager to share their discovery. The Great Spirit had come to live among his people.

Mishi-minauk-in-ong, the land of the great dancing spirits, became sacred to all the tribes. It was a place to bury their dead, so that their families would dwell forever under the protection of the Great Spirit. When they paddled near the island, they dropped packets of tobacco into the water to honor the spirits. On a visit, they offered treasures: belts of wampum, dogs, and other valuables to acknowledge the power of the manitous. If they pleased the spirits, their lands would be filled with game, their canoes with fish, and they would have protection from drowning and famine.

Gitchi-Manitou left the island when the white man came. Angered and saddened by their treatment of his people; he left the tribes under the protection of his smaller spirits, sometimes called *Imakinaks*. Then he hastened away to the cold distant sky, to live among the flickering flames of the Northern lights.

Indian Tribes

Over the years, many different tribes camped on the island's shores. To divide them by language similarities, they were either Sioux, Alqonquin, or Iroquois descendents. Some became prominent in the history of the area, with large numbers populating the northern wilderness. Other smaller tribes barely left their mark on the region. To someone unfamiliar with Indian ways, their different names and nations can be confusing. Especially since most tribes had a name for themselves that was different than the name assigned to them by Europeans. In addition, when a tribe was decimated through wars, famine, and disease they often united with an allied band, and absorbed their tribal name.

The tribes didn't have clear boundaries between them, and most wars were caused by the need to expand the hunting territory to feed a growing population. Because the terrain for each group might encompass eight-hundred to one-thousand square miles, inevitably there was intermingling— and it wasn't always peaceful.

There was no central leadership, each band or village had their own chief. Although he did not have absolute authority, his wisdom was honored and respected. Individual villages or entire tribes often formed alliances, usually among groups who spoke the same language and shared common enemies. Although they didn't have organized governments as we do today, these confederacies could be compared to the present-day cooperation between the United States, Canada, Australia, and England.

The *Asseguns* (Bone People) were one of the earliest in the region to live on Mishi-minauk-in-ong, and they had a tribal seat here. Of Sioux stock, they were prominent in the area before 1649. For years they battled both the Ottawa and Chippewa, and eventually fled to lower Michigan to escape their enemies. They were never heard from again.

The *Chippewa* were the fiercest Indians in the area. Originally known as the *Ojibwa*, the French corrupted the word to *Chippewa*. In Indian lore, the Chippewa, Ottawa, and Potawatomi were originally one tribe of Algonquin stock that came down from the north. They later divided, but maintained an alliance known as 'the three fires'. They battled the Iroquois, who drove them west to the Lakes Huron and Superior region. The Sioux were already there, but the Chippewa steadily pushed them west, into the region of what is now Minnesota and the Dakotas.

When the French first met the *Ottawa* in the St. Lawrence River area, they knew them as *Algonkins*. They quickly became French allies, but despite French assistance, the Iroquois drove them into the Michilimackinac area. Here they merged with other tribes and became known as the Ottawa. They were the tradesmen among the Indians; traveling from village to village in canoes loaded with furs, skins, rush mats, maize, tobacco, roots, and herbs. They were famous for their expert canoe handling, developed through their extensive voyages through the lakes.

The *Hurons* called themselves the *Wyandotte*. The French were amazed by their unusual hairstyles—shaved heads with just a two inch ridge of black hair running from forehead to neck. So they dubbed them Hur-on, a loose version of the French words for 'men with heads of boars'. This tribe was also closely allied to the French, and were great favorites of the Jesuit missionaries. Unfortunately, diseases such as smallpox decimated the tribe by the early 1640's. The tribe was of Iroquoian stock, but they had long ago separated, and were now bitter enemies of that nation. About 1648, hostile Iroquois raiders from the east began persistent attacks on the weakened Huron villages. The Hurons took refuge among the Tobacco Indians, but the Iroquois soon overpowered both tribes. They fled together to what is now Wisconsin, and the two tribes merged into one, calling themselves Wyandottes—although the Europeans still referred to them as Hurons. They remained in the area for years, engaging in periodic skirmishes with the neighboring Sioux. In 1666, the French made peace with the Iroquois, and the Wyandotte/Hurons slowly returned to the straits region. Most joined the French settlement at Point St. Ignace, and built a village with a wooden palisade around it for further protection.

Tobacco Indians (Tionontati) were once fierce enemies of the Huron, but they made peace and formed an alliance just before the Jesuits came to the area. The French called them the Tobacco Indians because they raised so much of that crop. As mentioned above, the Hurons took refuge with them and both tribes were driven west by the Iroquois. They returned as Wyandotte/Hurons to the Michilimackinac area around 1670.

Potawatomis were fierce enemies of the Huron. They originally lived in the upper peninsulas of Michigan and Wisconsin, but like all other tribes they ranged over a wide area through the years. They were strong allies of the French until 1763, and played a part in Pontiac's Conspiracy against the British. They later changed allegiance and fought on the British side during the American Revolution.

Although there was a sense of tribal identity among the people, an Indian's first loyalty was to his family. Clans lived and traveled together, occasionally breaking up into smaller bands. When the bands met, they usually knew one another's lineage at a glance. Facial tattoos of lines, circles, and varying colors proclaimed their ancestry.

Hiawatha's People

A man's job was to hunt, fish, fight, trade, build the houses and canoes. The women cooked, kept house, made clothes and pottery, raised children, farmed, and carried supplies on journeys. Many of the men were tall, some towering over six feet. All were dark-complexioned, with facial features varying between the tribes. For example: Chippewa were noted for their broad features, Huron for their hooked noses, and Potawatomi for their aquiline noses—and cheekbones that were very high—even for Indians.

Imagine one of those tall braves standing on the shore of Lake Huron, perhaps where Windermere Point is today. He has highly greased, straight black hair that is pulled back with a snakeskin cord. A few feathers are stuck in the cord and are trailing down his back. His face is carefully painted in streaks and circles of varying colors. It is warm, so he is naked from the waist up, and you can see white and red patterns drawn from clay across his chest and back. A treasured feather is set through his pierced nose, and two other feathers dangle from his ears. He is wearing only a breech cloth and mocassins decorated with a bright design of dyed quill work.

His wife approaches, and her only clothing is a short skirt decorated with bright shells and beads that covers her hips and thighs. Around her neck are several long strings of shells and bones. Her dark hair is knotted in two shiny braids, with a string of colorful stones wound into each plait. She is helping him to prepare for a journey, where he and the other warriors will retaliate against another tribe for a recent raid on their camp. She hands him a package that contains his pipe and tobacco, some snake rattles, and the wing bone of an eagle—to blow through in case of a thunderstorm. He reaches down and gathers his equipment: bow, arrows, knife, tomahawk, war club, and shield of thick hide, and quickly wades out to the waiting canoe. His wife walks to the wigwam they share and begins her wait for his return.

There is plenty of work to do to pass the time. Dried berries, roots, and maize hang in baskets dangling from the ceiling pole. She rummages among her storage baskets, ignoring quills, beads, and paints, until she finds her needle and cords. Today she will stitch together the deerskin shirt she had finished tanning last week. The time of cold weather is not far away, and she has much more warm clothing to make for her family.

In winter, the warrior and his wife will move to the mainland with their band, traveling to the same general area each year. Every family will build their own wigwam. The men will cut saplings and set them in the ground to form the frame, then bend the tops of young trees and twist them together into an arc. An opening is left for a door, and another at the roof, so that smoke from the fire can escape. More saplings are lashed horizontally around the outer shell to reinforce the frame. The final shape might resemble a cone or a dome, depending on family preference. A covering of rush mats woven from long grass, animal skins, or large strips of bark, is placed on the exterior. They are held in place by leaning other poles against them. The doorway and the smoke hole will be closed with skins in bad weather.

The women lay pine needles on the inside floor, to soften the ground and to help avoid the dampness. They set rush mats over the sweet-smelling needles, then make low bench platforms to be used as beds. These are built near the walls out of sticks and brush, and covered with skins and fur robes.

In the cooler weather, our Indian brave will wear a fringed shirt and buckskin leggings, decorated with a painted design. His wife has a long dress made from two skins stitched together at the shoulders, decorated in patterned quills and vermillion paint. Both have warm robes made of woven strips of rabbit fur, and turban style hats for very cold days. In the evenings, they can visit their neighbors and share stories around the fire. They love to play games, and often gamble with bone dice. The women work on making wampum belts, collars, or necklaces.

An Indian brave in winter attire.

Courtesy of Mackinac Island State Park Commission

Wampum was an important item among the Indians. It was used as gifts, in trade, and as a way of recording events or sending messages. Drilled beads (usually white or purple) were strung together and arranged in patterns that contained pictures or symbols and communicated information. They were sometimes painted a particular color to convey additional significance. For example: A black belt with a red hatchet meant war, and it would be sent among the tribes as an invitation to join in upcoming battles.

The early European explorers and missionaries sent back differing character descriptions of the Indians that they met. Some described them as friendly, charitable, peaceful, and hospitable. Others called them thieves, and hostile cutthroats. Like all groups of people, they had both saints and bloodthirsty killers among them. But often the representation was based more on misunderstanding and a conflict of cultures than on reality. While they might present dour faces to visitors, the Indians had a great sense of humor among themselves. A typical village was filled with shouting and laughter. Indian children were taught to control their emotions, and to never betray their feelings. It was considered a virtue to bear pain in silence. Yet they were well-loved, all Indians held children and family in high esteem.

There were continual struggles for territorial control among the tribes long before the white man came. They battled each other regularly, and nearly all tribes tortured their captives, had slaves, and practiced cannibalism (in the belief that they gained strength by eating their enemies). The Iroquois pushed the Chippewa and many other nations into the Michilimackinac area. They in turn drove the Sioux further west. In fact, it wasn't until the French came and eventually made peace with the Iroquois that many of the Indians felt some security. A typical warrior was well-armed and well-disciplined, a fierce, courageous fighter with great stamina. Europeans counted on them as allied troops in their various battles for the continent.

The Indians were intelligent and cunning, but they never understood the white man's concept of land ownership and his habit of planning for the distant future. The white man was always thinking about tomorrow—with visions of land conquered and fortunes made. The Indian felt that the land was without limit, they weren't as acquisitive, and they seldom planned further ahead than the next season. This is not a character failure, but a crucial difference in values. That, and their unfortunate ability to ally themselves to the losing side in every war, eventually caused them to lose their hold on their lands.

How many Indians were there in the region? No one knows for sure. The Chippewa were the largest tribe. In 1764, there were approximately twenty-five thousand Chippewa, and their numbers remained fairly steady over the years. The Hurons suffered the greatest losses. In 1615, there were twenty- to thirty-five thousand Hurons. In 1640, there were only twelve-thousand remaining. By 1748, the tribe had been reduced to between five- hundred and eight-hundred fifty members. They had been decimated by smallpox and wars with the Iroquois, and never regained their original strength. In 1812, there were only one-thousand Huron Indians in the United States. The Potawatomi were always a small tribe. There were approximately three-thousand in 1658, and their number stayed in the same general area for the next one-hundred fifty years.

In 1815, the Chippewa signed a treaty with the United States of America, and were put on reservations in Wisconsin, Minnesota, and North Dakota. The Hurons also signed treaties in 1815, and they received land in Michigan and Ohio. They eventually sold those lands and were relocated to Kansas, then to Oklahoma. Through various treaties in the 1800's, the Potawatomies ceded their lands and steadily moved farther and farther south. Eventually they ended up either at Lake St. Clair, or in the Iowa and Kansas region.

But long before that time, the Indian tribes in the area played a crucial role in assisting the white man when he came. First the French, then the British, relied on the Indians for help in exploration, as a vital source of trade, and as allied troops in their various battles for the continent. It was only later that he became an obstacle to the white man's need for more land.

Frontier Exploration

Explorers

Jean Nicolet was the first white man on record to journey through the straits of Michilimackinac. By 1634, Indian tales of a people who lived in the far west on the edge of a sea had reached Governor Samuel de Champlain, and he was convinced that these were the Chinese. Jean Nicolet and seven Huron companions were dispatched on the historic journey with a canoe heaped with gifts for the merchants of Cathay.

They left Quebec with a caravan of canoes. The men calling back and forth to one another boasting of their plans for the year, and of the celebrations they would have the following spring. After days of singing and laughter, the other canoes slowly dropped out—each group of men paddling away to their own destination. Nicolet and his men traveled alone for days following the northern coastline. They passed high grassy meadows filled with deer, and spotted wolf and bear on the edge of the dense forests. They poled through peaceful inlets in sunshine and gentle currents, and battled unexpected storms, high waves, and heavy winds. They detoured around dangerous rapids and tall waterfalls, and marched their heavy bundles and canoe through miles of portages between one river and the next. At night they camped on the rocky shores, slapping at the whining mosquitos.

A few days from Point Detour, Nicolet gazed at the blue water swaying toward the sun on the western horizon. Suddenly, the Indians began talking excitedly. Nicolet had lived among them for eleven years and knew their language well. "Mishi-minauk-in-ong," they said pointing. Nicolet turned to look at the legendary island. He had heard tales around the campfire about this home of the great spirits. It was just as he had heard it described, the high humped center, tall white cliffs, towering rocks—so different from the other islands they had seen. "Manitou's Landing Place," a companion said, pointing to a large rock in the shape of an arch. They watched the island as they paddled by, and the Hurons each dropped a handful of tobacco leaves into the water as a gift to the island spirits. Nicolet would like to have stopped to explore the island, but there was no time. The long sought land of Cathay loomed ahead.

Nicolet was a good man for this ambassadorial journey. He had come to New France as a fresh eighteen-year-old, and years of living among the Indians had built his discipline, courage, and stamina. He was a devout Catholic, and shared Champlain's vision of the possibilities that the China trade would bring to France. He was prepared to make a favorable impression. In addition to rich gifts, there was a silk ceremonial robe in one carefully wrapped bundle. It had been beautifully embroidered in brilliant colors—he would wear it when he reached the end of the journey.

About one week after they had passed Mishi-minauk-in-ong they entered a large bay and followed it to the mouth of a river. They could see smoke in the distant woods, and hear laughter and voices from a nearby village. The canoe landed and Nicolet solemnly donned his gown. He was instantly transformed from rough woodsman to a man of obvious importance and dignity. With a pistol in each hand, he started toward the village with his companions. Just then a group of Indians came out of the woods. Nicolet fired his pistols into the air, and the Indians stared in shock at the strangely dressed white man carrying crackling smoke sticks. Jean Nicolet stared back. He had discovered what is now Green Bay, Wisconsin.

He and his men were escorted to the Winnebago village, and among the feasts and dances and talks he eagerly questioned his hosts. They didn't know the distance to Cathay, but they could tell him that there were other tribes farther inland. After a brief rest, Nicolet set off again. He encountered several bands of Indians, but could only learn of a Great Water to the west. Although he was sure that the Great Water was the ocean that bordered China, Nicolet had to turn back. Supplies were low, and it was late in the year. He and his companions retraced their journey, never learning that the Great Water was the Mississippi. On his return, Champlain was disappointed. Although Nicolet was honored for discovering more territory for France, he wasn't given a hero's welcome. After all, he had failed to find Cathay. Nicolet settled down and married a Frenchwoman. He died a few years later while trying to save a drowning man.

The French had been searching for a route to China since the early 1500's, and this was the goal of their early explorations in North America. Jacques Cartier was the first explorer—he made it as far as the St. Lawrence River. But soon after that, problems at home delayed further expeditions. It wasn't until the early 1600's that the French king selected a young army officer to go to Canada and probe the size and shape of the land. The king still hoped for a new route to China, but the economic potential of furs in North America was also very exciting. Samuel de Champlain was the young man the king sent to open up the fur trade. He arrived as governor of New France, and founded Quebec with a group of settlers in 1603. He went on several treks, on one he sailed up the St. Lawrence but stopped short of discovering the Great Lakes.

In 1608, Champlain decided to put some young Frenchmen among the Indians to learn their languages. It was a way to discover more about the land without sending out expensive expeditions. One of these men was a seventeen-year-old named Etienne Brule. After only one year in the wilderness, Brule went completely native. He made his first report in Quebec dressed as an Algonquin, but didn't linger because he was exceptionally eager to return to his tribe. Although his transformation did not win him any friends back in Quebec, he did learn and see more than anyone else. He was the first

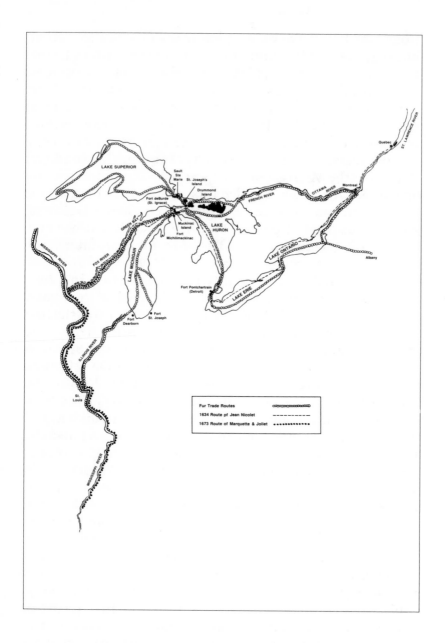

LAKE SUPERIOR

Sault Ste Marie

St. Joseph's Island

Drummond Island

Fort deBurde (St. Ignace)

FRENCH RIVER

OTTAWA RIVER

Montreal

Quebec

ST. LAWRENCE RIVER

Mackinac Island

LAKE HURON

Fort Michilimackinac

GREEN BAY

LAKE MICHIGAN

FOX RIVER

MISSISSIPPI RIVER

Fort Pontchartrain (Detroit)

LAKE ERIE

LAKE ONTARIO

Albany

Fort St. Joseph

Fort Dearborn

ILLINOIS RIVER

St. Louis

MISSISSIPPI RIVER

Fur Trade Routes	⊂∞∞∞∞∞∞∞∞∞∞∞⊃
1634 Route of Jean Nicolet	– – – – – – – –
1673 Route of Marquette & Joliet	••••••••••••

white man to see Lakes Huron and Superior, and although we have no recorded proof, there is a good chance that he passed through the straits of Michilimackinac long before Nicolet. In two decades of living with the Indians he probed a great deal of the wilderness, and in time he completely lost his loyalty to France. In 1629, he betrayed Champlain to the British. When Champlain was released four years later, he sent out word among the Huron that he wanted Brule delivered up for trial. The Hurons decided to punish him instead, and Brule was quartered, boiled, and eaten.

Champlain's governership had far-reaching effects on France's future in North America. He had founded a successful colony at Quebec during a time when similar settlements failed. His policy of putting young Frenchmen among the natives succeeded. It helped him gain important knowledge of the wilderness territories; and even more importantly cemented ties with Indians in the area. However, his greatest error may have been in 1609, while on an expedition to what is now northern New York. He was accompanied by some Huron and Algonquin Indians when they encountered a group of Mohawks. Champlain's Indians told him that the Mohawks were part of the Iroquois nation and were their ancient enemies. Champlain shot at them and killed two of their group. They had never seen guns before and fled to spread the tale of the unprovoked French attack. This began an animosity which grew and turned into bitter enmity. It made an Iroquois alliance with the British inevitable, and that alliance eventually caused the French to lose their hold on the continent.

Missionaries

The priests of the Society of Jesus had an essential role in helping France establish her hold on North America. The society shaped intelligent young men into a learned, well-organized, and disciplined group who followed the motto *For the Greater Glory of God*. Some have called this elite band the Catholic Marines, but the most common name for them is the Jesuits. All were volunteer missionaries, and many were

A trader bargains with some Hurons, while a Jesuit missionary watches.

Courtesy of Mackinac Island State Park Commission

from important and wealthy families. They were hard-working, dedicated men who had no doubt about the importance of bringing Christ to the Indians.

They started their work in North America in the early 1600's, and from the beginning established a pattern that led to their success. First they learned and recorded the native language. As they became fluent in the various dialects, they recorded Indian customs and descriptions of terrain, as well as chronicling the harsh realities of life in the wilderness. Many of the accounts they sent back to France were published. Soon their writings had excited the minds of many young Frenchmen who clamored to join the Jesuits. These writings were later called *The Jesuit Relations*, and were finally published in seventy-three volumes. Written between 1632 and 1673, they essentially covered the early years of the frontier empire. They not only provided an insight into the missionary work of North America, but supplied the French government with information that helped them settle and control the area. Father Vimont described the voyage of Nicolet in his 1642 letters, and the first account of a visit to Michilimackinac Island was by Father Jean Claude Allouez in 1669.

Their unflagging belief in the importance of their cause carried the earliest missionaries through incredible hardships. One of the first of these men was Father Jean de Brebeuf. He was a college graduate, the son of a wealthy farmer who requested a mission in Canada three years after his ordination. Arriving in 1625, the thirty-two year old priest wandered through indifferent villages for months; his only meal for many days a handful of coarsely ground corn mixed with water. Some Indians treated him kindly, but others were abusive. They stole his meager supplies, tormented him, and drove him out of their villages. But slowly, as he grew knowledgeable in their language and beliefs, he was able to convert many of the Huron tribe. He even composed a dictionary and catechism in the Huron language. He lived among the Indians for twenty-four years, except for occasional trips to France and Quebec. He traveled everywhere, and was even part of the caravan of canoes that left Quebec with Jean Nicolet. In 1649, a group of Iroquois captured him near Georgian Bay.

The Iroquois despised the *black robes* because of their close association with their hated enemies—the Hurons. Unlike other tribes, the Iroquois had an organized political system. They believed that the Christian teachings were undermining their government. The average Iroquois was encouraged to think of every *black robe* as the epitomy of evil, and treat him accordingly. Brebeuf was tortured mercilessly for hours and died from his wounds. He was one of the first of many Jesuits who later died horribly at the hand of the Iroquois. Some were held captive for months, even years, undergoing slow and painful tortures. The Catholic church honors many of these men as saints including: the lay missionaries John de Lalande and Rene Goupil, and Fathers Jean de Brebeuf, Charles Garnier, Isaac Jogues, and Gabriel Lalemant.

In the first missions, the Indians were somewhat intrigued by the *black robes* but often bored with their talks.

Frequently the Jesuits resorted to magic to prove their deeper knowledge to the tribes. One item that fascinated the natives was the clock. An early missionary wrote in Jesuit Relations:

> *"(The Indians)...all think it is some living thing. They cannot imagine how it speaks by itself; and when it is going to strike they look to see if we are all there and if someone has not hidden in order to shake it. They think it hears, especially if for a joke some one of our Frenchmen calls out at the last stroke of the hammer, "that's enough," and then it immediately becomes silent. They call it the Captain of the day. When it strikes they ask what it says. They ask about its food, and they stay a whole hour to hear it speak again."*

But the use of magic to gain respect and ward off violence could also backfire. Once they convinced the Indians that they had great powers, they were also blamed for anything bad that happened. When the village was hit by drought or famine, the Indians threatened and abused the missionaries. If a priest baptized a sick child and it died, many of them assumed it was because he had laid a death curse on it. The most difficult crisis was caused by their unwitting transmission of white men's diseases to the Indians. They themselves were somewhat immune, so when everyone in the village would fall ill with smallpox except for the priests, the Indians were convinced they had called down terrible spirits. The more the epidemic increased, the more they persecuted the missionaries. They were encouraged in this by their own priests and witch doctors, who resented the Jesuit usurpment of their power. When hunger or sickness became too much to bear, they beat them, stoned them, stole their belongings and turned them out of the village—if they were lucky. Many were tortured—one priest writing to his superior apologized for his handwriting—but he couldn't do any better because the Indians had only left him one finger.

In 1666, Father Jacques Marquette arrived in Canada. A former teacher and scholar in six languages, this sturdy, determined man had applied repeatedly for a missionary post in North America. His first assignment was to relieve Father Allouez at Sault Ste. Marie. This large mission was surrounded by friendly bands of Huron, Ottawa, and Chippewa. The Jesuits of the first generation had laid the groundwork, and there had been many Indian converts. It was a good, strong mission for the church.

A few days after he arrived, Marquette woke early and hurried to gather his things. A group of voyageurs and traders were leaving at first light and he wanted to join them on their journey. He checked his leather case...carefully arranging his bible, gold chalice and paten, holy pictures, medals, candles, altar cloth, vestments, and writing materials. He cautiously wrapped a sturdy bottle of grape wine and placed it next to a small packet of unconsecrated bread. These he would carefully measure, a small amount for each celebration of the Mass. He locked the portable case and quickly hooked his long black cassock closed. Strapping the case to his shoulders and back, he hurried to the waiting birchbark canoe. He greeted the boatmen, noting that some avoided his eyes. He would soon learn that this was common. In any group of men in the wilderness, some were eager to be with a priest and receive the sacraments, others resented their presence and influence on the Indians.

The canoe left quickly, the paddles barely disturbing the water as they moved. A quiet breeze blew little wisps of clouds along the deep blue sky. The canoe scuttled along in the opposite direction of the clouds. They followed the same route that Nicolet had taken thirty years before. Marquette was burning with excitement, remembering all he had read and heard about the western frontier. His easy-going nature quickly relaxed the men. Soon they were singing as they skimmed across the water, joking as they trotted over portages, telling stories around nightly campfires.

When Marquette arrived at the mission, Father Allouez stayed on for several weeks to break him in. Then he was on his own. He taught the catechism, patiently answered questions and joined in spirited discussions. He baptised, said Mass, distributed communion, heard confessions, and annointed the dying. In a very short time both the French and Indians in the area admired and respected him. A few years later he was transferred to the far western shore of Lake Superior at La Pointe. The Indians there were a mix of Huron, Ottawa, and Chippewa who were less receptive to having a priest among them. Marquette soon learned that his best intentions couldn't overcome all the differences between Christianity and Indian beliefs. A young brave who wished to become a warrior was trained to hate his enemies, and to be fiercely independent—never submitting to any man. Marquette found that he had to justify taking a vow of obedience, swearing to love his enemies, and struggling to submit his life to God's will. The proud, independent Indians were not eager to change their long-held values, and Marquette soon learned that there were no easy conversions among them.

While at La Pointe, Marquette spent many hours with a male slave who had been captured from the Illinois tribe. He taught the eager priest his native language and described his homeland in detail. Marquette's secret dream was to found new missions in yet unvisited territories. He carefully wrote down everything he learned, and his excited descriptions of the land were sent back to Quebec. In the meantime, Indian wars disrupted his plans. In 1670, the Chippewa in the area were fighting the neighboring Sioux. The other tribes were restless because they didn't want to be caught up in the war. In the east, the French had finally made peace with the Iroquois. The Straits at Michilimackinac were safe once again, and among the many bands returning to the area were the Indians from La Pointe and Father Marquette.

Soon after his arrival he met with Father Claude Dablon, the superior for all missions on the Great Lakes. Dablon had built a bark chapel on the Island of Michilimackinac in 1669, calling it the "Mission of St. Ignace," in honor of the founder of the Jesuit order, St. Ignatius Loyola. At first the island seemed like the perfect location for their work. Many tribes stopped there to trade during the summer, and it was already connected in the Indian mind with religion and spiritual beliefs. However, the growing season was too short for many Indian crops. It was also too isolated and inaccessible in the winter, without enough wildlife to sustain a population. After one year, Dablon decided to move the mission. When Marquette arrived, he instructed him to re-establish it on the Northern Peninsula, across from the island. Among the trader's cabins and Indian longhouses already there, Marquette and his Catholic followers built a new bark chapel, and the Mission of St. Ignace was once again in operation.

Frontier Exploration

Marquette's writing eventually helped to spark new interest in the Great Water that Nicolet had once described. Louis de Buade, Comte de Palluaue de Frontenac, the Governor of New France, decided to send an expedition west to explore the territory. He appointed Canadian-born Louis Joliet to lead the enterprise, and Marquette was invited to join. There hadn't been such an extensive trip to the west since Nicolet had tried to find a route to China in 1634. In the late spring of 1673, the twenty-eight year old Joliet and his party of five voyageurs received an enthusiastic welcome from Marquette when they arrived at the mission. Marquette carried his now battered leather case to the canoe, and helped the men load the remaining supplies. Soon he, Joliet, and the voyaguers were on their way, quickly leaving the Lake of the Hurons and entering the Lake of the Illinois. After stopping at Indian missions and villages along the way, they soon turned inland through the rivers of what is now Wisconsin. They traveled through woods and marshes, around islands and streams, carefully noting everything they encountered. A month after leaving St. Ignace, they saw a large wide river flowing to the south. They paused, and Marquette led them in a prayer of thanksgiving. They had found the Great Water.

The explorers were awed by the majesty of the river and careful of its rapid current. They slowly passed bluffs, prairies, rocks, forests—intently watching, but never seeing signs of people along the wild shores. It was an incredibly exciting feeling, to travel where no white man had been before. Round-ing each bend, they never knew what to expect on the other side. Joliet made careful maps of the water, land and stars, as well as recording the depth of the water, and the types of animals that they saw. Eight days after entering the Great Water the travelers met their first Indians, friendly Illinois who were thrilled to discover that Marquette could speak their language. Unfortunately, they couldn't tell the explorers how far it was to the southern sea. The natives did tell them of another river that lead northeast from the Mississippi to the Lake of the Illinois. Parting as friends, the Indians invited Marquette to return and bring his teachings to their people.

After traveling for several more weeks, they met a tribe of hostile Indians who wanted to kill them at once. The chief interceded, and as they talked and exchanged gifts they learned that these Indians had traded with the Spanish. The Frenchmen were worried about encountering Spanish troops. They were sure that the southern sea was not far, and rather than risk capture by the Spanish, they decided to return home. By now, they had traveled down the Great Water for a month, and when they turned around they were near the Arkansas River. Paddling against the powerful current slowed their homeward journey. After passing the Missouri River they turned onto the Illinois River, following it to the northeast. In the Illinois country, the little group split. Marquette stayed behind to preach to the Indians, and founded several missions. Joliet hurried back to Quebec to share his exciting report. In 1675, Marquette became ill and his Indian companions tried to get him back to St. Ignace. He died on the return trip, during a stop on the southeastern shore of Michigan. His Indian friends buried him there and carefully marked the spot. Two years later they returned and dug up his grave. They skinned and deboned him, bleached the bones, then carried them to St. Ignace where they were planted with great ceremony.

The Jesuit's work in North America slowly diminished over the next one-hundred years. They were the vanguard who had day to day contact with the native Americans and shared their lives. They supported the Indians through conflicts that often put them at odds with their fellow Frenchmen. One of the biggest sources of contention was liquor. The traders and soldiers encouraged the Indians to trade for it. The Indians liked the intoxicating beverage, but the priests wanted to keep it away. They were not only concerned about the un-Christian way the Indians acted when they were drunk; they felt that the effects of alcohol were destroying the Indian culture. On the other side, the soldiers, trappers, and traders wanted the Indians to concentrate on accumulating fur pelts. They felt that the Jesuits were distracting them from their work. They bombarded the government with complaints, and accused the Jesuits of not making enough conversions to justify their presence.

There is no exact record of the number of conversions the priests made. Despite the criticism of their fellow Frenchmen, the figures are not important. With the major difference in values and culture that Christianity represented, wholesale acceptance could not occur in just a few generations. In addition, most Indians were satisfied with their lives and not eager to change their system of beliefs. But the Jesuit presence gave them a positive image of the white man. They worked to protect the Indians from exploitation, and often served as spokesmen for the tribes to the French government. Despite their contributions, their persistent enemies were eventually successful, and the Jesuits were no longer allowed to send new missionaries. By 1773, only eleven remained on duty in Canada. The brave men who had learned the Indian languages; helped to map the entire region; built missions across the northern continent; suffered loneliness, hardship, and torture; and brought Christianity to a whole race of people; were no longer welcome on the frontier.

Expanding Fur Trade

Economic interests had replaced the need for religious conversions as the main goal of the French king and the Quebec government. Fur was the essential commodity of the era, just as oil is today. Governments struggled for influence in the region, juggled allies, and at all costs wanted to ensure the flow of pelts to European markets. By the 1600's, most of the fur-bearing animals in Europe had been heavily hunted. The beaver was almost extinct, yet the demand for furs hadn't stopped. In addition to providing warmth, the expensive garment was a means of flaunting wealth and status. The beaver was extremely popular. Each beaver hair is shielded by inter-locking scales that seal out water. When brushed, the material holds its shape through all kinds of weather. Beaver hats are an ideal, long-lasting, sturdy means of protection from rain and snow.

A great deal of money was needed to finance trapping expeditions in the wilderness, and to transport the large number of pelts the market demanded. Journeys had to be made to chart the territories; relations built with the Indians; traders sent to obtain the hides; soldiers dispatched to regulate trade; and an army of people persuaded to settle in new colonies in order to provide the necessary services. The French and English kings did not wish to underwrite the entire expense out of their national treasuries. To encourage entrepreneurs to invest in the industry, they offered exclusive territorial rights to the North American fur trade. In exchange for a monopoly on all furs trapped in a certain area for a given period of time, the investor would agree to establish a colony of settlers and to pay a percentage of fur income to the government in taxes. Through these grants, only the person holding the monopoly had a right to trade for furs in his designated area. In the early days, they were awarded on a small scale to individuals. The kings later expanded the monopoly rights by granting them to newly formed companies with heavier financial backing. The holders of these monopolies were given no help from the king other than their grant, and they were pretty much left alone to operate as they wished. That freedom made them very powerful, and their ventures were extremely profitable. It didn't take long before the acquisition of furs became essential to the French and British economies.

In the early days, the independent French trappers were called *Coureurs de Bois* (Rangers of the Woods). Later the term was applied to all Frenchmen who trapped or traded. These were tough men who worked on their own, skirting their way around the monopolies granted by the kings. Sometimes they were tolerated, at other times they were persecuted. For the most part, there was such a huge demand for pelts that they never had to worry about finding a buyer. They hunted all fur-bearing animals, but the beaver was the most plentiful and the most popular. Many coureurs caught them Indian fashion, a method carefully described by Alexander Henry in his biography:

> "To kill beaver we used to go several miles up the river before the approach of night...(and let) the canoe drift gently down the current without any noise. The beaver in this part of the evening came abroad to procure food or materials...The most common way of taking the beaver is that of breaking up its house... During this operation the (beaver) family made their escape to one or more of their washes. They had to be discovered by striking ice along the bank, and where the holes are hollow, sound is returned. After discovering and searching many of these in vain we often found a whole family together in the same wash...From the washes they must be taken out with the hands; and in doing this the hunter sometimes received severe wounds from their teeth..."

Imagine what it must have been like to work many long months in the dangerous and lonely woods. A silent ranger. Killing animals, collecting hides, fighting snow, cold, blizzards, unfriendly Indians, and competing coureurs.

Let's envision a coureur working the woods in what is now the upper peninsula of Michigan. He is weary after hours of trapping, and he now works at skinning the pile of dead animals. The air is cold and stinging in his nostrils. The dark woods are silent. Tall, black trees loom over him. Putting aside his knife, he reaches round to grab a bundle of sticks and builds a small fire. He digs through his pack, brings out a handful of Indian corn and adds a little water he has carried from a nearby stream. While it heats, he places some meat from his recent catch on a stick and props it over the fire. Except for his shorter height, he could be mistaken for an Indian. Dressed in bucksin leggings and leather shirt, he pulls a heavy robe of warm bear fur around him, while his long black hair hangs from beneath his thick wool cap. The Indian ways are the most practical for the life he leads, and he has long forgotten the feel of a soft, clean feather bed. Soon his dinner is ready, and while he eats he tallies his inventory in his mind. Pelts of beaver, fox, wolf, lynx, and raccoon are carefully bundled and stored in his secret hiding place. He would like to grab a few more deer, but it is already late in the season. He had traded away a beautiful deer-skin just a few months ago—but he needed new snow-shoes. His others had been lost during a terrible blizzard, along with many supplies and quite a few pelts. He hoped to return after the spring melt to search out the area, but knew that it was unlikely he would find them again.

As winter ends, he slowly moves his furs forward. He hikes with as many bundles as he can carry until midday, then erects a scaffold to protect the furs from snooping animals on the ground. Placing the bundles in the upper framework, he turns and marches back to his original camp. He repeats the trip, morning and evening for three days. When all of the bundles are piled on the elevated platform, he moves on to the next stage, building a new temporary structure and repeating the wearisome labor until he reaches the lake shore. From there, he finds the canoe he hid the autumn before, and carefully poles away to the nearest trading post. His eyes warily watch the sky. A sudden spring storm could mean disaster and the loss of his winter's work.

After arriving and unloading, he finds the trader is waiting for him. Quickly he learns his due, and receives a bill of credit good for future purchases. He buys a silver brooch for his wife and a pint of good whiskey, then hurries to his home in an Indian village near the trading post. His wife is an Ottawa and they have two children. She carefully cooks the deer meat he brought while he relaxes with his pipe in the smoky wigwam. That week, many other coureurs have come in, and the traders are doing a fast business. With the pelts sold and the feeling of prosperity in their minds, they celebrate each evening. One of the traders has a fiddle, and as the sun disappears each night he strikes the joyful notes that remind them of home. They dance with the women, sing mournful songs, or wrestle with their Indian companions by the leaping firelight. Liquor flows freely, and men fight, shove, jostle, joke—and drink and gamble away the gains from their months of hard work. Many will be penniless by the end of summer, then it will again be time to disappear into the woods.

Although the government didn't like their independence, it wasn't consistent in dealing out punishment to the coureurs. In the late 1600's, the exclusive monopolies given to the fur companies became more stringently enforced. That decision eventually caused enormous repercussions for the French. Two coureurs named Grosseilliers and Radisson showed up in Montreal in 1660, with a rich load of furs, and descriptions of lands filled with beaver in the Northwest. The French officials reacted by confiscating their furs and fining them for hunting without a license. The angry explorers turned to King Charles II of Britain and offered him their knowledge of the area. They quickly received his royal patronage. In 1670, The Hudson's Bay Company was formed to develop the land, and it became one of the most powerful fur companies of all.

On their first English-backed venture, Grosseilliers and Radisson sent back a shipload of furs so profitable that it was the talk of Britain. In 1676, the Hudson's Bay Company paid out 650£ sterling for pelts. They sold those furs for 19,000£ sterling. Soon many coureurs and Indians dropped their French ties and began taking their furs to the English because they offered better trade goods. Stunned by the success of the Hudson's Bay Company, the French first tried to compete by trimming prices. The stiff competition led to skirmishes in the backwoods between competing coureurs and Indian trappers. In time it grew to armed conflicts and the French-Indian wars. The French had tried to regulate the volume of trapping, but the English removed all controls. This led to huge numbers of immature animals being killed and year-round trapping, which decimated the supply.

The men who handled transportation in those early days were called *voyageurs*. These sturdy men had huge shoulders and arms built up from fourteen hours of paddling each day; and strong, muscular legs from carrying the canoes and bundles across portages. Two men carried the canoe, while the others carried two ninety-pound packs on their backs. They would trot the entire portage, whether it was five or twenty miles. Among them, a man was measured by his endurance and stamina. These bold, rough men were paid in pelts, the going rate in the 1760's was one-hundred pounds of beaver pelts for one year's work.

Their birchbark canoes were similar to the Indian style. The one-fourth inch thick bark was sewn with spruce fibres, then made water tight by pouring hot pitch over the seams. The bark was then stretched over a thin frame of cedar reinforced with cross bars. The ends were an upturned gondola-shape to deflect the icy sprays of rapids. Many were gaily painted and decorated with drawings and colorful designs. Each canoe was forty feet long and five feet wide; and it carried ten to fourteen men with five tons of trade goods and support equipment. Their main food was Indian corn that had been boiled, mashed, and dried. Each man was allowed one quart per day and one pound of fat for the voyage. They only had room to carry twenty to twenty-five days rations each way, so they had to move quickly. On average, they traveled forty miles per day, and they often covered two-thousand miles on a round trip.

They were famous for their singing—dipping their paddles to the rhythm of their songs to make the hours fly by. They could paddle forty to sixty strokes per minute yet barely

A French voyageur of the 1700's.

Courtesy of Mackinac Island State Park Commission

disturb the water. Since they often traveled in brigades of twenty to fifty canoes, the sound of six-hundred men singing as they moved across the water must have been astounding. As they neared port, they sometimes decorated the canoes with ribbons and feathers. Speeding toward land with rapidly moving paddles, they loved to show off for the crowd lining the shore. H. H. Bancroft described it as an amazing spectacle to...

> *"...Stand upon the bank and witness the arrival of a brigade of light canoes, dashing up with arrow-swiftness to the very edge of the little wharf; then, like a Mexican with his mustang, coming to a sudden stop, accomplished as if by miracle by backing water simultaneously, each with his utmost strength then rolling their paddles all together on the gunwale, shake from their bright vermillion blades a shower of spray, from which the rowers lightly emerge as from a cloud."*

When Governor Frontenac arrived in 1672, he granted Robert Cavelier, Sieur de la Salle, a fur monopoly. LaSalle was a former Jesuit student, who later mastered eight Indian languages. His monopoly was for the trade from the ports of Lachine and Montreal on the St. Lawrence. He also went on several exploratory expeditions in the wilderness. On one trip, he traveled through the straits of Michilimackinac, south into Lake Michigan to the Illinois River. On another, in 1681, he explored the Mississippi to the Gulf of Mexico—and claimed for France the region from Quebec to the Gulf.

He and Governor Frontenac shared the vision of a chain of fur trading posts throughout the Great Lakes with forts to provide policing support. In their plans, they saw Quebec as the gateway, and posts at Montreal, Lake Ontario, Sault Ste Marie, St. Ignace, Detroit, southern Lake Michigan, and at St. Louis as the complete circle for total control of the trade. They wanted to expand fur shipments beyond canoe capabilities, and use ships for transport. LaSalle built a small ship named the *Griffin* in 1679, but it sank on its first voyage after leaving Green Bay loaded with furs. The loss was a heavy blow to their plans, but they soon recovered. For a while it seemed they would beat out the British competition as they slowly built their group of northern trading centers.

Fort de Buade

The Mission of St. Ignace had been on the southern point of the upper peninsula for thirteen years before the first French troops were permanently stationed there. Seven years later (around 1690), they built Fort de Buade. Its purpose was to control the fur trade in the straits by having regular troops monitor trade and trapping licenses. The fort would protect French interests from the encroaching British, as well as provide a center for meeting with Indian allies and building relations among them. In 1683, the Jesuits had a run-in with the French military at the fort. The missionaries tried to stop the officers and soldiers from trading brandy to the Indians. They failed to make headway locally, so they sued the military in the French courts. Through this suit the missionaries succeeded in getting the brandy traffic suppressed to some degree. But their action made them many enemies among both the French and the Indians in the area. In 1694, Antoine de la Mothe-Cadillac was sent by Governor Frontenac to take charge of Fort de Buade with a garrison of two-hundred men. Ignoring the priests, he quickly got permission from the king to once again increase liquor sales to the Indians.

Six years later, a combination of continued British encroachment and a slight depression in the French fur market caused King Louis XIV to order the post abandoned and all trade halted. He revoked all local trading licenses and told the Indians to take their furs to other authorized posts. The soldiers and trading facilities were moved to Fort Pontchartrain, now known as Detroit. The French felt that this location would provide a better base for blocking British access to the Great Lakes. Many coureurs and Indians refused to follow the French. They remained in the area and continued to trap and trade illegally. The Jesuits abandoned the mission in 1706, burning the chapel to protect it from desecration by hostile Indians.

The boom and bust cycles of the fur industry had a tremendous effect on the lifestyle of the Indians in the Northwest. The fur market languished from the 1640's to 1660's, because of repeated Iroquois attacks against the tribes allied with the French. It fell again in the years between 1698 and 1715, as the result of trade controls put in place by Louis XIV. The Indians had changed their traditional way of life. They now spent much more time hunting for furs so they could obtain knives, traps, kettles, beads, cloth, blankets, whiskey, and guns. In time, it became the basis for their economic life—just as the French and English economies came to depend upon it. When the fur trade dwindled, many Indians almost starved. They had quickly forgotten their traditional skills, and now relied on tools and trade from the Europeans for their survival.

After Louis XIV died in 1715, the government in Quebec once again allowed independent coureurs to be licensed, and lifted the trade controls on furs. By then, the French were back at Michilimackinac—this time on the other side of the straits.

War
At The Straits

Fort Michilimackinac

With the closing of Fort de Buade, British traders began arriving in St. Ignace even before the caravan of military canoes had disappeared into southern Lake Huron. They were welcomed by those who remained in the Michilimackinac region, men who appreciated the convenience of having trade merchandise available nearby. However, the trappers and traders found themselves harassed by the Fox Indians, fierce enemies of the French, who grew bolder without the protective presence of military troops. In a series of devastating raids, they soon closed several important trade routes.

King Louis XIV eventually realized his error, and ordered troops back to the straits to regain control of the area. By 1712, a handful of French soldiers were camped across from St. Ignace on the northern tip of the lower peninsula. They quickly recruited Huron and Ottawa warriors to help drive the Fox Indians from the region. Their military presence reinforced their country's domination of the territory, yet the small force could do little more than pose a threat to illegal trappers and Indian aggression. They primarily concentrated their efforts on driving British traders from the region.

Twenty additional troops arrived to strengthen the guard in 1715, and they swiftly began the construction of Fort Ste. Phillipe de Michilimackinac on the sight of their original camp. They enclosed two acres of sandy ground with an eight-

Rowhouse at Fort Michilimackinac.

een foot stockade of sharply pointed cedar logs. Sentry boxes armed with cannon were placed above the pickets in each corner of the compound, as well as over the two gates. The northern gate offered easy and protected access for unloading canoe cargoes. It was located along the lakeshore, and on windy days the waves would fly against it. The land gate shielded the southern entrance and was primarily used by trappers and Indians living around the fort.

Long, low buildings were constructed inside the compound with each divided into five units separated by thick wooden walls. These rowhouses were to be residences for soldiers, traders, and their families. When the stronghold was secure, some men sent for their wives and children in Quebec or Montreal. Others took Indian wives and started new families on the frontier. Dwelling in the northern wilderness could be a dramatic change to anyone accustomed to living in a more refined culture. There were no shops, schools, doctors, theatres, museums, and a limited number of people to socialize with. Every bolt of cloth, needle, pin, cup, chair, table, bed, and toy had to be transported great distances over lakes, rivers, streams, and portages. If something broke it might take six months or a year to replace it. Many wives tried to enhance the appearance of the rough quarters by adding special adornments—a beautifully crocheted quilt, hand-painted china plates, an ornate silver tea set—which provided a touch of elegance to remind them of a more refined world thousands of miles away. As trade expanded, a steady stream of goods helped to improve their standard of living by offering more of the comforts of home.

The women spent their days caring for the home, raising children, and performing hundreds of tasks from spinning and crocheting to gardening. Some trader's wives would travel with their husbands when they wintered among the Indians. The men performed their work, whether it was for the military or the fur trade. In their spare time they drank, played cards, whittled, fished, and hunted. Their social life included dinners, holiday celebrations, weddings, funerals, and visits back and forth to the surrounding Indian camps. Since the garrison was always a small one (in 1749 there were still only twenty enlisted men and a few officers), the little group had to make a diligent effort to maintain cordial relations among themselves. It was the commanding officer's responsibility to make sure that any dissension or discord between residents was stamped out at once.

The soldiers were paid in powder and bullets—there wasn't much cash in the wilderness. They could either offer these directly to a trader and receive credit for other purchases; or bargain independently with private trappers and Indians for fur pelts, the legal tender of the day. The fort was such an ideal center for commerce that by 1722, there were as many traders living there as there were soldiers. Each man who traded was an entrepreneurial frontiersmen who risked hauling his merchandise through wild and dangerous regions for a chance of incredible profit. He had to be a shrewd judge of his customers needs, for there was no room for surplus stock.

He also had to be sure that his goods would appeal to Indians, soldiers, officers, coureurs, and trappers, as well as both men and women. He had to learn Indian languages, and convince everyone that he was honest in his dealings. Many wintered among the tribal villages, deep in the back country. They gave up any comfort and security the fort might offer for a chance to make year-round sales, and to get first crack at the pelts as they came in. All transactions were done on credit. In the fall, men obtained their traps, ammunition, food, and clothes. Each man's purchases were charged and recorded in pictograph symbols that everyone could read. In the spring, each man paid his account with pelts, and was given credit toward future purchases for the excess furs turned in. After the trading season slowed, the traders traveled east with their cargoes and bought supplies for the coming year. Every trip was a risk. They could lose a load because of a canoe overturning, a sudden thunderstorm, Indian attacks, or theft. However, the abundant profits made the risks worthwhile.

War At The Straits

Over the next forty years competition between the French and British continued to grow with occasional clashes among rival woodsmen. When war seemed inevitable, the French took steps to secure Indian support. In 1753, Commandant Louis Beaujeau hosted a gathering of twelve-hundred chiefs and warriors from sixteen tribes. He managed to form a desperately needed alliance which would help to resist the British threat. Warriors from the Michilimackinac area fought in many battles with the French during the French-Indian War. In 1755, they helped defeat General Braddock in Pennsylvania; in 1756, a group led by Charles Langlade (a half-breed from Michilimackinac) battled the English from New York to Virginia; in 1757, combined French and Indian forces captured Fort William Henry in New York; and from 1759 to 1760, Langlade and his Indian warriors fought bravely in the final battles at Quebec and Montreal. But even in victory there was disaster. Langlade and his band of Indians had brought English captives from Fort William Henry to Michilimackinac. Some of the

Soldiers march out of Fort Michilimackinac—note the Indian teepees in background (a re-enactment).

Courtesy of Mackinac Island State Park Commission

British were infected with smallpox, and soon hundreds of men, women, and children in the fort and surrounding Indian villages died from the epidemic.

The final blow of the war was the fall of Montreal in 1760. The French surrendered, and all of Canada was given to Great Britain. The hard-won territory reached much farther south than it does today—including present day Michigan, Wisconsin, Ohio, Indiana, and Illinois. Commandant Beaujeu immediately evacuated his garrison at Fort Michilimackinac and they fled to Louisiana, the last stronghold for the French in North America. Charles Langlade was left in charge of the fort, which he subsequently turned over to the British three years later.

The English thought the French retreat signaled the end of hostilities, but they made a serious mistake by not making peace with the Indians. Disdainfully waving off the important role the tribes played in many battles, they continued to

see the Indians as savage, second-class citizens. They despised
the French habit of fraternizing and inter-marrying among the
tribes. The Indians recognized this aversion, and were determined that the French surrender hadn't ended the war. In addition to their long-held loyalty to the French, the arrogant
attitude of the English probably made it inevitable that the
Indians would consider them their enemy.

The first Englishman to arrive at Michilimackinac was
the trader Alexander Henry. On his voyage west in 1761, he
was so unwelcome among the Indians that he tried disguis-
ing himself as a French-Canadian. Soon after he appeared at
the fort the pretense failed, and he spent several days using
his trading merchandise to bargain for his life. Just when the
hostile Indians had decided to confiscate his wares; Captain
Henry Balfour and his British troops arrived to take possession of the fort. The transition was a smooth one and they
quickly brought order to the region. It helped that the English were willing to start with generous terms. The villagers
were informed that the French could continue to retain their
property, and practice their Roman Catholic faith (which was
persecuted in England).

However, the British didn't do enough to appease the
Indians, and their hostility against the new regime continued
to grow. They felt that the British were cheap with their gifts;
their traders cheated them; and that the soldiers kept a
haughty distance from their people. An Ottawa chief by the
name of Pontiac formed an Indian alliance to wipe the British off the face of the continent. He developed a well-organized
plan worthy of any European general, and in a very short time
his followers captured Fort St. Joseph (Niles, Michigan), Fort
Sandusky (Ohio), Fort Miami (Fort Wayne, Indiana), and Fort
Ouiatenon (Lafayette, Indiana). Fort Pitt in Pennsylvania was
held for a short time, and Pontiac himself led a long siege of
Fort Pontchartrain in Detroit that eventually failed. Because
of the great distances between the posts and the slow communications of the period, the English at Michilimackinac
had no way of knowing about the attacks, or that their fort
would be next.

Depiction of the June, 1763 massacre at Fort Michilimackinac.

Courtesy of Mackinac Island State Park Commission

On June 2, 1763, the English were celebrating King George III's birthday. As part of the celebration, Chippewa and Sac Indians played a game of baggitiway. Each player carried a curved four-foot bat that was used to catch or throw a wooden ball. The object of the game was to throw the ball to the post of the other team, which was located on the opposite end of the playing field. In the effort to make goals, any tactics were allowed and vicious fights often broke out among the players. It was a popular inter-tribal competition, and a game could go on for hours or even days. The officers and enlisted men watched the lively contest, wagering on their favorite teams... never realizing that Chief Matchekewis of the Chippewas had a surprise for them. Suddenly the ball was tossed over the wall of the fort. Seemingly caught up in the spirit of the game, the Indian players streamed towards the gate, stopping to grab weapons from under their wive's blankets along the wall. Before the British knew what was happening, the players turned

on them yelling their war cries, and began furiously butcher-
ing every Englishman they could find. The surprised garrison
had no time to resist. Within minutes, sixteen soldiers and
one trader were dead and the rest taken prisoner.

The French-Canadians in the fort did nothing. Although
the English bitterly resented their non-interference, it seems
likely that if they had tried to rescue the English they too
would have been killed. It wasn't their quarrel so they stayed
neutral. Alexander Henry was taken captive after hiding
through the night in Charles Langlade's attic. After some
harrowing experiences he was released into the custody of
Wawatam, his Indian friend. Fortunately, in the previous
year Wawatam had adopted him as a brother. The relationship was recognized among the Indians, and that—as well
as the many gifts he offered—bought Henry his freedom.
The other prisoners weren't as lucky, five more solders were
later killed and eaten. Others were sold or traded among the
Indians who eventually returned the prisoners to the British
in Montreal.

The Indians were thrilled with the success of their attack,
but worried about British retaliation. They soon decided to
move to the more easily defensible position of Michilimackinac Island. They quickly paddled across the straits, and after
making camp determined that they had three-hundred and
fifty warriors available to fight if attacked. After several days
of false alarms, two large trading canoes from Montreal happened to pass the island. The Indians captured them and discovered a large liquor supply. The celebration began, and
Wawatam knew that he couldn't guarantee Alexander Henry's
safety. That night he led him up the high ground of the island
to a small cave. Henry lay down to sleep at once. In his biography he describes what happened the next morning:

> *"On awakening I felt myself incommoded by
> some object upon which I lay; and removing it found
> it to be a bone. This I supposed to be that of a deer,
> or some other animal,...but when daylight visited my
> chamber I discovered with feelings of horror that I was*

*lying on nothing less than a heap of human bones and
skulls which covered all the floor.''*

Henry spent two nights in the vicinity, but on the second
he slumbered under a nearby bush. When Wawatam returned
on the third day he apologetically explained that he had drunk
so much at the celebration that he had passed out and slept
away the time. He was surprised when Henry showed him
the bones (as were the other Indians of the village). None had
ever heard of the Cave of Skulls, but many had opinions about
its history. Some felt that the people had drowned there in
a flood, others believed that they were massacred by a warring tribe. Henry felt it was a receptacle for prisoners who had
been cannibalized, since he noticed that at Michilimackinac
the Indians had carefully deposited the bones of their victims
in a special area after the rituals. Throughout the winter, Alexander Henry stayed under the protection of Wawatam and his
family at their mainland camp. The following summer he
returned to Montreal, and spent many years as a successful
trader in the upper Great Lakes region.

Pontiac's plan could have turned into a sensational victory. Unfortunately its ultimate success relied on French reinforcements. He was sure that once they proved to the French
that the English were still vulnerable—and that the Indians
could take their forts—they would rejoin their native allies
and break the peace. Out of twelve forts in the Midwest, nine
were taken, but none were held for long. The French restraint
caused them to lose their last opportunity to regain the northern territory. The British didn't retaliate against the tribes,
each group had learned valuable lessons about their own vul-
nerabilities on the frontier. Over the next year both sides made
compromises that allowed peace terms to be settled between
them. A year after the Indian attack the British were once again
at Fort Michilimackinac, and by 1765, even Pontiac had made
a treaty with the British. The new fort commandant responded
quickly to previous Indian complaints of swindling traders.
He set fixed exchanges for pelts. You could obtain a large blanket for three beaver skins or four buckskins. For six feet of

Costumed interpreters portray two voyageurs preparing their meal.

Calico cloth, a payment of two beavers or three buckskins was required. One good beaver could buy a pound of gunpowder, but for a silver brooch you only need pay with one raccoon.

War Hero Takes Command

In August of 1766, a war hero on both sides of the Atlantic took command of the fort. Major Robert Rogers was over six feet tall, lean, muscular, energetic, and tough. More comfortable in buckskins than in uniform, he wasn't a typical Crown officer. The American classic *Northwest Passage* is based on Rogers' exploits, and some believe that the character of 'Hawkeye' in *The Last of The Mohicans* was also based on his life. He had been a scout during the war in the upper New York area, and could fight with a bow, scalping knife, or musket with equal ease. His cunning gained him respect on both sides, and with his company of Rangers he waged a successful guerrilla campaign against the French and Indian forces. By 1758, he was promoted to major and put in charge of all the scouts in the British army. He was honored for his brilliant assaults, and his triumphs brought him attention in the colonies and among the English at home. At the end of the war he had settled down to write a book, when he was called back to action during Pontiac's uprising. He and his hastily gathered Rangers fought their way to Fort Pontchartrain (Detroit), where they relieved the besieged troops and broke the Indian assault. In 1765, he was given command of the Great Lakes outposts, and after wintering in Detroit he moved to Michilimackinac.

Rogers was an ambitious but easy-going man with a magnetic personality who always managed to win the admiration and respect of his subordinates. He soon won the approval of the Indians and traders in the area. They appreciated his management style (similar to that of the French): lavishing gifts upon the Indians, allowing his men to do entrepreneurial work on the side, and freeing up trade regulations for traders and trappers in the area. He wasn't perfect. He was an extravagant spender and careless record keeper—which didn't sit well with his superiors. His greatest dream was to discover a northwest passage to the Pacific Ocean. Soon after arriving at Michilimackinac he financed an expedition to search for the route, led by Jonathon Carver. It had great profit potential because the British government had offered a reward of 20,000£ for discovering a water route across North America. The expedition traveled for a year, covered four-thousand miles, and visited twelve nations of Indians—but never found the passage. On his journey Carver notified all the Indians he met that there was to be a great council at the fort the following year. In 1768, thousands of Indians came to Michilimackinac to meet and build relations with the British. At the council, Rogers made peace between the Sioux and Chippewa, and established trade alliances with all of the tribes. At the end of the meetings, he spent a whole day passing out gifts of blankets, ornaments, tobacco, and gunpowder.

He had a far-reaching plan to expand trade in the region by setting up posts in areas closer to the tribal villages. He

Chopping wood was a tiresome chore in the eighteenth century, as this costumed interpreter demonstrates.

firmly believed that installing traders nearer to their villages would inspire the Indians to work harder. The instant access would allow them to quickly cash in their pelts for goods all year long. It was also a way to keep them on the British side, and their pelts in British hands. To Rogers, the procedure needed to ensure the plan's success was to make Michilimackinac into an independent province under his own control. However, it wasn't a good diplomatic move, and his superiors were shocked by his bold grab for power. Meanwhile, Rogers had gone heavily into debt for the expedition, and for the magnificent gifts he lavished on the Indians. He became involved in illegal rum trafficking at the fort for personal profit. The English government sent out an inspector to examine the liquor trade, and the inspector caught Roger's men smuggling rum. The inspector and Rogers had a verbal battle that resulted in the commandant locking the inspector in the guardhouse.

When the inspector was finally freed, he returned to the government filled with irate complaints against Rogers.

Rogers audacious plans for expansion, extravagance with Indian gifts, poor financial record keeping, and illegal rum sales came to the attention of General Thomas Gage, the commander in chief of British forces in America. He sent Ensign Robert Johnston to Michilimackinac to place Rogers under arrest for high treason. Soon after Johnston arrived, winter set in. Rogers was put under house arrest until he could be removed in the spring. But rumours of an Indian plan to free him caused Johnston to put Rogers in irons. In May, still in irons, he was put on a schooner and sent to Montreal. There he was acquitted of treason, but not restored to office.

Although Rogers' actions clearly weren't acceptable to his superiors, he was a typical British officer of his time. Officer's commissions were bought and sold, and all members of the military were poorly paid. Soldiers and officers alike were expected to make their fortunes through plunder, bounty, and initiative at their post. But Rogers had either over-reached, or had too many enemies in the high command. After his trial he went to London, where his creditors put him in debtor's prison. Eventually he was released and granted the retirement pay of major. He returned to America, and when the Revolutionary War broke out, he took the British side. Unfortunately, when he lost a skirmish at White Plains, New York, the Army took away his command. He then turned to the American side, but he wasn't welcomed despite his experience. He returned to England with the defeated British army at the end of the war. He spent another term in debtor's prison, and died a hopeless alcoholic in 1795.

The Fort at Michilimackinac went downhill after Rogers left. The surrounding pickets were damaged by winds and dashing waves. Half the garrison was illiterate and all the men were demoralized. They spent most of their time in Indian dress, and drunkenness was common. The men lost their interest in advancing the fur trade, and occupied themselves with Indian women, gambling, fighting, and drinking.

The American rebellion of 1776 soon threatened the area. The rebels captured Montreal in the same year, but the British soon drove them back. They had to keep the trade routes open—both for the fur profits to finance the war, and for the access to the Indians. As was traditonal among the tribes, they had to pay the Indians to fight on their side—and if the Americans blocked the ships filled with Indian gifts, the British would lose their allies. With the help of the Indians, the British were able to keep the essential fur trade flowing throughout the Revolution. Soldiers from Michilimackinac accompanied canoe caravans into the wilderness and back through the St. Lawrence to Montreal. Yet the British unease over Indian loyalties and concern about their exposure in case of an American attack led them to a bold decision. Move the fort to a more defensible position—the Island of Michilimackinac.

CHAPTER 4

Fort Mackinac

The Fort and The American Revolution

British attention was focused on the eastern colonies throughout the Revolutionary War. The men at Michilimackinac were lucky to receive any supplies, and communication was erratic at best. Their job was to keep the fur trade open and to hold their territory, the English government couldn't promise them much support. In 1778 and 1779, George Rogers Clark and his American troops advanced through the Illinois country to the south. They captured Kaskaskia, Cahokia, and Vincennes from the British. Detroit was next.

Since they didn't receive many official dispatches at the fort, the isolated community thrived on rumors. A trader stopping by one day would tell them: "Clark's taken Detroit and he's on his way here." A few weeks later a trapper might visit with a different tale: "Clark and his men are marching through Wisconsin and they'll turn toward Michilimackinac any day." Worst of all were the stories of Indian unrest. After being on the losing side in the last war, the tribes didn't want to err again. As American troops won more and more battles, individual bands and villages started taking a neutral stand. And without Indian support, there was no way to hold Fort Michilimackinac if attacked.

Major Patrick Sinclair made it to the fort in the fall of 1779, after three years of trying. He had been captured by Americans and deported when he first arrived to take his

post in 1776. He had served in America during the French-
Indian wars, and after the conflict he captained the schooner
Gladwin. That vessel carried supplies to besieged Detroit,
and transported Major Robert Rogers to Michilimackinac.

Sinclair arrived on a crisp fall day when the brightly colored leaves and blue sky furnished an illusion of calm, dis-
guising the threat of war that hung over the post. Major Arent
Schuyler de Peyster was thrilled to see him. He hated his command at the isolated fort, and left as soon as he briefed Sinclair on the situation there. Sinclair was a frank, tough, steady,
instinctive commander, and his intense blue eyes seldom
missed a thing. He was stunned by the poor condition of the
fort, the morale of the men, and its inadequately secure position. The morning after his arrival he walked to the lakeshore
and gazed out over the lake. He watched the breaking waves
and listened to the call of the seagulls in the clear air. When
he glanced across the water he saw a turtle-shaped island in
the distance. He immediately recognized its possibilities as
a natural fortress, but was concerned about its susceptibility
to blockade. He spent the day getting to know the people of
the community, and he talked to each about the island across
the water. The next morning he rowed over, and soon he was
writing to General Haldimand in Quebec:

> "I stopped at Michilimackinac Island for several
> hours in a very fine Bay well covered by the little
> white wood island. The situation is respectable and
> convenient for a Fort."

He went on to point out the strong defensive position the
island could maintain against any attacks. The excellent harbor
would be ideal for sheltering military and trading vessels.
He requested approval to move his forces to the island. A few
weeks later, he forwarded a more detailed plan that included
sketches of the terrain and the proposed fort. He wrote:

> "I employed three days from sun to sun in
> examining the island...on which I found great quan-

*tities of excellent oak, elm, beech, and maple, with
a vein of the largest and finest cedar trees I ever saw...
The soil is exceedingly fine with an abundance of
limestone..."*

Moving The Fort

With winter setting in, he had no hope of hearing from
General Haldimand until the following spring. But the threat
of American attack and the poor morale of his men couldn't
be ignored. He took the initiative and sent work crews to the
island as weather permitted. Over the long winter they cleared
land and chopped trees. When the straits froze, they began to
haul buildings and supplies on sleds. The Church of Ste. Anne
de Michilimackinac was one of the first structures dragged
across the ice. It was raised on a plot in the middle of the village, where Market and Hoban Streets meet today. Sinclair
moved the church first because he wanted the settlers and
traders at his new location; both for commercial purposes and
for the additional manpower they brought for building the fort.
A government house was quickly built near the present site
of Stuart House on Market Street. A broad-faced hill one-
hundred and fifty feet above the harbor was enclosed with a
ten foot stockade of cedar posts. In May, the permission to
transfer the fort to the island arrived from General Haldimand.
Sinclair began immediate negotiations with the Chippewa to
purchase the land. Buildings flew up as the talks continued.
By July 13, 1780, the troops were living in blockhouses in each
corner of the compound. A barracks, storehouse, guardhouse,
officer's quarters, and powder magazine quickly followed. A
lime kiln was built in the nearby woods, and the soldiers
hauled the processed limestone back to the fort to make the
thick, enduring walls that seem to rise naturally to protect
the structure.

Traders, trappers, settlers, soldiers, and Indians traveled
back and forth between the old and new forts every day. They
hauled homes, personal possessions, food caches, and military stores. Not everyone dismantled their entire house for

relocation, but hard-to-replace items such as nails, doors, and windows were never left behind. On the island they built log homes, sealing the cracks with mortar and whitewashing the walls inside and out. They used cedar bark shingles on the roof and enclosed their yards with cedar fences. Every newcomer had to provide twenty pickets of wood for a barrier to be built around the village. Unlike the previous fort, the civilians would live separately from the military. They built a fourteen foot high wooden stockade to protect their homes, and if we measure it by today's sights—it ran from the middle of Marquette Park, across to the Grand Hotel golf course, down French Lane to the lake at Windermere Point, then along the lakeshore to the Visitor's Center and back up into the park. Every man on the island (including visiting traders) was asked to take an oath of allegience to the king. All male residents from sixteen to sixty were also required to enlist in the island's militia.

On May 12, 1781, several Chippewa chiefs made their marks on a deed of title, and for 5,000£ (or about $3 an acre) they relinquished their claim to the island of Mishi-minauk-in-ong. Once everything had been salvaged from the old fort, anything left was destroyed so that the Americans couldn't use it. The British flag came down for the last time and was transferred to the island. The fort that had served France and England for more than sixty-five years was now just a pile of ruined timbers in the blowing sand.

Sinclair had wanted to name the new fort after his superior, but General Haldimand refused the honor. He wrote that it was unwise to change the name of a place that had been used commonly among the people for a long time. He did allow Sinclair to leave his name on the little bay below the fort, although the designation *Haldimand Bay* never became widely used. The official name of the fort remained Michilimackinac, although it was later shortened to *Mackinac*.

The Revolutionary War raged on, but the men at Michilimackinac had no way of knowing that George Rogers Clark couldn't obtain adequate reinforcements to expand his western campaign. The planned attack on Detroit and push to

Michilimackinac never materialized. Long before Sinclair understood this, he had to deal with the more immediate problem of unhappy Indians. Many Chippewa did not agree with the sale of the island. Since their chiefs did not have absolute authority, they didn't see the agreement as final. In additon, other tribes were used to having free access to the island and didn't appreciate the British ordering them around. Sinclair quickly sent to Detroit for cannon which arrived eight days later. When the ship pulled into the harbor she fired a massive artillery salute. The unhappy Indians got the message and never confronted the British about title to the island.

Support for the British varied among the tribes. Some tried to stay neutral while others wavered, changing sides at each show of power. Many others, veterans of the previous war and Pontiac's Conspiracy, were recruited by Charles Langlade and fought for the British. The Crown outfitted the warriors, provided for their families, and re-supplied them when they returned. Some British officials resented the use of Indian mercenaries, and had trouble comprehending Indian expectations. They never understood that distributing blankets, shirts, tobacco, kettles, guns, and knives was not just buying loyalty. It was a way of assuring the Indians that the British were powerful enough to be generous. Such benevolence was costly, and it appears that every fort commander had trouble justifying expenditures for Indian relations. Sinclair was continually accused of extravagance, and was relieved of his command in 1782.

His replacement didn't fare much better. Captain Daniel Robertson held his command for five years, and when the war ended in 1783, he was ordered to cease any unnecessary spending. His definition of necessary was different from his superiors. It was not uncommon for four-thousand Indians to arrive each summer for trading, and they still expected British hospitality. Rather than anger such a large group, Robertson continued to distribute gifts. He was a practical and reasonable man who handled the fort under a barrage of criticism during a very difficult period. Today his name is tied to many romantic legends. Over the years "Robertson" was corrupted to

Fort Mackinac today.

Courtesy of Thomas M. Piljac

"Robinson" and varying tales refer to *Robinson's Folly,* a spot on the east bluff of the island. The British still held the fort when Robertson left in 1787, four years after the end of the hostilities.

The War Ends

British officials were shocked and dismayed to learn that their government had relinquished the straits in the Treaty of Paris. The Mackinac fur business comprised three-fourths of all the trade in the Mississippi Valley—and there was always the possibility that the new American government would fail. General Haldimand devised a strategy that helped them to keep their hold on the area for thirteen more years. Each time the young United States government sent an official to receive the forts, the British reply was that they were "awaiting official orders from the king." Later they would cite any supposed

U. S. violation of the pact as justification for their own. Finally, a commerce treaty negotiated by John Jay set a final withdrawal date of June 1, 1796.

Three months later, one-hundred and ten American troops arrived under Major Henry Burbeck. The first American forces at Michilimackinac were carefully designed to sufficiently impress the British and Indians as to U. S. capability in holding their lands. The first detachment included four officers, one company of Artillery and Engineers, and one company of Infantry. Major Burbeck set a guard of nine privates and one non-commissioned officer. All guards were to remain outside except for rain and snow, and watch for intruders and fire. They were always to have their muskets ready, and could not allow any civilian into the fort without the approval of the officer of the day. When not guarding, the soldiers drilled, took target practice, and kept their equipment and grounds in shape.

Because they had already been battling with France for three years, the British didn't want to start another American war. Over the following month they slowly withdrew to nearby St. Joseph's Island and built a small post. As part of their strategy to maintain their lock on the valuable commerce of furs, they encouraged the Indians to continue resisting any American attempts to gain supremacy in the region.

Americans At Mackinac

Americans Gain Control

Most Americans believed that the Indians who fought against them were little more than hired mercenaries. When the British-American treaty was signed in 1783, they were expected to either leave the United States—or settle down peacefully under the new government. But Indian participation in the war was for more than personal gain. They had a genuine grievance, which grew even larger in the years after the hostilities ended. More and more American settlers were encroaching on their lands.

They continued fighting a guerilla war, and (as was their custom) they didn't differentiate between killing soldiers and civilians. They raided villages, burned homesteads, and murdered many of the inhabitants. A trapper in a dark, deep forest worked under a constant threat of a sudden tomahawk blow to his scalp. A trader paddling along an isolated river risked capture, torture, and painful death. The American Army was hard-pressed to bring the problem under control until 1794, when General Anthony Wayne broke the back of the Indian resistance at the bloody battle of Fallen Timbers in northwestern Ohio. The confederacy of tribes finally announced their willingness to make peace, and the following summer they gathered at Fort Greenville (Ohio) to negotiate a treaty. The agreement set boundaries for U.S. and Indian lands, with the straits and Mackinac Island acknowledged as

An early 20th century view of the town and harbor from the fort. Note steamships lined up at the docks.

Courtesy of Mackinac Island State Park Commission

American territory. Chief Matchekewis (who led the 1763 attack on the British at Fort Michilimackinac) added Bois Blanc Island to the American lands as his personal gift to the United States Government. In return for signing the treaty, the Indians received a lump sum of $20,000 with a promise of $8,000 a year in future payments.

After the British departed from Mackinac Island in 1796, they tried to maintain their control of the fur trade by luring business to their new headquarters on St. Joseph Island. They had an edge on the American competition because the sales and distribution of most fur pelts on the northern frontier were supervised by British-owned companies. At Mackinac, the Americans were left to try and unravel years of British influence and develop their own commercial network. Their only real advantage was location, the island was both the ideal and traditional place to transact business in furs.

In one plan, the U. S. tried to squeeze out private traders by offering trade goods at government cost. Unfortunately, it was shoddy, second-rate merchandise. Even more damaging was the government's idealistic but doomed policy of refusing to offer liquor for trade. Independent traders with no such scruples simply went into the woods and gave the trappers the opportunity to obtain rum or whiskey for their best pelts. U. S. Government stores were only offered lower quality furs for their inferior wares. The plan was eventually abandoned, and independent traders continued to thrive. Despite the failed policy, the government made a great deal of money through its control of the island. In 1804, the U. S. Customs House brought in $60,000 in government revenues.

Fort Mackinac

The mission of the American troops on Mackinac Island was to protect U. S. interests and assure friends and enemies of their ability to govern the region. Military companies came and went, but life for the individual soldier varied little throughout the years at this military post. We've created a fictional diary of an eighteen-year-old soldier during his first year on the island, to offer an idea of what the men of the garrison faced during their stay.

May 5th

Our company arrived on Mackinac Island today. There's a limestone fort on a high hill above the harbor with a garden and stables below. A small village is near the lakeshore and I heard that plenty of fur men stop here during the summer. I hope I'll like it because I'll be here for the next two years.

After we marched up the ramp and into the compound I was surprised by the way the place looks. Most of the buildings are run down with peeling paint and the gate pickets are leaning in some places. The only buildings that look sturdy and safe are the blockhouses—and

A musket firing demonstration at Fort Mackinac.

that's where the other company is staying. We sleep in the barracks, all forty of us in one big room. Our beds are rough wood platforms with straw mattresses, and I'll be sharing mine with Joe, who reminds me of grandpa. I guess I'll welcome his extra blanket come winter. I feel sorry for Pete. He and his wife and kid all share one bunk in the same room as the rest of us. They put up a cloth curtain around it, but they're not going to have much privacy. None of us will. There's a stove not far from our bunk, and some tables, chairs, and benches scattered along the walls. There's not much to this place, but most of the men didn't have anything better back home.

Later I talked to a fellow from the other company here. He said the food isn't too bad most of the time. Breakfast is usually coffee, bread, and bacon or fish. Lunch is the big meal with meat or fish, soup and vegetables in the summer; and lots of stews in the winter. At supper we have bread and coffee. Then we each get a ration of salt every day, and one-fourth pint of rum, whiskey or brandy. If I want milk, eggs, butter, whiskey, or beer I can buy it from my pay at the commissary.

June 1

Today I had police duty which means I picked up rubbish, swept the buildings, and fixed a few broken shingles. That's a lot better than working the water cart—hauling all those barrels down, filling them up, then getting the heavy load back up the steep hill. Another job I don't mind is chopping trees. Although it's tiresome work I like getting away from the post and out into the woods. We're cutting extra right now because they're going to add on to some of the buildings. I'd rather do that than paint the captain's house, he's out there every day telling them what to do. Joe (my bunkmate) is on farm duty today, feeding the pigs and chickens, milking the cows, brushing the horses, and mucking out the stable. He grumbles whenever he has to do it, says if he wanted to take care of animals he'd have stayed on the farm.

July 2

It was so hot today and all we did was drill. My uniform was soaked and my feet were swollen in my boots, but we kept marching back and forth over and over again. Seems awful pointless to me, but the sergeant says it keeps up our discipline. You'd think they could come up with a better way to do that. Then we tried some bayonet charges and had target practice. It was hard to keep from dropping my musket because my hands were so sweaty. The captain didn't like anything we did, and he did a lot of yelling at parade tonight. I'm sick and tired of cleaning my gun and marching around and having drills and parades all the time. Even worse are all the inspections. Every time I turn around they're checking our weapons, tools, the barracks, or our uniforms. It seems like officers spend all their time finding things wrong with us.

August 10th

We worked hard today sawing planks and cutting shingles. Some men had to fill the carts with stones and move them to the post. There's a lot of fellows who are pretty mad, saying "we're not soldiers, we're slaves." The men cutting the new road back in the woods complain the most. They've been working real hard and then an ax was broken—no one knows how—but now the whole company's got to pay for it. They hold back part of our whiskey rations to get the money.

Men drink a lot here. It seems like someone is always getting into trouble for being drunk, or for something they did when they drank too much. Like the fellow last month who drank a whole bottle of whiskey then told the captain to 'shut up' during an inspection. Most of the time they get whipped in front of all of us at parade. Right now, two men are in the black hole under the guardhouse because they started a big fight at a saloon in town. They just get bread and water and no pay while they're in there. Worst of all, we're all restricted to barracks for two weeks because of it.

September 8th

Me and a few friends took a walk along the island's paths with some pretty village girls today. It was nice and sunny and one of them made it a point to ask me if I'll be at the big dance next week. I hope so. I'll be there if nothing goes wrong and we're all restricted to the barracks. Or if the captain doesn't get too nervous about all the Indians still camped here and mount an extra guard. After we took the girls home we went down to the saloon by the docks. An old voyageur was telling some good stories and I listened to him for hours. He had real interesting tales about Indians and ghosts and spirits in the woods. I started to get spooked but I want to try and write them down sometime.

Fort Mackinac soldiers stand at rest on the parade grounds. A young boy poses next to the third soldier from the left.

Courtesy of Mackinac Island State Park Commission

October 10th

I've been on guard duty. I like doing that because I can watch the boats and people come and go. It's pretty when the weather's nice, especially now with the trees all scarlet, green, and gold. Some men complain about lugging their heavy musket around, it weighs about fourteen pounds. But I don't mind, it's good company. Night guard is very peaceful, I just sit and look at the stars and try and imagine what they are and where they came from. The only bad thing is that I get real hungry, it's a long night when you only have bread and coffee for supper.

Today I watched from the north wall while some women did the laundry. I never paid much attention when ma did it back home, but it's a lot of work. These women have to bring in money, they're married to enlisted men and the army doesn't feed families. So they sweated over big steaming pots in the cold, lifting, stirring, twisting all the blankets, sheets, and uniforms, then laying them on the grass to dry. If I was married I wouldn't have my wife here, it's no place for a woman.

There's a prisoner in the guardhouse who's in real trouble. He's been whipped before for getting drunk, but this time they caught him running away. He stole a canoe and was paddling across the lake when he ran right by the lieutenant who was coming back with a fishing party. They whipped him and put him in irons and when he gets out he'll do two months hard labor. He told one of the guards that he wanted out of here because the Army is nothing like he thought it would be. He's right about that.

November 8th

It can get pretty lonely here now, and I'm worried about what it will be like when winter sets in and the lake freezes. Then there are no more boats until spring and we have to hope that our food can last until the ice melts. We had our first snow last week. Everything was bright and sparkling white against black trees and green pines. I looked at it so long that little red and green dots started jumping around in front of my eyes.

The sutler was hauling up his winter supplies today. I saw crates of tobacco, pipes, knives, razors, whiskey, and beer. I hope he has a good amount of paper and ink. I'm going to go over later and check.

December 12th

Everything is frozen here. We're surrounded by ice and snow as far as you can see. Out on the lake the giant piles look like little blue mountains when the sun hits them a certain way. It's too cold to do anything, but we had to go out yesterday and cut more wood. I thought my fingers would fall off they were so cold, I don't think I'll ever feel warm again. Then we had to drag the wood here, slipping and sliding all over the icy trail. The man next to me had his finger crushed when a log dropped on it.

It's even cold here in the barracks, but we keep the coffee pot going on the stove and drink plenty to stay warm. Some of the men are playing poker—one of them has already lost a month's pay. I played checkers with Joe earlier, but now he's talking politics with the sergeant. Last night we had some singing, Pete's wife has a nice voice. When she sang some of the old ballads a few of the men had tears in their eyes. We all get homesick sometimes.

February 19th

There's been lots of griping about the officers here. They get nice big quarters and we're all cramped together. They get good food and no one holds back their liquor rations over every little offense. It seems like all they do is order us around and write reports. They get invited to all the fancy dinners and dances that the rich people throw in town. We do the hard, dirty work and they get paid more. It's not fair. Some men say I could be an officer because I read and write good, but I wouldn't want all the men to hate me.

The other day a fellow was sentenced to the guard-house for disobeying orders. But I don't think he even heard the lieutenant because the wind was howling so loud. Last week they stripped away our corporal's stripe at parade because they said he stole a blanket. Even if he did it's awful cold here at night and it's hard to blame a man for wanting to be warm. Everyone is edgy and we all drink a lot—to forget, stay warm, and because there isn't much else to do. I took a walk in the woods today and that helped clear my head, but the snow was so deep it wore me out. I think we need spring to get here fast.

March 20th
The hardest thing to get used to in Army life is having no freedom. If I want to go to town, for a walk, or even ice-fishing I have to have a pass. They own me twenty-four hours a day. Worst of all, there's not much to do here when I do get out. I have a few friends in the village but some families think all soldiers are trouble and they keep away from us. There aren't many girls here and most of them are part Indian, the prettiest ones all set their caps for the officers.

It's awful easy to go crazy here. Three men from our company did—they had to be to go running off like that in a blizzard. The captain sent out a search party but they never found them. I think they died in the cold. This is a cruel place to be in the winter.

April 14th
The first boat made it through today and it sure was a welcome sight. People started running to the beach from every direction, shouting and waving as soon as it came around Bois Blanc Island. We marched down as soon as we could and got everything back up here. There's piles of newspapers and letters and fresh food and supplies. We all feel real good, like we're part of the rest of the world again. It was great to hear from everybody back home.

I'm glad winter's over, even if it does mean longer hours of work.

But spring is here now, and Saturday there's a dance in town to celebrate. I'm ready to have a good time. Best of all, I've almost made it through my first year in the Army.

War

When England and France went to war in 1803, they tried to isolate each other economically by attacking neutral American trading ships. Britain was the worst offender. Her Navy set up a blockade off the east coast and seized over five-hundred American vessels in four years. Some American seamen were killed in the attacks and many others were impressed (forced to serve) in the British Navy. At the same time, the British in Canada were inciting the American Indians to revolt. They provided money and military supplies to Tecumseh, a Shawnee chief, who had formed an Indian confederacy against the white man in the early 1800's.

Despite their belligerence, the British were not trying to pull the United States into the war. England was desperately fighting for her national survival against Napoleon's forces, and it was critical for her to stop American trade to the French. In addition, there was a powerful American movement to annex Canada during those years. By forcing our government to deal with an Indian insurrection, they hoped to distract American intentions of expansion.

Today, the reasons for British provocation are understandable when seen through the calm perspective of history. At the time, just twenty-five years after the Revolutionary War, Americans were outraged over British assaults, harassment, and interference with our national sovereignty. President James Madison had hoped to maintain a neutral course through his second term of office. However, within a few months of his inauguration he bowed to internal pressure and signed a declaration of war against the British on June 18, 1812.

Neither country was ready to fight. The British forces were thinly dispersed with only 5,000 troops scattered across all of Canada. There were just 6,700 regulars in the U. S. Army, and the U. S. Navy had only sixteen ships. The American military was poorly organized, and the communications network was so bad that no one notified the American commanders on the western frontier that the war had begun. In Detroit, General Hull (the commander of the Michigan territory) didn't receive the news until early July. The Commander of Fort Mackinac, his subordinate, still hadn't been notified two weeks later. Some believe that the failure in communication was treachery; others say that the Secretary of War transmitted the information by ordinary post. In any case, the British commanders knew about the declaration of war long before their American counterparts.

On St. Joseph Island, British Captain Charles Roberts and his garrison of forty-seven redcoats immediately received orders to capture Fort Mackinac. He quickly assembled a force of French-Canadians and several hundred Indians, and on July 16th, he set sail for Mackinac Island with six-hundred men. In the interim, Lieutenant Porter Hanks, the American Commandant on Mackinac, had heard rumors of hostile Indians gathering on St. Joseph Island. He asked Michael Dousman, a prominent trader, to visit the island and investigate the situation there. Dousman left that night. Fifteen miles out he ran right into the British combatants. They took the bewildered trader prisoner, and he was completely stunned when he was told that the two countries were at war. Still in shock, he revealed that the American forces on the island didn't know that war had been declared.

The English captain was concerned that his Indian allies would harm the Mackinac villagers once the fighting started. When Indian warriors took part in a battle, they often slaughtered everyone in their path. They were not trained in the gentlemanly rules of conduct that British and American soldiers tried to follow, and they didn't always obey when ordered to leave civilians alone. Captain Roberts took Dousman aside and proposed to release him as soon as they landed on Mackinac. In return, Dousman, on his word of honor, must only notify civilians to take cover and tell no one connected with the fort. In a time when a man's word of honor was an important guarantee, Dousman agreed to the arrangement.

The invasion force landed at 3 a.m. on the western side of the island (at the site that is still called British Landing today). Dousman left at once and went door to door warning the residents, who hurried away in the early dawn to the protection of a thick-walled distillery near the base of the west bluff. He kept his promise and did not notify the military of the British presence.

The British advanced toward the heights under cover of darkness, laboriously hauling their two creaking, clanking, six-pound cannon through the tangled brush and up the steep hills. The struggling men groaned, sweated and cursed their way to the top of the island. Their destination was a hill one-half mile behind Fort Mackinac that towered one-hundred feet above it. The fort had been built to protect the island from a southern attack, and its northern side (back) was its weak link. With the guns in a commanding position, and the Indians stationed in the woods on the right and left flanks, the British sent a message to the American commandant demanding that the fort be surrendered.

Lieutenant Hanks was surrounded, outnumbered and outgunned. He had fifty-seven men against six-hundred; a limited water supply inside the fort; and cannon bearing down from above. There was no chance for a victory, and any resistance was likely to incite an Indian massacre. He relinquished the fort, and the American troops were allowed to retreat, unarmed, to Detroit. In Lieutenant Hanks report of the surrender he states:

> *"On the 16th I was informed by the Indian interpreter that he had discovered...that several nations of Indians then at St. Joseph intended to make an immediate attack on Michilimackinac...I immediately called a meeting of the American gentlemen at the time on the island, in which it was thought proper to dispatch a confidential person to St. Joseph, to watch the motions of the Indians.*

Captain Michael Dousman, of the militia, was thought the most suitable for this service. He embarked about sunset, and met the British forces within ten or fifteen miles of the island, by whom he was made prisoner and put on his parole of honor. He was landed on the island at daybreak, with positive directions to give me no intelligence whatever. He was also instructed to take the inhabitants of the village, indiscriminately, to a place on the west side of the island, where their persons and property should be protected by a British guard, but should they go to the fort, they would be subject to a general massacre by the savages, which would be inevitable if the garrison fired a gun.

This information I received from Dr. Day (the post surgeon), who was passing through the village when every person was flying for refuge to the enemy. I immediately, on being informed of the approach of the enemy, placed ammunition, etc., in the block houses, ordered every gun charged, and made every preparation for action. About nine o'clock I could discover that the enemy were in possession of the heights that commanded the fort and one piece of their artillery directed to the most defenseless part of the garrison. The Indians at this time were to be seen in great numbers on the edge of the woods.

At half past eleven o'clock the enemy sent in a flag of truce demanding a surrender of the fort and island to His Britannic Majesty's forces. This, sir, was the first information I had of the declaration of war. I, however, had anticipated it, and was as well prepared to meet such an event as I possibly could have been with the force under my command, amounting to fifty-seven effective men, including officers. Three American gentlemen, who were prisoners, were permitted to accompany the flag. From them I ascertained the strength of the enemy to be nine-hundred to one-thousand strong, consisting of regular troops, Canadians and savages; that they had

*two pieces of artillery, and were provided with lad-
ders and ropes for the purpose of scaling the works
if necessary.*

*After I had obtained this information I consulted
my officers, and also the American gentlemen present, who were very intelligent men; the result of which
was, that it was impossible for the garrison to hold
out against such a superior force. In this opinion I fully
concurred, from the conviction that it was the only
measure that would prevent a general massacre. The
fort and garrison were accordingly surrendered."*

The British gained a great deal from this early hard-hitting
maneuver: a fort in a strategic location; damage to American
morale; renewed respect in the eyes of the Indians; and massive stores of merchandise captured on the island and taken
from ships in the harbor. They had command of the upper
Great Lakes—and now Detroit and lower Michigan lay
exposed. They awarded their Indian allies with prizes of
blankets, guns, tobacco and other goods. Each British soldier
who took part in the invasion received a bonus of 10£. For
keeping his word, Dousman was given a grant of land near the
'British Landing' area. American citizens who wished to
remain on the island were given one month to either leave
or swear allegiance to the British. Dousman was allowed to
remain without taking the oath. Others who refused had to
abandon their homes and property until the end of the war.

President Madison planned to end the conflict quickly
by invading Canada. New England was the most logical base
of attack, but there was a great deal of opposition to the war
in that region. Many States even refused to call up their
militias. To overcome this obstacle, the military devised a
three-pronged attack over the border. In Detroit, General Hull
was ordered to lead his forces into Canada in mid-July. But
his offensive was bogged down by Indian resistance and a fragile supply line. When he heard that Michilimackinac had been
captured he feared that all the Indians from the northern frontier would be coming down on him, so he pulled his forces

back to Detroit. The rest of the planned Canadian invasion failed just as miserably. One month later, British Commander Brock marched into Detroit with a combination of regulars and Tecumseh's Indians. Even though Hull's garrison outnumbered Brock's forces, Hull was so demoralized by the other defeats that he gave up without a fight. The garrison that had surrendered at Fort Mackinac were among the men forced to relinquish the fort at Detroit.

The war raged on. Battles were fought on land and sea throughout the eastern United States and both sides suffered many losses. Then the American Navy managed to trap several British ships at Lake Erie, leaving the British land forces completely cut off from their supply lines. After several failed attempts to escape the American blockade, the British commander decided to fight his way out. On September 10, 1813, he engaged five American vessels under the command of Captain Oliver H. Perry. The American victory came after a ferocious battle, brilliantly directed by Captain Perry. He quickly wrote to General William Henry Harrison on shore: *"We have met the enemy and they are ours."*

Within three weeks, the starving British were in full retreat, and Perry and his men were ferrying troops across the lake to pursue them. The Americans caught up with the fleeing British in southern Ontario on October 5th. A fierce battle was fought at the Thames River (near Chatham), and the U.S. troops virtually annihilated the British and their Indian allies. Tecumseh was killed and six-hundred British troops were captured. The British lost their hold on Detroit, and the Indian Confederacy collapsed with the death of Tecumeseh. The Americans now had a clear path to the upper Great Lakes. General Harrison began to move his forces north, but they had to halt for the approaching winter.

On Mackinac, Captain Bullock (the British Commander) kept his men busy preparing the heights above Fort Mackinac for a new defensive position. Every islander (including civilians) was required to contribute three days labor to the construction effort. Fort George (named for the English king) was a simple dirt and picket fortification surrounded by a reinforced wooden wall. Inside were a two-story blockhouse and a bomb-proof storage building. Unfortunately, it couldn't be a permanent station because it lacked its own water supply. But it was a perfect observation post, and it was completed in July of 1814.

By then Colonel McDouall had arrived with fresh troops and supplies to take command. He immediately set up night watches, and had artillery placed at various points outside of Fort Mackinac. One battery was placed on the east bluff, another located where the Grand Hotel is today, and a third commanded a hill just west of the fort. All faced the beach for extra firepower in repelling any invasion force that might appear.

Not long after British defensive efforts were completed, a fleet of five American schooners appeared on Lake Huron. They began their offensive by attempting to shell Fort Mackinac, but their guns couldn't angle up high enough to hit the ramparts and their shells dropped into the gardens below. They then decided to place artillery on Round Island across from the harbor. A squad of men debarked and selected a spot, but the watching English knew what they were up to and sent over a party of Indians. The Americans had stopped to pick some fresh berries, and when they suddenly saw the approaching warriors they fled. One man was captured, and an officer at the fort sent out a few soldiers to protect the prisoner (since there was a good chance the Indians would kill him when they reached the shore).

Later a fog drifted in and the vessels pulled back, hiding in the impenetrable mist for a week. When it lifted the American ships moved to the west side of the island, anchoring near British Landing. Before the attack began, the ships bombarded the shore with cannon. They then landed with a force of more than seven-hundred men led by Colonel George Croghan. The plan was to quickly overwhelm the enemy forces and take possession of the heights behind Fort Mackinac, forcing a surrender. The invaders moved quickly uphill through the thick woods and rough trails. They reached a large open field (part of the farm the British had given to Michael Dousman), and were immediately driven back by a shattering blaze of artillery from the waiting British and their Indian allies. While the Americans tried to dig in, the defenders blasted away with four booming cannon and a clattering barrage of rifles. Major Andrew Hunter Holmes attempted to lead his battalion in a flanking movement around the enemy positions. He was a gallant Virginian, protege of Thomas Jefferson, a man who's future held great promise until he was killed in the first wave. Colonel Croghan ordered his forces to pull back. The Americans retreated, covering the evacuation of the wounded with intense fire. They clambered through the brush and down the steep hills to the beach. The defenders pursued and the men re-boarded the ships under a hail of bullets. The vessels quickly sailed away and transferred the wounded to schooners waiting off Bois Blanc Island. Fifteen Americans died and fifty were wounded in that short battle.

The next American attempt to regain the island was through the establishment of a naval blockade. Without a British naval presence in the area, the garrison and civilians were unable to re-supply. Two American ships, the *Tigress* and the *Scorpion* blocked key routes to intercept any British vessels attempting to reach Mackinac. Soon food supplies on the island had been reduced to dangerous levels. Bread sold for $1 a loaf and horse meat replaced beef as hunger set in. Faced with certain starvation, the British conceived a daring plan.

Lieutenant Worsley took seventeen sailors of the Royal Navy (who had recently lost their ship to the Americans) and fifty other volunteers through the American lines. On a dark night they quietly rowed up to the *Tigress*, which was guarding the Nautawasaga River route near St. Joseph Island. The British slipped aboard and took possession after a hand-to-hand fight. Still flying the U. S. flag, they used the *Tigress* as a lure and sailed boldly up to the American vessel Scorpion, which had no reason to be alarmed by the *Tigress'* presence. The British quickly swept down, opened fire, then boarded and seized the ship. The American crews were sent back to Mackinac as prisoners. With the capture of their ships, the Americans lost their only hope for retaking the island.

The blockade was broken and Britain regained control of the straits.

Peace

In 1814, Britain had been continuously at war for more than twenty years. When Napoleon's forces collapsed and the French sued for peace, the British took steps to end the American conflict as well. On December 24, 1814, the United States and Great Britain signed the Treaty of Ghent which agreed to end hostilities and return all the land that was captured on both sides. The two nations also set up a commission to determine the exact border between the United States and Canada. Until then they had recognized a general boundary, but many areas (including some islands in northern Lake Huron) were still disputed territory. The war helped the young United States to re-establish her supremacy. In addition, it crushed the Indian resistance in the Great Lakes region. Now, the American government was firmly in control.

The British garrison was notified of the treaty and told to withdraw their forces by July 1, 1815. The unhappy British commandant searched for an island location at the Canadian border so they could continue to compete for control of the fur trade and Indian friendship. He finally selected Drummond Island, forty miles from Mackinac. But he was unable to evacuate his forces by the deadline because of a shortage of boats. When the American troops arrived to take possession of Fort Mackinac, they agreeably camped on the field below the limestone fortress and raised the American flag above the grounds. Soon after, the British removed to Drummond Island and erected a small fort and a trading post. These were considered temporary structures. Plans were drawn for a large military and commercial center, but funding was witheld until the final borders were confirmed.

On Mackinac, continued Indian threats and further disputes with the British kept the garrison on their guard in the years immediately following the war. To ensure that they were never again taken by surprise, the Americans strengthened Fort Holmes (formerly Fort George)—named after the brave

An early twentieth century reconstruction of Fort Holmes, as it may have looked when the American garrison completed their fortifications in 1815. The structure fell into disrepair and was torn down in the 1960's. Today, only the sturdy timber walls remain.

Courtesy of Mackinac Island State Park Commission

officer who died during the 1814 invasion. The finished fort was inpenetrable. It was surrounded by a tangle of trees running up a slope that shielded the main walls from cannon fire and human advance. Inside the main walls was an eight foot ditch—just in case anyone made it that far. All brush and trees were cleared in a large area surrounding the fort, to ensure that any attackers would be easily spotted. The gate was put on the east side, overlooking the bluff so that one had to circle the fort to enter the gate.

The two nations slowly settled into a peaceful era, and by 1817 security concerns had dwindled and Fort Holmes was no longer manned. The thriving fur business was now the most important focus of interest for both the U. S. Government and private citizens on Mackinac Island. The British lost their last hold on the area in 1828, when the joint commission for setting boundaries ruled that Drummond Island was part of the United States. Once again the British had to evacuate their fort and trading post. Their influence on the fur trade was already waning, and with this move they relinquished their sixty-five years of dominance in the Great Lakes.

CHAPTER 6

Important Business Center 1815 to 1875

The American Fur Company

At war's end the American Congress banned British companies from operating in the United States. This left the expanding fur industry wide open for American entrepreneurs, and John Jacob Astor quickly stepped in and filled the gap. He snapped up the American operations of the British Northwest Company and The Mackinac Company at bargain prices. The purchase brought him more than land rights, equipment, buildings, and trading posts. He now had an army of experienced clerks, agents, traders, trappers, boatmen, and interpreters who were eager to please their new employer. Astor's American Fur Company already owned a string of posts along the western frontier, and he used the power of his enlarged organization to ruthlessly squeeze out many independent operators. Soon the American Fur Company had a virtual monopoly on the trade.

Mackinac Island was an ideal location for the company's new headquarters. It was a natural stopover for boatmen delivering pelts to the eastern markets and for voyageurs moving trade goods to the west. The island promptly became an important business center, the equal of Detroit and St. Louis. Demand for furs had never been higher, and with pelts selling at a 900% markup, everyone prospered. The American Fur Company alone was handling three million dollars a year in furs. Shops, saloons, lodging houses, and other businesses

An 1890's view of the fort from the island docks.

Courtesy of Mackinac Island State Park Commission

thrived on the profits generated by the American Fur Company employees, independent woodsmen, and Indians that came to the island during peak summer season—eight thousand in all.

We can envision a young man who arrives one summer day in the 1820's to take a job at the American Fur Company warehouse. His boat slips into a harbor packed with vessels of all shapes and sizes: there are trading schooners, heavy mackinac sailboats, and huge steamships lining the nearby docks. The sun is warm and bright, flashing and sparkling off the blue-green water. A slight wind gently rocks a group of small sailboats, anchored side by side. The nearby piers are heaped with merchandise, and bales of furs are being loaded onto an east bound schooner. Newly arrived boxes of food and crates of furnishings are piled high onto several horse-drawn carts. The land slopes upward from the beach, and on the heights the white buildings and thick stone walls of the fort gleam in the bright blue sky. Soldiers move along the entrance ramp to the post, and two officers on trotting horses head toward a stable on the grounds below. As far as he can see, Indian wigwams covered with brightly colored designs line the beach. Two half-naked Indian men carry a slender birch-bark canoe to one of the larger teepees; squaws bustle around cooking fires, and children dart happily through the camps.

The babble of voices is incredibly confusing, it seems like everyone is laughing, shouting and calling to one another in a different language. Soon a large hooting blast from a nearby ship startles the young man from his reverie. He picks up his satchel and begins walking toward the town. Wooden houses and storage buildings are clustered along the waterfront and across the dusty street. Some are rickety, crumbling, and weather-beaten with sagging roofs and doors, while others are newly built of fresh white pine. After questioning a passing soldier, he turns, walks up a short hill, and soon sees the sign for

the American Fur Company retail store on the corner.
Stepping inside, it takes a minute for his eyes to adjust
to the dark, crowded room. There are shelves and boxes
everywhere loaded with guns, powder, blankets, knives,
axes, tobacco, jewelry, kettles, and hundreds of other
items. A crudely printed sign catches his eye. It lists the
payment rate for pelts:

Mink	$ .25
Lynx	$ 1.37
Beaver	$ 4.00
Black bear	$ 4.50
Silver fox	$10.00

The clerk behind the counter directs him to the
warehouse office. With a friendly nod, he returns to the
street. There are several large homes here, surrounded
by picket fences and pretty gardens. He quickly finds the
three-story warehouse in the middle of the block. A constant flow of men is moving in and out of the doors.
Inside, the air is thick and musty, reeking from the gamey
smell of animal hides. He sees men dividing furs; separating them by size, color, and quality, then tossing them
into piles. Walking toward the back of the building, the
dust and dirt are so thick he is coughing before he arrives
at what is obviously the 'cleaners' work area. He finds
his new boss and presents his letter of employment. "Not
much for a cleaner to learn," he is told, "just gotta beat
'em till the bugs and dirt are gone. Then they bale 'em
a hundred pounds at a time," the man pointed to another
group of men, "and haul 'em up for storage." He could
hear the constant creaking of pulleys lifting the heavy
bundles. "Good thing you came early," he was told.
"There's still room for you in the dormitory out back.
Put your things over there and you can get to work."

When the day ended, the tired, thirsty young man
headed toward the waterfront with the other warehouse
workers. The night was cool and clear, and stars filling

Young men gather at an island pub in the 1800's.

Courtesy of Mackinac Island State Park Commission

the black sky seemed very close and very white. The rubble-filled street was packed with rollicking, boisterous men. Trappers in buckskins and beaver caps, off-duty soldiers, merchants in broadcloth suits, and Indians in flashy costumes all wandered, shoved, shouted and stumbled in and out of houses and saloons. Throbbing drums from the camps on the shore competed with the scraping of fiddles. Men bellowed songs, whooped, laughed, and stomped to the music with heavy thumping feet, and the sounds seemed to pour into the air from every direction. Occasionally he could hear sharp, angry words and scuffles, but most revelers seemed intent on having a good time. He would soon learn that the celebrations lasted all night, every night, until autumn.

Settling in a crowded tavern, he learned from his companions that a lot of clerks planned to make a name for themselves with the company, advancing to handling sales and manning trading posts in the winter. "If you're willing to spend the cold months alone, among Indians who can't make it to Mackinac each year," they told him, "you might get ahead and make some money for yourself." They also filled him in about company management. The big bosses to watch out for were Robert Stuart and Ramsey Crooks. Stuart lived in the tall white house near the warehouse, and was a powerful, tough company agent. Crooks didn't live on the island, but he was there on business frequently and stayed at Stuart's house. Mr. Astor (who owned the company) never came to the island, but his son William was living over at Grand Cottage for the summer.

Everyone knew about John Jacob Astor, and he was one of the reasons the young man had come to the island. He wanted a chance to make a fortune, just like Mr. Astor had done. Astor had been a German immigrant who learned the business from the bottom up, starting as a pelt cleaner. Then he married a rich New York socialite who knew a good fur when she saw one. Astor used her dowry to start his own company, and her valuable judgement in buying the best pelts. Between his American Fur Company and New York real estate holdings, he was one of America's first millionaires.

About ten years after our young man came to Mackinac Island, John Jacob Astor shrewdly decided that the fur trade had peaked. In 1834, he sold The American Fur Company to a group of businessmen that included Ramsey Crooks. Not long after that, the industry fell apart. Years of over-trapping had made it virtually impossible to acquire prime quality pelts. In addition, beaver hats and furs of all types were no longer considered fashionable. By 1842, the American Fur Company had left the island. Astor died six years later, leaving his various businesses and a twenty million dollar fortune in the hands of his son William.

Commercial Fishing

The American Fur Company buildings stood abandoned,

and the remaining papers and records were used for scrap. Island businesses closed, families went hungry, and everyone struggled to make ends meet. Then, a few clever men realized that the speedy steamships could move a new commodity to populated areas very quickly. With the surrounding lakes teeming with trout and whitefish, Mackinac businessmen had a new product to sell. The straits became a huge center for the fishing industry. Fish were caught, then dried, sorted, packed, salted and stored near the island docks. When the steamers arrived, the wooden storage barrels were hoisted onto the ships and hurried to eager markets in Chicago, Detroit, and other midwestern cities. The industry had a short boom period, but never became the driving force in the area that the fur trade had been. Commercial fishing still continues in the straits on a smaller scale today.

People of Mackinac

Because the American Fur Company and Fort Mackinac virtually dominated life on the island, it's easy to forget that there were many residents who had nothing to do with either enterprise. There were independent businessmen, fishermen, traders, and families who lived on the island year-round. In the early 1800's most were descended from French-Indian parents and grew up with the benefits of a dual culture. Almost everyone was multi-lingual; speaking French-Canadian, a little bit of English, and one or more Indian dialects with ease. Of the many interesting and important people who made their home on the island, there were two women of Indian descent whose fascinating life stories have been recorded in some detail.

Elizabeth Mitchell liked nothing better than to play a lively game of whist with her friends. They were the best of Mackinac society, the officers and prosperous traders and their wives. They gathered often to play cards in her elegant Astor (Market) Street home. On a typical evening they bet, gossiped, laughed, and played game after game while the clock ticked away on the mantle and candles flickered shadows on the walls. Firelight danced in the reflection of the highly polished furniture and occasionally caught a glimmer from a ringed hand holding the cards. The tall, dark, merry Elizabeth loved parties. On other evenings she might preside as a sparkling hostess for a dinner, wedding, or formal ball.

Her mother was Chippewa, her father French, and her husband (Dr. David Mitchell) was an officer in the British Army. He resigned his commission shortly after the fort was moved to Mackinac Island, and now operated a prosperous trading business. Elizabeth managed the home and servants, raised twelve children, cared for her beautiful flower gardens, and used her influence among her Indian relatives to make sure they offered her husband their best pelts.

The family was torn apart by the War of 1812. Both husband and wife sympathized with the British, and David joined them on St. Joseph Island shortly before the British invasion of Mackinac. Meanwhile, Elizabeth stayed behind to run their retail store on the island. After the war, she continued to manage the island operations while David relocated to Drummond Island, refusing to live under American rule. They visited back and forth, and she died on Drummond in the winter of 1827. Her body was returned and buried on Mackinac Island the following spring.

Magdalaine La Framboise was a fifteen year old Ottawa maiden when Joseph La Framboise, a member of a prominent French trading family, visited her family's village on the mainland. He soon fell in love with the beautiful, graceful Magdalaine, and a year later their daughter Josette was born. The family traveled together on trading expeditions, wintering in the isolated woodlands among the tribes, and summering on Mackinac Island. They were happy and prosperous until tragedy struck in 1809. At their winter camp, Joseph was killed by an Indian who felt he had been cheated. Magdalaine buried her husband and put aside her grief to care for the children and continue operating the business. When her husband's killer was caught by other Indians of the village, they took him to Magdalaine so she could have her revenge. It wasn't easy, but as a pious Catholic, she felt she must forgive him. The other Indians didn't, and the man led the rest of his life as an outcast.

As a businesswoman she could bargain fluently in many languages, and was respected for her honesty and integrity. She became very wealthy and her children were sent to the finest schools in Montreal. In 1816, her daughter Josette married Fort Commander Captain Benjamin Pierce, brother of future President Franklin Pierce. It was an unforgettable celebration: the women in brilliant silk dresses, high-heeled shoes, and ribbons and flowers in their elaborately styled hair; the men handsome in their uniforms or their best broadcloth suits. Couples danced to the rousing violin music, the room a kaleidescope of whirling bright red, blue, brown and yellow skirts. Her good friend Elizabeth Mitchell declared that it was a triumph of Mackinac society. Magdalaine would treasure the memory of that day for many years.

Josette settled happily into the commanding officer's quarters at the fort. Within a year, she died during childbirth. Magdalaine helped to raise her grandchild in her white two-story home on Huron Street. In 1818, she sold her trading business to the American Fur Company, and devoted her time to helping others. Since the island had been without a resident priest for years, she worked to revitalize the Catholic faith of the islanders by holding prayer meetings and giving catechism lessons. The present Ste. Anne's church and gardens are currently located on lots she donated to the parish. She died in 1846 at the age of sixty-six, and was buried under the altar of Ste. Anne's with her daughter Josette. Her tomb was later moved to the center of the garden next to the church, where it remains today.

Two men who lived on the island in the first half of the nineteenth century became world-famous and were pioneers in their respective fields. Much of their most important work was done on Mackinac Island.

Dr. William Beaumont was Post Surgeon at Fort Mackinac in 1821. On June 6, a young voyageur named Alexis St. Martin was accidentally shot at close range while in the American Fur Company retail store. Beaumont was called at once and removed the balls of shot from his stomach and applied a dressing. He later said that he didn't expect the young man to live through the night. When he returned the next day, he was surprised to find his patient improved. He cleaned the injury again and carried him up to the fort. Although weeks passed and St. Martin's health returned, his wound didn't close (although a flap of flesh eventually grew around it). It soon occured to Beaumont that he could watch the stomach at work through this opening. He began a series of experiments on St. Martin, and broke new ground with his discoveries. He wrote:

> "I can look directly into the cavity of the stomach, observe its motion, and almost see the process of digestion. I can pour in water with a funnel and put in food with a spoon, and draw them out again with a siphon...It would give no pain or cause the least uneasiness to extract a gill of fluid every two or three days, for it frequently flows out spontaneously in considerable quantities; and I might introduce various digestible substances into the stomach and easily examine them during the whole process of digestion..."

Beaumont did a series of fifty-six experiments on St. Martin. By suspending raw and cooked meat on silk strings into his stomach, he discovered how long it took to digest certain foods. By studying the stomach fluid he could examine food left in for varying periods of time to see how it changed during digestion. Among his revelations were:

1. Meat digests more easily than vegetables.
2. Food should be chewed thoroughly for easier digestion.
3. Oily food is difficult to digest.
4. The temperature of the stomach is 100 degrees.

Although Beaumont supported him financially during the research, St. Martin was not always a willing subject. Over the twelve years of experiments St. Martin would disappear periodically. On one occasion he moved to Canada and started a family. Whenever he needed more money he would show up on Beaumont's doorstep and allow the research to continue. After Beaumont concluded his work and published his findings in 1833, St. Martin returned to his family in Canada. Beaumont received many commendations for his studies. He retired from the army in 1839 and moved to St. Louis, where he practiced medicine until he died in 1853.

Henry R. Schoolcraft was a writer, linguist, traveler, explorer, and geologist. Yet he came to the island in 1833 as the Government Agent for Indian Affairs. During his eight year stay, Schoolcraft used much of his spare time to write books and articles that were published in both the United States and Europe. He had an international reputation and received a prize from the National Institute of France. He was quoted by Darwin in *Descent of Man*, and had corresponded with Thomas Jefferson, John Adams, and James Madison. Henry W. Longfellow later based his famous poem *"Song of Hiawatha"* on Schoolcraft's Indian writings.

The Indian Agent's position was a political appointment, and he lost it in an 1841 power struggle. When Robert Stuart was named to replace him, Schoolcraft left the island and traveled through Europe, devoting much of his time to writing. He penned his best known work from the mountain of notes he had accumulated in thirty years of contact with the Indians. It was published in 1851 under the patronage of the U.S. Congress, and called *Ethnological Researches Among the Red Men*. In six large volumes (with over three hundred color engravings) he describes legends, customs, habits, traditions, spiritual beliefs, and ancestries of the Indian people. It is still considered to be one of the best reference works ever done on eighteenth and nineteenth century Indian life. Schoolcraft wrote many other books, and died in Washington D. C. in 1864.

Agent For An Economically Depressed People

Schoolcraft quickly learned that the surrounding tribes had been destroyed economically by the collapse of the fur industry. They would come to his home near the harbor with tales of traders hounding them for debts, and of white settlers encroaching on their lands. Many earned a little money by fishing or supplying wood to the steamships, but those jobs didn't provide a broad enough economic base for all the people. In May of 1836, he set up a conference between the tribal leaders and U.S. Government agents in Washington D.C. After days of discussion, the chiefs agreed to sell more of their lands. They sold about twenty-million acres for two-million dollars and a promise of annual annuities and government assistance for setting up shops, schools, and farms. They were left with a reserve of 227,000 acres of land. A small clause in the treaty also allowed for the construction of a dormitory on the island, to remain open for at least ten years. It would be a lodging house for Indian leaders when they came to the island to collect government payments.

Late in the summer of 1836, four-thousand Indians (143 chiefs and their bands) gathered on the island to collect their first annuity payments. The cluster of wigwams stretched along the lake shore from Robinson's Folly to the west bluff. Indian maidens in beautifully decorated dresses promenaded together, while young warriors competed in rousing games of skill. Old men sat near the fires, exchanging news and talking about the annuities. All hoped they would receive practical items of good quality. They'd been cheated in other treaties, and it was not always easy to keep the young men from the warpath when it happened.

When it was time for the distribution to begin, the carts and wagons entered the camp creaking from their heavy loads. As everyone hurried toward them the chiefs and leaders struggled to bring some order to the crowd. Soon flour, pork, rice, corn, tobacco, traps, kettles, axes, knives, shovels, blankets, coats, shirts, stockings, and bolts of calico had been unloaded, and the chiefs supervised the division of goods. Other bands would receive their shares over the coming weeks. When the final parcels had been divided among the last groups, it was time to leave for the winter camps. This year, everyone paddled away happily. With plenty of food and goods to trade, this winter would not be a desperate one.

Schoolcraft knew that the payments weren't enough to provide a new economic base. He sadly predicted that it seemed the Indians fate to "...fritter away their large domain for temporary and local ends, without making any general and permanent provision for their prosperity."

The Indian dormitory opened in 1838, after various disputes over the $4800 building cost. It was located near the harbor, next to Schoolcraft's house and just east of the fort. A manager was hired to care for the quarters and two of the four rooms on the first floor were set aside for him. Upstairs there were Indian lodgings, while a kitchen and storage area occupied the cellar. Over the years there were many controversies over the use and management of the building. Many felt that it wasn't being properly utilized by visiting Indians. The dormitory was closed in 1846, and stood empty for the next twenty years. In 1867, it became the island's schoolhouse, and remained a school until 1964. Today, the building is a museum, restored to the dormitory era.

Fort Mackinac

The fort continued to operate as a military post, but by the late 1830's the danger of outside attack had diminished. Between 1837 and 1858, there were six years when the fort was emptied of troops who were critically needed in the western United States. For most of that period, one soldier remained behind to care for the fort buildings.

In 1861, the troops were called away from the fort to fight in the Civil War. The fort was used for a short time during the war to house confederate prisoners who were guarded by Michigan Volunteers. A regular Army unit did not return until 1867. Over the next twenty-eight years it remained an active military post.

Growth of Tourism

In June of 1819, the first steamship on the upper Great Lakes, *Walk-in-the-Water* visited Mackinac Island. The people of the island watched excitedly as wisps of smoke appeared

Cattle graze on the public pasture at the turn of the century. This land is the Grand Hotel golf course today.

Courtesy of Mackinac Island State Park Commission

on the distant horizon. As the ship came into view, troops from the fort marched down to greet her. A cannon boomed from the steamer as she pulled into the harbor, and it was answered by artillery from the fort. The waiting soldiers were joined by an excited crowd of residents, visitors and Indians, all jostling for a better view of the brightly painted vessel and its turning paddle wheels.

Steamship traffic soon brought more and more tourists to Mackinac. By 1838, it was a well-established resort, with visitors being turned away due to a lack of sufficient accommodations. One early attraction was the chance to see 'real, live Indians' before they all disappeared onto reservations. Many stores offered *Indian Curiosities* as souvenirs, such as corn husk dolls, woven mats, mocassins, miniature canoes, and baskets of all shapes and sizes. But it was enthusiastic writing about the island's natural beauty that brought it to the widespread attention of Americans and Europeans alike. In 1837, Mrs. Jameson (an English author) wrote:

> *"It is a bijou of an island. A little bit of fairy ground, just such a thing as some of our amateur travelers would like to pocket and run away with (if they could) and set down in the midst of their fish ponds; skull-cave, wigwams, Indians and all."*

In 1846, author William Cullen Bryant wrote:

> *"I spoke in one of my former letters of the manifest fate of Mackinaw, which is to be a watering place. I cannot see how it is to escape this destiny. People already begin to repair to it for health and refreshment from the southern borders of Lake Michigan. Its climate during the summer months is delightful; there is no air more pure and elastic, and the winds of the south and southwest, which are so hot on the prairies, arrive here tempered to a grateful coolness by the waters over which they have swept. The nights are always, in the hottest season, agreeably cool, and the health of the place is proverbial. The world has not many islands so beautiful as Mackinaw..."*

Businesses that catered to the new clientele sprang up in the village. James Doud opened his grocery store at the head of the main dock. In 1845, Dr. Bailey's National Park Drug Store offered gifts, medicine, and general merchandise. In 1875, Wendell's Customs House offered snowshoes, Indian-made baskets, souvenirs, books, and maple sugar. Charles Fenton, a former officer at the fort, had his impressive Indian Bazaar near Bailey's Drug Store. The shop sold corn husk dolls, woven mats, baskets, cigars, candy, and post cards. An opera house upstairs provided additional entertainment for island visitors.

The world was changing, and the people of the island skillfully adapted to the new times. In just one generation they went from complete economic dependence on the fur trade, to making money from visitors who asked for nothing more than a chance to enjoy the healthy and peaceful atmosphere of the island.

Vacation Resort

CHAPTER 7

Western Mecca
of The Rich
1875-1900

Growth As A Tourist Attraction

After the Civil War, a new wealthy class of men and women were eager to enjoy their affluence. Their fortunes were made in supplying the military of both sides, and in the various new industries springing up across the nation. These 'newly rich' no longer converged on the eastern seaboard. Families with huge spendable incomes could now be found all over America as settlements expanded in the west and new cities rose on the frontier. Although it was still desirable to accumulate wealth, it was also a mark of success to have ample time for leisure activities. Their more comfortable existence allowed them to promote the arts and enlighten their lives with music and literature. They didn't hesitate to journey away from home to shop in large cities, visit friends and relatives, tour European capitals, and spend the summer months in a beautiful location.

In the days before air conditioning or electric fans, everyone wanted to escape their surroundings during July and August each year. The cities were oppressively hot and dusty, pollution hung thick and heavy in the air. The continual cycle of family and social obligations had grown tiresome. It was time to pack up and flee to a spot that would restore health and vitality—ideally near a cool, restful lake. But the need to get away didn't include a desire for isolation. They wanted to share their vacation with people who had similar economic and social positions. Easterners regularly flocked to Newport and Nantucket. Although many prominent midwestern families traveled to locations in Michigan and Wisconsin, as yet there was no mecca for the rich in the west.

It was almost inevitable that they would discover Mackinac Island. Its fresh pure air, cool natural springs, peaceful woods, delightful views, and fascinating history made it a perfect destination. Until the 1870's, there had been a modest number of summer visitors, but the island was relatively inaccessible to most travelers. However, once railroad and steamship companies expanded into the straits area it became possible to take a steamer from Detroit to the island in three days. Travelers from Chicago could board a train and arrive in Mackinaw City two days later. Before 1878, they would hire a boat to transport them to the island, but in that year a regularly scheduled ferry service began operations. Word about the wonders of Mackinac began to spread. It was helped along by promotions from railroad and steamship companies who were anxious to increase their passenger traffic. They commissioned brochures, booklets and newspaper articles to publicize the island's charm. Doctors were encouraged to recommend the island to their patients. Dr. R. H. Mills went so far as to say: "No better place can be found for sickly chlorotic girls and puny boys; worn-out men and women, whether suffering from overworked brain or muscle."

Entire families, accompanied by their harried servants and mountains of trunks, would arrive on the island for a stay of several weeks or months. Most lived at one of the island's hotels, and became such regulars that they demanded (and received) the same rooms year after year. Some even left clothing and equipment in their hotel rooms over the winter, never doubting they would be waiting for them the following summer.

Many stayed at the Island House and Mission House Hotels. The rival establishments both opened in 1852 and attracted families who returned each year. The Mission House was a former boarding school, located one block northeast of the Mission Church. The Island House is located across from

The paddle wheeler "Flora" made regular stops at Mackinac Island. Here, she is ice bound off of Cheboygan in March, 1882.

Courtesy of Mackinac Island State Park Commission

A Victorian family visits Mackinac Island in their sailing yacht.
Note steamship in background.

the harbor and is still flourishing today. In town, guests could
enjoy the Lake View Hotel...back then it truly had a view of
the lake because there were no buildings across the street. The
Mackinac House and The Murray Hotel were right in the middle of Main Street. In the 1870's, the former American Fur
Company buildings on Market Street were joined together by
a three-tiered porch and opened as the John Jacob Astor House
Hotel. There were other smaller hotels and lodging houses
scattered about, and some visitors rented private homes. The
going rate in the 1880's was $50 to $100 a year for an unfur-
nished home, and $200 to $300 a year for a furnished one.

   Demand for lodgings often exceeded supply. The time had
come for residents, businessmen, and property owners to consider the course of the island's future. Should the limited private property be developed into more hotels? How would that
affect its unique character? Some strongly desired more tourist

attractions to bring much needed income into the area. Others were worried that Mackinac's unique appeal would be quickly destroyed by over-development.

Mackinac National Park

Conserving resources and preserving land were new and unusual concepts in the late nineteenth century. Nobody worried much about the effects of pollution. Lakes, forests, and vast tracts of land still seemed without limit. Yet in 1872, a group of far-sighted citizens convinced the U.S. Congress to safeguard vast western acreages of mountains, gorges, geysers, hot springs, and forests by declaring Yellowstone to be our nation's first national park. With the same idea in mind, a group of islanders led by Senator Thomas Ferry (who was born on the island) worked to preserve it from unnecessary change. They convinced Congress that its historical significance, natural beauty, and unique atmosphere should be protected for the joy, benefit, and pleasure of the people. In 1875, Congress proclaimed most of Mackinac Island to be our second national park.

It was primarily a paper transaction. The government already owned the land, and the soldiers stationed there were assigned the task of caring for the park. An additional company of troops was sent to the fort to expedite the transformation. At that time there were only 28,565 troops in the U.S. Army, and many were busy fighting Indians on the western plains. Ferry and his supporters must have had powerful connections. However, the move wasn't totally unjustified. The two infantry companies had plenty of work to do. They cleared roads for carriages and smoothed trails for hiking. They moved brush, shoveled snow, and policed the 1,100 acre park. Their mandate to protect the property was often a major task, for the concept of preserving resources was still a new idea. They had constant confrontations with island residents over the destruction of park trees for firewood. They had to be alert for souvenir-happy tourists who didn't think twice about stripping bark from the trees, pulling up wildflowers, or chipping off a piece of Arch Rock or Sugar Loaf as a keepsake of their visit.

Fort Mackinac and the lands immediately surrounding it were not included in the national park. The fort was still an active military post and the soldiers were subject to drills and inspections, as well as being responsible for upkeep of the buildings and grounds. During those years, construction of additional housing for officers, a commissary, storehouse, bakehouse, and a bathhouse at the fort was completed. Since they were not authorized extra-duty pay (overtime), their work on the park had to be accomplished in conjunction with their regular chores.

The fort commander doubled as park superintendent in the early years, and he received many inquiries about the land on the east and west bluffs. Because the park was always short of funds, he hoped to generate income by granting leases so that summer cottages could be built. However, he was caught in a bureaucratic maze. He couldn't lease the lots until they were surveyed, but the government refused to authorize funds for that purpose. The stalemate ended nine years later when Lieutenant Calvin D. Cowles, a surveyor, was assigned to the fort and given the duty of surveying park lands. The national park finally began issuing leases in March of 1885. Lot rent was set at $10, $15, or $25 a year and the lease expired after ten years. Renters had to fight for an additional clause that allowed them to renew their contract at the end of the term. The leases were written to closely regulate all improvements on the lots. To meet the requirements an applicant had to:

1. Provide letters of recommendation showing themselves to be of fine moral character.
2. Agree to a minimum construction cost when building their cottage. In 1886 it was $800, and by 1889 it was $2,000.
3. Submit all building plans to the park superintendent for approval before construction could begin.

The initial results were disappointing. Prospective cottagers were concerned about the restrictions imposed by the park contract. Many who had been especially eager to have summer homes built had already purchased property in the newly developed area of Hubbard's Annex. Between 1885 and 1888, twenty-three leases were signed, but only seven cottages were built. The other sixteen forfeited their rights, which caused the park superintendent to begin demanding two years lot rent in advance for the 1888 leases. In the mean time, the government authorized the sale of lands on nearby Bois Blanc Island to help supplement park funds. The money was needed for general operations, improvements, and the construction of a set of stairs to the east bluff and a twenty foot observation tower at Fort Holmes.

In 1894, the War Department decided to close Fort Mackinac and re-assign the troops. There was an alarmed outcry when word of the ruling reached the island. Although they understood that military troops weren't necessary to maintain a summer resort area, the citizens had a legitimate cause for concern. Until then, the presence of the national park had protected the island from entrepreneurs and developers out to make money off of the tourist trade. [For example: In 1894, J.H. Roberts of Grand Rapids wanted to build an electric railroad along all of the island's streets. That plan was actually approved by the Village Council, but fortunately the park administration turned it down.] Now they learned that the government had already considered plans for selling the lands at public auction. At that time, few federal officials believed that the government should spend money to maintain parks (as yet there was no National Park Service), and they were eager to unload their responsibilities. Recognizing this, a group of residents, businessmen, and property owners joined forces once again, this time under the leadership of Senator James McMillan. They managed to obtain federal approval to have the national park and the forts transferred to the State of Michigan, making Mackinac its first State park. It was the best solution to ensure that the lands and buildings would continue to be protected.

On September 16, 1895, the last company of soldiers lowered the American flag and marched down the ramp from the fort. Behind them lay the ghosts of memories, the echoes of all the men who had served there. Patrick Sinclair, who recognized the superiority of the location and ordered a strong-hold built on the heights above the harbor. The British troops who dragged the furnishings of their old fort across the icy straits. The men who built the first structures and the tower-ing limestone walls. The commanding officers who clung to it for thirteen years after the Revolutionary War. The Ameri-cans who finally gained the post through a treaty, only to lose it in a surprise attack. Others who fought and died to recap-ture it in the War of 1812. The British garrison that repelled the invasion and lived through a hungry blockade. The many commanding officers of both countries who struggled to main-tain relations with the thousands of Indians who came to the island every summer. The enlisted soldiers of both countries who constructed roads and buildings, fulfilled their duties, and spent hundreds of lonely hours on the ramparts. After more than one hundred and ten years as a military post, Fort Mackinac was closed.

Development of Cottage Communities

While the park superintendent was struggling to have the land surveyed, a cottage community sprang up on the south-western heights of the island. The developer was Gurdon S. Hubbard. He had visited the island often during the early nineteenth century, initially as an American Fur Company employee. In 1828, he bought out the company's Illinois interests and eventually became a leading organizer of the new city of Chicago. In 1855, he purchased eighty acres of land on Mackinac Island. Although he built his wealth in many differ-ent industries, a series of financial setbacks and the great Chicago fire of 1871 destroyed his fortune. Among his few remaining assets were his Mackinac Island cottage *The Lilacs*, and his undeveloped land.

To generate desperately needed income, he decided to sell lots to individuals interested in forming a resort community. His plans called for a 'common' area central to all of the homes. An eating house there would serve three meals a day, and the building would also serve as a lodging quarters for guests, and a center for informal gatherings. The 'common' area would also include a stable, tennis courts, and a small park with a bandstand. Hubbard borrowed the money to have the land platted and surveyed, and began advertising lots for Hubbard's Annex. The timing was perfect. The island was swiftly becoming a fashionable vacation destination, and now families could have their own summer residence on the island. The first lots were sold in 1882, and within one year eight cottages had been built in the Annex. Three more were completed before the first cottage was raised on the west bluff. Many of the early dwellings were built by Charles W. Caskey, who had constructed homes in other resort areas and had a fine reputation for doing quality work. Caskey fell in love with the island, and built an Annex cottage for his own family in 1884. In 1887 he secured his name in island history by building the Grand Hotel.

Hubbard died just four years after selling his first lot. With his passing, the communal aspect of the Annex faded away. Remaining lots were sold and developed, but the focus was now strictly on private residences.

In 1885, the first cottages were finally built on national park lots. All three were on the east bluff, and two of them were built by Caskey. In 1886, William Westover owned the first house on the west bluff. Almost all of the early cottages in the Annex and on the bluffs were quite simple, but they didn't stay that way for long in those pre-income tax days. While the orginal designs were often from standard pattern books, the new owners began hiring high-priced architects to design cottages that suited both the land and their needs. Within a few years, almost all of the early cottages were expanded into more elaborate structures. Most cottagers preferred a design that included large windows, porches, and verandas to bring the outdoor beauty into their homes. The selected styles varied—Queen Anne, Victorian, Colonial, Shingle—but all were built of wood because of its availability.

People who could afford to build a summer home on the island were accustomed to pleasant surroundings. They brought their fine furnishings, china, silver, servants, horses, carriages, and the wardrobes of clothes needed to follow the fashion of changing outfits three to six times a day. By the 1890's, the island was the ideal destination for those who liked to dance, socialize, and pleasurably pass the time. There were other resorts for people who didn't appreciate that kind of atmosphere. And because the same families would vacation together each year, close bonds of friendship were formed among the visitors. Everyone took part in as many activities as their age and temperament would allow. There were dances and formal balls at the Grand and Island House Hotels. Some afternoons would pass in a pleasant game of bridge, others at a band concert or on a shopping expedition to the mainland. They invited one another to dinners and afternoon teas, and some cottagers held parties on their private yachts for every-one's enjoyment. Many went on fishing expeditions to the nearby Les Cheneaux Islands. They also took time to appreci-ate Mackinac; walking or riding along wooded paths, picnick-ing on the shore, bicycling or horseback riding with friends. The more athletically inclined would play tennis, and by 1898 they could golf at the newly opened Wawashkamo Golf Links.

Who were the people who built these early cottages? They were a roll call of successful businessmen and com-munity leaders in the Midwest. Among them were Hugh McCurdy, a Michigan probate judge; Francis B. Stockbridge, lumber millionaire and future U.S. Senator from Michigan; Alexander Hannah and David Hogg, who owned an important distillery company in Chicago; William Hughart, President of the Grand Rapids and Indiana Railroad; Delos Blodgett, a prosperous lumberman from Grand Rapids; Dr. L.L. McArthur, a leading Chicago surgeon; Ernst Puttkammer, coal merchant; John, Michael, and Edward Cudahy, Chicago meatpackers; and the Reverend Meade C. Williams, future author of: *Early Mackinac, The Fairy Island* (1897).

While the cottage community helped to establish the island as a vacation resort, the number of summer visitors was still quite small. In 1886, the Island House could accom-

In the early years of the twentieth century this group of women gathered in their finery to have their picture taken on a scenic bluff.

Courtesy of Mackinac Island State Park Commission

modate only 150 guests; the Mission House 200; and J.J. Astor House, 200 as well. Even with private rentals and the twenty-four cottages on the Bluffs and in the Annex, lodgings on the island were still quite limited.

Grand Hotel

Hubbard was never able to build the resort hotel he had dreamed of when he made his plans for the Annex. But the idea had taken shape in the minds of other men who recognized both the benefits to the island and the profit potential. However, an enterprise of this magnitude required powerful financial backing. At just that time, the railroad and steamship companies were concerned about declining profits in timber transportation. They were searching for ways to increase passenger traffic on their lines. Recognizing the benefits of mutual co-operation, officers of the *Michigan Central Railroad*, the *Grand Rapids and Indiana Railroad*, and the *Detroit and Cleveland Steam and Navigation Company* met to discuss the idea. They agreed to listen to a presentation from John Oliver Plank, whose family had been in the hotel business for years.

Plank believed that the island was an ideal location for a resort hotel. He wanted to create an atmosphere of opulence, grandeur, and magnificence to attract the wealthy spenders most likely to travel long distances. His plan was for a long, narrow building of Michigan white pine. It would be four-stories high and fronted by a large porch and stately columns. It would stand on a clearing one-hundred feet above the shore with a commanding view of the straits. The land was owned by Francis B. Stockbridge, who had promoted the idea of a resort hotel and was more than willing to sell. Plank went on to describe his plans for the interior. Regular sleeping rooms, suites with private bathrooms, parlors, salons, reading rooms, and a huge dining area. A cupola on the roof would offer an open viewing area, and on a clear day visitors could see all the way to Cheboygan.

The financiers agreed to the plan, and formed a consortium to finance the construction. Plank invested some of his own money in the project, and was given a short-term lease to operate the hotel in return. The group selected the name *Grand Hotel,* and planned to open as quickly as possible.

Plank hired Charles W. Caskey to build the resort—and Caskey was ready for the challenge. By March of 1887, he had horses hauling wagonloads of supplies across the icy straits. Fifteen carpenters began their work with snow still on the ground, and by April 25th, they were hammering on the second story. The job was completed in less than four months and the hotel opened in July of 1887. To the surprise of his partners, Plank changed the name they had selected. The building's new sign read: *Plank's Grand Hotel.* The hotel would remain open for eight weeks each year, and rooms would cost $3 to $5 per night, meals not included. Despite planted articles in the press about huge crowds at the opening, the first season was slow. As Plank struggled to build a clientele over the next three years, he was constantly battling with his partners over hotel operations. In 1890, they bought out his interests and his name was removed from the building.

The owners hired a new manager, James R. Hayes. His style was to make the hotel a whirlwind of activity, and to create the perception that this was where the action was— where the best people would spend their summer. He brought in casinos, hired a dancing teacher, sponsored nightly hops and elegant balls, encouraged physical activity such as tennis, bicycling, and golf, and imported the best bands for afternoon concerts. He focused his attention on attracting midwestern society, reasoning that visitors with distinguished eastern names would be less likely to abandon Newport and Nantucket for their summer vacation.

He charmed members of the press, and worked hard to make sure that their stories made the hotel sound like it was the center for society's best. Despite his efforts, Hayes failed to make a profit. He was hindered in part by the very following that he wanted to attract. If a socially prominent person left early, so did everyone else. In addition, it wasn't easy for any enterprise to make a profit in a short eight week season. Although Hayes left in 1900, the Grand was finally beginning to establish a fashionable reputation.

Since its opening, members of Chicago's wealthy families—the Swifts, Armours, Cudahys, Palmers, and Fields made the hotel their summer vacation destination. Important Detroit names such as the Whitneys, Algers, and Newburys could be found on the register each season. The Grand Hotel was only one-half the size it is today, yet it became the drawing card for the rich and powerful, and those who dreamed of someday joining their ranks.

An Island Sojourn

Let's envision what it was like to visit the island in the late 1800's. A young woman and her brother are planning to spend a month with their cousins who have rented a home on the island. They travel in style on a luxurious steamer, taking meals in an elegant dining room and relaxing in a wood-paneled salon with rich Persian carpets and cheerful flowers on the tables. During the sunny afternoons they lounge in comfortable chairs on the deck, and pass the time comparing notes about the island with other passengers.

As the ship arrives, the young lady hurries to her stateroom to gather her things. Hearing a knock, she flings the door open, assuming it's the porter to collect her luggage. Instead she discovers a stranger standing there. He props the door open with his foot and immediately starts to pitch his personally guided tour of Mackinac. He promises that she'll see the best views and learn everything of interest, and he won't stop talking long enough for her to refuse. Fortunately her brother arrives with the porter and they chase the man away.

When the two travelers arrive on deck they are stunned by the confusing melee around them. Passengers are struggling to disembark amid porters trying to unload the ship. They are held back by a massive crush of people on the dock: friends waiting to greet new arrivals, islanders waiting for parcels, and outbound passengers waiting to board. The crowd is boxed in by a group of horse-drawn carriages, each driver bellowing the benefits of his island tour. Despite attempts by the ships officers to clear them away, each refuses to move without a paying passenger. The youngsters look toward the end of the ship when they hear a loud snapping hiss, just in time to see a young officer aim a firehose at the carriages. Shouts and curses fly over the flood of water as drivers struggle to keep their horses under control and innocent bystanders are drenched in the shower. But the tactic works and within minutes traffic begins pouring off the docks. The young girl and her brother locate their cousins, and they all hurry away in the family carriage.

The next morning the two visitors set off with their cousins to explore the island's sights. They admire Arch Rock and have their picture taken there; enjoy the magnificent view from Fort Holmes; are awed by the palatial Grand Hotel; then dare each other to enter the Crack in the Island. They return home by a peaceful path across the old battlefield and through the dense woods.

That afternoon, the girl puts on a stylish ruffled gown, complete with ribbons, flounces, and a matching hat. Twirling her parasol, she sets off with her cousin for a short drive to a friend's house on the bluff. They move quickly through cluttered rooms filled with bric-a-brac to a wide, sweeping veranda. Seated on thickly cushioned wicker chairs, they sip lemonade and catch up on news and gossip, while a whirl of activity continues in the house behind them. The cook is busy preparing dinner and grumbling because the ice man is late with his delivery. While the maid polishes the ornately carved tables, the children's nurse tries to keep them under control. A hired man is chasing a meandering cow from the garden, and in the stable a young boy carefully brushes down the horses.

That enjoyable visit was just the beginning of a pleasurable round of activities. They took a ride on the ferry

Algomah one afternoon for a delightful tour around the
island. They bicycled along the wooded paths, pointing
out favorite sights. There were fun-filled afternoon pic-
nics on Round Island, where they admired the newly
built lighthouse. They toured the empty fort and strolled
through the shops in town. One afternoon they spotted
Samuel Clemens striding up the hill to the Grand, on his
way to his lecture at the hotel. On Sunday evenings they
often took a carriage ride, using the newly built gravel
road around the island. The contrasts were delightful: on
one side of the road there was the serenity of lapping
waves, the cry of seagulls, the dim outlines of the other
islands, and distant boats. On the other side was the
towering fort, and rows of houses with beautiful gardens,
trees, and shrubberies lining the walks. They tried to time
the drive to arrive at the southwest shore at sunset. As
slices of the horizon slowly disappeared in the shadows,
the blue expanse of water and sky melted into unforgettable shades of red/pink/blue and gold. The last of the
light quickly disappeared. They were suddenly left with
just the endless water and the barely visible gray line
of the mainland. The night wind picked up, the lapping
lake seemed louder, the twinkling lights of the Round
Island lighthouse came into view. They drove home still
wrapped in the memory of the tranquil scene.

On other evenings they went to parties, concerts,
and dances at different hotels. One afternoon they
watched an exciting baseball game between a group of
island workers and a team of summer guests. Toward the
end of the season they joined almost everyone else on the
island at the Grand Hotel grounds for the Field Day
celebration. It was a fun day with horse and bicycle races,
swimming contests, rowing and climbing events, and
other antics all in the spirit of merry mischief.

The day soon came for their departure and they sadly
boarded the steamer that would take them home. They
remained on deck with many others, determined to keep
the island in sight for as long as possible. As they absorbed

A large crowd on the docks waits to greet the steamer "North West" on her regularly scheduled visit to the island.

Courtesy of Mackinac Island State Park Commission

A view from the docks showing the east end of town in the 1880's. The tall building next to Bailey's was Fenton's Bazaar. At one time there was an opera house in the upper story.

Courtesy of Mackinac Island State Park Commission

their last views of the enchanted fairy island, they vowed to return again and again.

Island Community

In just one generation, the island developed from an important trading center to a fabulous vacation resort. It was still a destination for large numbers of people during the summer, but wealthy families came instead of Indians and fur company men. However, the two groups shared a common goal during their visits—both expected to have a good time. The new visitors: tourists combing shops during a six-hour steamship layover; families visiting for the summer at their favorite hotel; and cottagers who made the island their second home; looked for entertainment that was more varied and refined than their predecessors.

Restaurants, ice cream parlors, photographers, bicycle rentals, and horse- buggy liveries were now scattered among the gift shops and saloons. Bands came to play for afternoon concerts and evening dances, while boatmen offered lake tours and fishing excursions. Descendents of the early French and Indian families continued to supply the workforce, supplemented by mainlanders eager to cash in on the summer bonanza. The transition from one economic base to another was complete as the island entered the twentieth century. But there had been many changes in the world in a very short time. The telephone, electric lighting, running water, radio, phonographs, motion pictures, and motor vehicles were altering society in profound ways. The question remained, could the island retain its unique character amid all the changes?

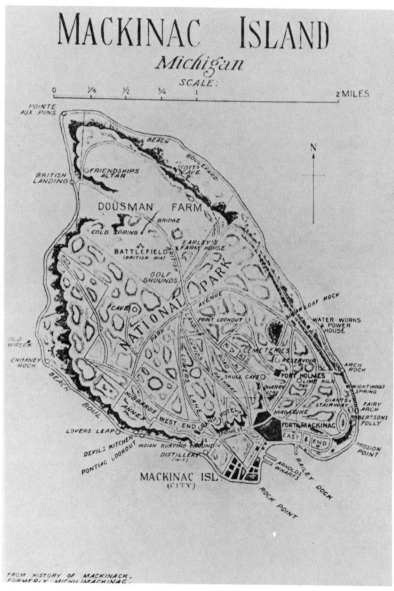

A 1909 map of Mackinac Island. Although several attractions such as Scott's Cave and Giant's Stairway no longer exist, much of the island remains the same.

CHAPTER 8

Transition To Modern Times 1901-1941

Motor Vehicle Ban

If Mackinac had cars traveling through its peaceful woods, trucks rolling along Lake Shore Road, and buses rumbling down Cadotte Avenue; it wouldn't be as appealing to the hundreds of thousands who visit the island annually. The absence of mechanized vehicles (when few of us can imagine being without them) helps to enhance the tranquil atmosphere of the island. It's a charming escape for us to come to a place where there are no exhaust fumes, loud mufflers, honking horns, or traffic jams.

Surprisingly, motor vehicles have been banned from the island since their earliest days. The movement started in 1896, when 'horseless carriages' were just a popular toy among the wealthy. Buggy-for-hire drivers made their living by transporting island visitors from place to place, as well as escorting them on tours around the island. Draymen hauled all of the cargo from the docks to businesses and homes. These horsemen were concerned that the new vehicles would soon make their jobs obsolete. The men banded together and petitioned the Village Council, asking them to refuse to grant licenses for the:

"...Purpose of operating or running...a horseless carriage...(and that they) take such action as may be

A long line of carriages-for-hire stretches down Main Street.

Courtesy of Mackinac Island State Park Commission

necessary to prevent the operating use or running of any vehicle known as a horseless carriage on the streets or roads of this village...''

Their petition was approved, and three years later the State Park Commission adopted its own resolution to prohibit motorized vehicles within the park limits. Since there is very little privately held land, the regulations effectively excluded them from the island.

The buggy-for-hire drivers were always an important force on the island, and these restraints were not the first measure that offered them protection. In the mid 1800's the Village Council began issuing licenses for buggies and drivers, the fee to be paid half in cash, and half by performing maintenance work on the roads. The Village Council helped to drive away non-residents who were coming in and encroaching on business by charging outsiders a huge tax—about double what resident drivers had to pay. They were harrassed by constantly changing regulations over such items as the width of buggy wheels, and threatened with fines and jail terms. By the 1880's, most outside drivers had given up and found other employment.

There were also disagreements between the drivers, the city, and the State Park. In the early 1900's, a dispute occured over the park's ability to levy a tax on the drivers in addition to the one they were already paying to the city. The challenge went all the way to the State Supreme Court, and in a landmark decision the park won. Although the drivers occasionally joined forces to fight such issues, they were not a united group. Most of the time they competed fiercely for their customers, and a troublesome few were dishonest, gave disappointing tours, drove passengers in unsafe carriages, and mistreated their horses. There were no set fees for transportation—everyone negotiated on the spot and took what they could get.

Over the next thirty years city and park officials became very concerned about the negative impression that some drivers were presenting, and their effect on future tourism. They continually urged the men to form an association that would set standards for all drivers to follow. These tough, independent, competitive men were not interested in uniting—believing instead that it was "every man for himself." Finally, in 1932, the State Park Commission forced their hand by refusing to issue any more licenses unless they formed an association. The men grudgingly agreed, and the *Mackinac Island Carriagemen's Association* was formed. The first officers were Alex Gillespie, W.K. Chambers, Carl Cushway, and J.D. Flanagan. Under their guidance, the association set fixed prices for drivers and adopted rules to regulate the conduct of its members. To ensure that the horses were receiving proper care they designed rest and feeding schedules for the members to follow. The organization made an effective start, but the drivers were more united in name than they were in spirit.

In 1948, State Park Commissioner Bill Doyle worked with Arthur Chambers, Alex Gillespie, Harold Cushois, Dunlevy Flanagan, and Orville Steel to organize a more powerful and effective alliance. They developed a plan for safer carriages and equipment, better trained drivers, standard pricing, set up a ticket office to stop street solicitation, and selected the name *Mackinac Island Carriage Tours Inc*. In time the men realized that it was to their mutual advantage to work together. The organization still exists today and operates most of the passenger buggies on the island.

The first fifty years of the twentieth century had passed before the horsemen were able to form a workable alliance. It also took more than the early regulations to keep motor vehicles off of the island. In truth, the laws were so full of loop-holes that a few violated them with impunity. However, most islanders didn't want cars, trucks, or buses and pushed for tighter ordinances. The city and park bans were finally re-written in the 1930's. Under the new rules, the use of motor vehicles would only be allowed if permits were obtained from both the city and the Mackinac Island State Park Commission. E.M. Tellefson tested the rule in 1935 by bringing his Buick to the island. The Governor of Michigan was out for a drive in his carriage one day, and noticed the car parked near Tellefson's home. He made sure that Tellefson was prosecuted, convicted, and fined to set an example for any others tempted to bring their cars to the island.

The laws were meant to keep motor vehicles off the island, but the issuance of permits allowed for exceptions to the rule. In the 1930's, Chrysler was permitted to introduce their car line on the Grand Hotel porch. Over the years occasional permits were issued for construction vehicles, movie filmings, and special events. Today there are emergency motor vehicles here (police, fire, ambulance), and construction and road workers are allowed to operate vehicles in some areas during the spring and fall . In the winter months, the ban is eased considerably and most islanders travel about in their snowmobiles.

The newly renovated Island House Hotel in the early 1900's.

Courtesy of Library of Congress

Transition To Modern Times

From its earliest days as a vacation destination, islanders (residents, businessmen, and summer cottagers) tried to maintain a sensible balance between preserving the island's old-fashioned atmosphere and allowing the addition of modern conveniences. They may have opposed the introduction of motorized vehicles, but they actively sought to have telephones, electricity, and running water provided. Until the early years of the twentieth century, most islanders had to haul their drinking water from springs, and catch rainwater in barrels for bathing and washing. The only exceptions were a few east bluff cottagers who paid to have water piped from the fort spring to their homes. When the municipal water works finally opened, water from Lake Huron was pumped to a reservoir near Fort Holmes, then distributed to residences and businesses with the help of gravity. In that same era an electrical power plant opened, its generators fueled by oil imported from the mainland.

The island lost the services of the Military Hospital and post surgeon when the fort closed in 1895. If anyone was seriously ill or injured, it was a long trip across the straits to the nearest hospital. As tourism increased it seemed only a matter of time before the dangerous lack of medical facilities resulted in an unnecessary fatality. The point was driven home to Dr. L.L. McArthur, a leading Chicago surgeon who came to the island each summer for a well-needed vacation. One day in the early 1900's he had to perform an emergency appendectomy in the John Cudahy home. Frustrated because he had to operate in an unsterile environment without the proper surgical instruments, he launched a drive to have emergency medical facilities made available on the island. The State Park Commission quickly offered the use of the old Post Hospital building, as well as funds to stock it with supplies. Other donations poured in and soon two administrative boards had been formed: one to manage the funds, another to raise additional money for ongoing support of the medical center. The *Beaumont Emergency Operating Room* provided vital care on the island for many years. Because the early board members invested the donations very wisely, interest from the original fund helps to support its replacement. *The Mackinac Island Medical Center* opened in 1953, and it continues to offer both emergency and outpatient care to islanders and visitors each year.

In addition to these improvements in the quality of life, there was a tremendous building boom during the early years of the twentieth century. Homes and cottages rose on the remaining available lots. Many were outstanding examples of architectural brilliance, but none could match the magnificence of Stonecliffe. Michael Cudahy, of the wealthy Chicago meat-packing family, hired the Doud Brothers to build this lavish Tudor mansion in 1904. Surrounded by more than 150 acres on the western heights, it served as a perfect summer retreat for a number of years.

A huge crowd gathered on September 1, 1909 to celebrate the dedication of Marquette Park. Here, the new statue of Father Marquette is unveiled.

Courtesy of Mackinac Island State Park Commission

A mile and a half away from Stonecliffe, the town was expanding to meet demands for more lodging space. The Lake View Hotel enlarged its accommodations, adding two new wings by 1901. The stately Chippewa Hotel was built on the lake shore in 1902, on the sight of the old Wendell's Customs House. A private home on the opposite end of Main Street was remodeled by the Doud family, and opened as the Windermere Hotel in 1904. Former State Park Superintendent Samuel D.

Poole transformed a private home on the lake into the Iroquois Hotel, opening for business in 1907. The Island House Hotel doubled in size by adding a west wing in 1895. In 1912, a dining wing was added to the east side of the structure. The *Mansion on the Hill* (as the Grand Hotel is sometimes called) built a new tier of rooms above its large porch. By the 1920's they had also added a golf course, swimming pool, and installed the latest in automatic sprinkler systems.

While explosive growth was taking place among the businesses, the State Park Commission continued to work to improve visitor attractions. After rejecting numerous requests to build a hotel on the grounds below the fort, they decided to turn it into a park. The last of the old stables were hauled away, and a blockhouse was moved to Fort Holmes. Gravel walkways were designed and laid out, and stone benches set in strategic locations. Weeds and brush were cleared away, and grass, trees, shrubs and flowers were planted in their place. Peter White (a former member of the park commission) led a drive to have a statue of Father Jacques Marquette placed in the new park. More than $2,000 was raised through private donations and the statue was ready for the park's dedication on September 1, 1909. William R. Day, summer resident and U.S. Supreme Court Justice, spoke at the opening ceremonies. He said he hoped that the thousands who came from:

> "...Towered cities and busy marts of trade to find health and recreation on the island shall learn as they look upon this statue new lessons of duty, self-reliance, and that faith in high ideas which characterized every act of Jacques Marquette from early manhood to the grave."

In the 1920's, the State park acquired six-hundred more acres of land, most of it through the purchase of two farms that had been owned by the Early brothers. Those lands included the old battlefield area, and the site of Wawashkamo Golf Links.

Victorian couples view the Marquette Park dedication ceremonies from the fort. Note the carriages lined up below the park—a familiar scene to visitors today.

Courtesy of Mackinac Island State Park Commission

As the island's reputation grew, more people crossed the straits to see if Mackinac really was a fairy isle. There were new vistors staying for a few days; ferry passengers stopping for an hour or two; the wealthy summer cottagers and their servants, family members and friends; and yachtsmen who found the island a pleasurable port of call.

Destination: Mackinac Island

On a hot July day in 1927, a man leaped into the cold transparent waters of the harbor. Around him a group of thrilled, relieved sailors were splashing and shouting. After two days and 333 miles they had finished the exhilarating race from Chicago to Mackinac.

Sailing Lake Michigan was an extraordinary experience because of its unpredictable and constantly changing weather. The crew left Chicago with plenty of fanfare on a bright, breezy day. A few hours later the boat was buffeted by strong winds and he found himself trying to do emergency repairs on the rudder while rocking in the huge waves. Another man sent off one of the homing pigeons with a dispatch, and the bird seemed to toss in the air like a scrap of paper as it tried to flap away. After gulping down dinner, he tried to rest. The lake was calmer now, but he was cold and too tense to sleep.

On the second day there was no breeze at all. The sun beat down on them, swarming lake flies were a constant distraction, and everyone was on edge. He was sure that they were stuck in the only quiet pocket on the lake, while their competitors were rushing towards the finish line. He watched for the sails of other boats and was almost hypnotized by the steady bars of blue, gray, and green water. It wasn't easy to stay alert.

Things picked up for them at Gray's Reef Passage. They spotted racers and even a few cruisers, and you could feel the tense excitement in the air. As they hit the straits everyone was wide awake, and when they sighted Mackinac Island a cheer went up. He carefully moved through the steps they had drilled over and over again and tried to maintain his concentration. Then they shot across the finish line past the flags, crowds, white buildings, and booming guns on the shore. They docked the boat and took the traditional leap.

Since the race commission used a handicap system to balance any differences among the vessels, it would be a while before the winner was announced. They hadn't arrived first, but the first boat wasn't necessarily the winner. There were two top prizes this year: the Mackinac Cup for the winning racer, and the Chicago-Mackinac trophy for the winning cruiser.

He joined a few chums in the search for a place to stay, they desperately needed a bath and a nap. After stopping at all the hotels in town, they tried a lodging house they'd heard about and managed to get rooms. They were too keyed up to rest for long, and soon they joined friends from the other yachting crews. They all headed into town and picked up a few jugs of moonshine. Drinking, singing, and telling tall stories, they strolled up the island streets. One of their group knew about a speakeasy at the Indian Village, and they headed that way. No one worried much about it still being Prohibition, this was a place to have fun, and most everyone made sure that their customers were happy.

They had a good time, there were all kinds of bets and games going everywhere they stopped. He had already lost one bet made in Chicago, gambling that his boat could beat the Amorita's record. The four-sail schooner had made it to the island in just 31 hours and 14½ minutes in 1911. The Amorita didn't win the Mackinac Cup that year due to the handicap system, but it still held the record for the fastest sail to the island. Once again, no one had topped it.

After sleeping away most of the next day, the 'official' parties began that night. They danced to Jazz for hours with some very pretty young ladies, drank, sang, and finished the evening at a private gambling casino where he proceeded to win more than he'd ever made in a year, then lose it back again. He later learned that he wasn't alone. The owner of his yacht had a special membership card to the private casino at the Grand Hotel and he lost a bundle that night.

He awoke early the next day and decided to hike around the island's outer road. As he started out toward town, he could hardly make out the buildings. They shimmered, barely visible in the heavy mist. A long line of horses and buggies stretched along Main Street, waiting for the first ferries to dock. The horses ignored him, patiently munching their breakfast while he strolled by. The sounds of the creaking early drays and the crunch of hooves on gravel soon faded away, and he was left with

Sailing yachts anchor off of Haldimand Bay.

Courtesy of Mackinac Island State Park Commission

just the company of the peaceful lapping waves and seagulls darting in and out. By the time he reached British Landing the sun had burned away the mist, and it looked as if it would be a sparkling, golden day.

He ran into a few acquaintances and decided to join them, turning on the road inland through the heavy trees. After a short walk they found the broad expanse of the 1814 Battlefield and could see the early golfers at Wawashkamo across the way. While laboring up a steep hill a group of gleefully shouting children on bicycles sped past them. A little while later they were passed by a carriage of young ladies enjoying a morning ride. They eventually found Fort Holmes and wandered up the trail. The sweeping panorama around them was peaceful and serene, and they climbed the tower for an even broader view of the straits and surrounding islands. One of their group had been here before, and he promised to take them to Sugar Loaf. After a few wrong turns they found the trail and soon encountered the towering rock. Another group arrived soon after with a photographer, and the young men took turns climbing to its summit and having their photograph taken atop the pinnacle.

They strolled back to town and enjoyed a hearty lunch. The man decided to visit the shops in town, he

Island visitors stroll along the lake shore on the east end of town. Ste. Anne's Church is in the background.

Courtesy of Mackinac Island State Park Commission

wanted to take back souvenirs of this special place to his mother, brother, and fiancee. He strolled into John W. Davis and Sons and discovered it was more a general store, with groceries, dry goods and hardware. He did examine some pieces of fine china, but decided he wanted a less fragile gift. The afternoon was spent going in and out of the stores, which offered high quality linens, the finest cut glass, beautiful figurines, and art works. He finally selected an embroidered balsam-scented pillow for his mother, a toy wooden sailboat for his brother, and an ornate pine box with many delightful hidden compartments for his fiancee.

That evening the crew had dinner together and talked about the trip home. They were leaving in the morning and our voyager was confident he would be back—the island would be an ideal location for his honeymoon. The caravan of yachts sailed away the following day, next year already on their minds.

Scout Guard of Honor

After Fort Mackinac closed as a military post, many island visitors enjoyed touring the grounds and buildings and learning about its history. As an alternative to hiring guides, Roger M. Andrews (vice-chairman of the Mackinac Island State Park Commission), developed a plan to use Michigan boy scouts who had attained Eagle status in their place. They would be taught the history of the island, then serve as escorts throughout the compound. They would also enhance the fort's atmosphere by raising and lowering the flag each day, blowing reveille and taps, and firing the cannon at sunset. The plan was approved, and in 1929, eight scouts were appointed as a Scout Guard of Honor to serve on the island from August 1 to September 2. The scouts would sleep at the fort barracks and be paid $5 a week plus expenses. They would work in four hour shifts, leaving plenty of free time for exploring, bicycling, swimming, and horseback riding. Among that first group of scouts was sixteen-year-old Gerald R. Ford of Grand Rapids, future President of the United States.

The *Scout Guard of Honor* proved to be so successful that it became an annual event. In 1934, the program was opened up to Eagle Scouts across the country, and they began serving in relays throughout the summer months. In that same year they took on the additional job of 'guard duty' for the valuable historical objects now housed in the fort's museum. They also formed a fire patrol, drilling and practicing to protect the wooden buildings in the event of fire. In that same year, a plan for a new scout barracks on the parade grounds behind the fort was approved. CCC workers and scouts worked together to construct the building, but due to a shortage of funds the forty man barracks wasn't completed until 1937.

The Man Of The Grand

In 1919, a young man came to the Grand Hotel as a clerk and went on to become one of the most powerful and influential forces on the island. W. Stewart Woodfill was born in Indiana in 1896. As a child he had seen the Grand on summer trips to northern Michigan, and now that he was finished

The stately Grand Hotel rests high on a hill overlooking the straits. This gracious, six-story resort has been on of the most popular island attractions throughout the twentieth century.

Courtesy of Grand Hotel

with college and military service he was eager to work there. When his job application was accepted, he later said: "My Scot heart was greatly warmed by this arrangement, because I could live at the hotel without paying for the privilege."

He worked long hours as a desk clerk and learned all that he could about the hotel. The next year he was allowed to assist the auditor, Eugene J. LaChance. He impressed his superiors with his keen intelligence and enthusiasm. When J. Logan Ballard, the hotel's owner died, he was named manager. Woodfill soon decided that he wanted to buy the hotel, a very large goal for a young man who was not independently wealthy. In 1925, he put together a partnership with Ballard's younger brother Joseph, Eugene LaChance, and himself. Through some clever maneuvers he managed to obtain the necessary financing, and the three men agreed to an arrangement that had Woodfill managing the hotel's operations, and LaChance and Ballard as silent partners. Woodfill's strategy for success included renovations, improvements, and showmanship. Under his guidance the seasons of 1925 through 1927 were great years for the Grand Hotel. Yet Woodfill was sure that the boom couldn't continue, and the three men were in constant disagreement about that and other issues. In 1927, Woodfill sold out his interests. Since his partners didn't have the cash to pay him, he accepted notes for his stock and became one of the hotel's principal creditors.

Woodfill's decision was timely. Battered from the effects of poor management and the stock market crash of 1929, the Grand Hotel went bankrupt in just a few years. It passed into receivership in 1931 with operating debts of over $100,000. Although the hotel opened in 1932 (the only hope creditors had of recovering their money), the season was a terrible failure and the Grand was put up for auction in March of 1933. There was only one bidder, W. Stewart Woodfill.

His family thought he was crazy to pour his own money back into the hotel. He later said:

> *"They suggested a bucket be secured, a sterling silver bucket if need be to please my expensive tastes,*

*and that my money be put into it and poured down
the sink. This would shorten the ordeal of losing my
money and make it much easier."*

It certainly wasn't easy to turn the hotel into a profitable business in the midst of the Great Depression. Room rates were down to $3 a night, and a pleasant meal could be enjoyed for only $2. Woodfill tried to improve the services at the hotel, but at times he had problems even paying his employees.

Like other astute managers before him, he did what he could to keep the hotel's name in the papers. In one bid for attention he submitted to *"Ripley's Believe It Or Not"* the 'fact' that the Grand Hotel porch was 880 feet long, the longest in the world. Ripley used it in his nationally syndicated features in 1936 without checking or asking for proof. The fallacy wasn't discovered until the hotel was undergoing massive renovations in 1982. When some engineers measured the porch they discovered it was only 628 feet long.

With the help of government support programs the American economy slowly began to improve. The Grand Hotel managed to have reasonably good seasons from 1934 to 1937. Then in 1937, the stockmarket plunged once again and the tourists stopped coming. According to Woodfill:

*"While 1938 was a very poor season at Grand
Hotel, 1939 was truly grim. The night of July 11 can
well be recalled. There were 411 employees on the
payroll but only 11 paying guests!"*

The Great Depression

Naturally the Great Depression had a profound affect on the island. All businessmen suffered from the lack of tourism and some were forced to file bankruptcy. People just weren't vacationing during those desperate years. If two-hundred visitors were on the island in one day it was considered a huge crowd. Still, there were some bright spots. In 1934, they celebrated the 300th anniversary of the island's discovery by Jean Nicolet. There were concerts, parties, balls, and lots of publicity for Mackinac. The Governor and many other dignitaries came to visit, and tourism picked up for a short time. However, the steadiest jobs on the island during the worst years were those in the CCC (the government funded work force). In addition to working on the scout barracks, they built the boardwalk leading out from town along the lake shore. In 1936, they rebuilt Fort Holmes to its original formation, and worked on Fort Holmes Road leading up to the heights.

Homeowners and cottagers were also hurt by the Depression. Many of the original wealthy cottagers had lost their fortunes in the stock market crash, and by the late 1930's their homes had been abandoned and were in disrepair. By this time lot rentals for State Park lands were running $500 to $600 a year. Since the State couldn't afford to keep up all of the buildings, State Park Commissioner Bill Doyle convinced the commission to lower rental rates to $60 per year. They also put the deserted homes up for sale. Buyers came forward and snapped up the homes at bargain prices. They cleaned, repaired, and rebuilt the properties and soon most were back to their original elegant state.

Once again, things were improving on the island. In 1938, the city bought the ramshackle Mackinac House Hotel on Main Street, tore it down and put in a small city park. The visitors started coming again. 1940 was a good year for business, and 1941 was even better. Then came Pearl Harbor.

CHAPTER 9

Contemporary Mackinac 1942-Present

The War Years

When America entered World War II, thousands of men and women went off to fight. Those that stayed home were encouraged to take jobs because workers were desperately needed in many vital industries. The government asked everyone to limit travel, and businessmen were encouraged to delay their conventions. Railroad and shipping lines were busy transporting men and materials. Gas, oil, and tires were rationed along with butter, sugar, meat, and cheese. It was not a time for pleasurable vacations.

Without revenues from tourism, the island businesses would fail. But Woodfill was determined to find a way to keep the Grand Hotel open. When he heard that a few southern hotels were being used as military convalescent centers, he went to Washington to suggest that the Grand be utilized for the same purpose. Realizing that any facility leased by the government would have to remain open year round, he even included a plan for heating and insulating the hotel in his proposal. Although no one could doubt that the beauty of Mackinac would help to revive ailing troops, the island was too remote for any kind of large scale transportation. Eventually a few sailors from the Illinois Naval Hospital were sent to the Grand, but that was all that ever came of the program. In spite of this setback, Woodfill still managed to keep the hotel open.

He cut the staff, trimmed expenses, and turned the main dining room into a cafeteria. Enough guests continued to arrive
each summer to pay expenses during those lean years.

Most island visitors during the war were either wealthy
older couples who stayed at the Grand, or day visitors who
were residents from the surrounding area. *Mays* was the only
fudge shop to open their doors for business each day. They
managed to offer a small supply in the midst of sugar rationing, and they limited sales to one pound per person. A day's
supply was usually sold out in about one hour. Other businesses suffered even more, and many were forced to close until
tourists began to return in larger numbers.

After a few years, Americans needed an escape from the
rationing, blackouts, long hours of work, telegrams from the
war office, and stories of enemy submarines off of American
shores. It's not surprising that some managed to slip away for
a well-needed vacation, and the island was a perfect getaway.
By 1944, tourism was on the upswing and Mackinac's falter-
ing economy began to recover.

Throughout those years Woodfill continued to try various promotional strategies to increase traffic to the island. Like
Jimmy Hayes before him, he charmed members of the press.
Soon, flattering articles about the Grand Hotel and Mackinac
Island began appearing in newspapers and magazines across
the country. When he learned that the island was being considered as a location for a movie, he offered his full co-
operation. The result was the 1946 film *This Time For Keeps*,
starring Esther Williams and Jimmy Durante. Although only
part of the movie was actually filmed there (many scenes that
were supposed to be on the island were actually staged in
Hollywood) it was still great publicity. The film was never
a huge box office sensation, but many people who might never
have heard of the Grand Hotel or Mackinac Island discovered
their appeal through the movie.

Moral Re-Armament

An organization known as Moral Re-Armament came to
the island during the early war years. They acquired Stonecliffe

and purchased the Island House, Mission House, and many private homes to lodge more than three-hundred of their members. This international group was led by Dr. Frank Buchman, and tried to combat the horror of war with the concept that each individual should take responsibility to bring about moral and spiritual improvement to the world. They tried to encourage love, honesty, purity, and unselfishness among themselves and others.

Throughout 1955 and 1956, the group sold off their other properties and constructed many of the buildings that are now Mission Point Resort. By 1960, they had added a modern production studio, sound stage, and theatre to the complex. It was used to make feature length films promoting the Moral Re-Armament philosophy. In 1966, the buildings were turned into Mackinac College, which offered an education based on the principles of Moral Re-Armament. But the college was weighed down by financial problems and management disagreements. It closed in 1970, and was sold to evangelist Rex Humbard. The college was eventually converted to a resort hotel and has had several owners since Humbard. Although the Moral Re-Armament organization is no longer on Mackinac Island, it is still active in Europe and in other parts of the United States.

Mackinac Bridge

An amazing 1,595 foot bridge was completed across New York's East River in in 1883. Soon many people in Michigan began speculating about constructing a similar suspension bridge across the Straits of Mackinac. But it quickly became evident that an identical structure wouldn't work for the straits, which were much wider and subject to heavy winds. The idea continued as a long-held dream, and other plans were discussed over the years. In 1920, the Michigan State Highway Commission designed a series of tunnels and causeways that would allow travelers to cross in short bounds. However that concept was much too expensive to become a reality. In 1928, a thirty-million dollar bridge was proposed, but the high cost and the onset of the Depression killed any consider-

The Mackinac Bridge stretches five miles over the straits to connect Mackinaw City and St. Ignace.

Courtesy of Mackinac Bridge Authority

ation of the idea. Another feasibility study was begun in 1940, but World War II intervened. After the war, Senator Prentiss M. Brown of St. Ignace, and W. Stewart Woodfill of Mackinac Island, worked to convince others that a bridge across the straits would benefit the entire State. It became an important issue in the 1948 gubernatorial campaign, supported by the eventual winner, G. Mennen Williams. In 1950, Governor Williams finally formed the Mackinac Bridge Authority to raise money, select the design, and supervise construction of the bridge.

The board examined submissions from leading bridge designers, and approved a plan presented by David B. Steinman. This sixty-year-old engineer had already designed four-hundred structures around the world. His plan called for one-third of the five mile span to hang suspended by cables from high towers. The design also included an innovative feature that left openings in the grid along the bridge floor. This would make it easier for wind currents to pass through the structure. Winter winds on the straits have been known to exceed 80 mph, so Steinman's unique design was constructed to withstand a 125 mph gale.

The bridge would be financed by a new concept in bond issues. Studies of traffic volume concluded that if crossing motor vehicles would pay a toll, enough income would be generated to repay the bonds. The Mackinac Bridge Authority issued $99.8 million in bonds to finance the construction. They accepted the bids of two companies and both immediately initiated preparations for the giant project.

Merritt-Chapman & Scott received the contract to build the underwater foundation for $25,735,000. Their men worked under the surface in specially built cofferdams that held back the water. Before they were finished they had poured 900,000 tons of concrete; 720,000 tons of which were laid underwater (in some places as much as 200 feet deep). U.S. Steel was awarded the contract to erect the superstructure for $44,532,000. They built the 552 foot high, 6,500 ton cable towers, at a cost of $3,625,000 apiece. The support cables alone are 24½ inches in diameter and contain 42,000 miles of wire.

Back then everything was a gamble. The promise to have the bond repaid was based on estimated traffic. No one really knew if the bridge would withstand the heavy winds. The belief that the foundation would hold was based on the assessments of engineers and geologists. The creation of every tower, cable, wire, and bolt relied on the mathematical accuracy of the designer's drawings. Skeptics were still saying that it was insane to spend millions of dollars on an unproven concept, to connect two rural towns with a combined population of less than three-thousand people.

They broke ground in 1954. Before the bridge was completed three years later, 2,500 men would work on the construction. These men did a truly impressive job. They worked deep under the water or balanced precariously above it. They struggled through wind, rain, ice, heat, and fog. They dealt with changing tides and rough, choppy water. And some of them died while they worked.

Frank Pepper (a diver) was inspecting Pier #19, one-hundred and fifty feet under the water. He rose to the surface too quickly, and died in the decompression chamber. James R. LeSarge was working on Pier #20, the foundation for the north main tower. He fell inside the reinforced steel form and his head struck several steel braces during the fall. He was believed dead before he hit bottom. Albert B. Abbott was walking on an eighteen inch wide beam above the water. He fell and drowned. While working on the superstructure, Mack C. Baker and Robert Koppen were placing a chain link fence to be used by the cable spinners at the top of the north tower. A restraining line broke, and the two fell five-hundred and fifty feet to the water. All of their names are engraved on a bronze plaque on Pier #1 in Mackinaw City.

The bridge opened to traffic November 1, 1957, and was formally dedicated in June of 1958. Its designer, David B. Steinman, read a moving poem at the dedication. Today, it is still an unforgettable site of lofty spans and twin towers that rise delicately yet magnificently above the straits. The bridge is five miles long, the distance between anchorages is 8,614 feet, and there is a 3,800 foot stretch between the two main towers. The road is 199 feet above the water at midspan, and the depth of the water below is 295 feet.

According to Lawrence A. Rubin, former executive secretary of the Mackinac Bridge Authority, if the bridge wouldn't have been built in the 1950's, we probably wouldnt have one today. Inflation and high interest rates would:

> *"...Put a three-hundred million dollar price tag on the bridge, requiring a toll of $30 per car to be self-liquidating."*

Mackinac Island Leaders

There are many people who contributed to the growth and improvement of the island during the twentieth century. Some worked tirelessly for charitable causes, others devoted hours to the work of councils, committees, commissions, and boards. It is impossible to name everyone that deserves recognition for their efforts. The people mentioned here are examples of the strong leadership the island has been fortunate to attract throughout the years. There are many others that have been inspired to devote their time, energy, and resources to the betterment of Mackinac Island.

We've already spoken of **W. Stewart Woodfill** and his importance to the success of the Grand Hotel. He is the man who finally turned it into a profitable and enduring enterprise. He also worked to improve the rest of the island and the straits area, believing that everyone gained from mutual co-operation. His support of the Mackinac Bridge was important to its eventual construction. He served as chairman of the Mackinac Island State Park Commission, and obtained the early funding for the massive renovation project on Fort Mackinac and other historic attractions. In addition, he took time to help the next generation see his vision for preserving and improving the island. His impact reached to every area of the island, the State of Michigan and beyond.

Harry Ryba is an American success story. He sold his Mackinac Island Fudge at fairs, shows, and carnivals before opening his first shop here. When he leased his original store in 1959, the landlord predicted that he would fail because there were three other shops on the island. Instead he used ingenious marketing and promotional techniques—such as making fudge in the window and piping the aroma outside. It didn't take long before crowds were forming outside his store each day. From those simple beginnings he opened additional fudge shops and continued to expand into other areas. He went on to own many important island businesses such as: the Lake View Hotel, the Island House Hotel, Ryba Bicycles, the Dockside Inn, the Pancake House, and part of Star Line Ferries. In addition to creating successful business enterprises, he has been called Mackinac Island's unofficial lobbyist. He has worked hard to protect the island from anything that would harm its unique appeal.

Robert Doud worked toward the betterment of the island in many ways during his lifetime. He served as Mayor of Mackinac Island and was on the City Council for over forty years. He was also a member of the Mackinac Island State Park Commission and served a term as its superintendent. He focused his efforts on improving the island for both residents and visitors. Among his many accomplishments: he was instrumental in having the new school built on Lake Shore Boulevard, and in forming a commission that cleared away many old shacks and landscaped the town properties. His warm, keen intelligence and sage advice gave direction to the island for many years. He died in 1987.

W.F. (Bill) Doyle served on the Mackinac Island State Park Commission for forty-five years, and for many of those years he was commissioner. He was an important force in getting the carriagemen united into the more effective Mackinac Island Carriage Tours; in having lot rents lowered and cottages resold during the Depression; and in keeping motor vehicles off the island. His conservative viewpoint helped to both improve the island and preserve its unique atmosphere.

In 1958, **Dr. Eugene T. Peterson** came to the island as director of historic projects for the Mackinac Island State Park Commission. He brought in archeologists, anthropologists, artists, and authors to develop a solid foundation for the new park expansion and development program. By 1966, he was park superintendent, and under his guidance the huge restoration program on Fort Mackinac was begun, as well as the reconstruction of Fort Michilimackinac, and the archeological development of Old Mill Creek. To encourage visitor understanding of the island, he wrote the text for one of the State Park guidebooks, as well as *Mackinac Island: Its History in Pictures, Mackinac In Restoration,* and several other books about the island. His wife Marian worked with him as the park's business manager, handling budgeting, collecting revenues, completing paperwork for bond issues, and managing the office. Both retired in 1985.

R. Daniel Musser became President of the Grand Hotel in 1962. He joined the organization as a young man in the early 1950's under the direction of his uncle, W. Stewart Woodfill. Woodfill never tolerated failure and told Musser that he would work him twice as hard as his other employees simply because he was his nephew. While Musser worked his way up the organization he and his uncle maintained a formal relationship. Woodfill called him 'Mr. Musser', and Daniel called his uncle 'Boss'. He shares Woodfill's philosophy about mutual co-operation among people and businesses in the region, and he works hard to promote and improve the entire straits area. As head of the Department of Public Works Commission he was an important force behind planning for the badly needed water and sewage systems, as well as obtaining funding for the project.

He continues to maintain the hotel's dignified tradition while keeping it a profitable business enterprise. He and his wife Amelia convinced Woodfill to begin a massive renovation and redecoration of the Grand Hotel in the mid-1970's. Until then, the hotel's interior decor had been quite disappointing, and the building was in disrepair. The transformation made it a tremendously attractive place to stay.

When Musser heard that the hotel was being considered as a backdrop for a motion picture, he dispatched a sales representative to Hollywood to offer his full co-operation. When the site was almost rejected because of lack of available rooms for the cast and crew, Musser offered to lodge them at the Mackinac Hotel (now Mission Point Resort) and provide all of their meals. The deal was clinched when he pointed out that the Mackinac Hotel had a complete sound stage, television studio, and technical facilities that Universal Studios could lease. In 1979, the movie *Somewhere In Time* with Jane Seymour and Christopher Reeve was filmed on Mackinac Island. This romantic film had many scenes filmed at the Grand and in other island settings. It was released in 1980, and has given the hotel and the island incalculable publicity.

Margaret Doud has been mayor of the island for thirteen years, and during her tenure many important improvements have been made on Mackinac. Her tireless efforts have helped the island to gain modern municipal water and sewer plants, as well as increased employment, city revenues, and higher standards for businesses to follow. She also manages the Windermere Hotel, serves on various boards, and helps with many charitable events. Daughter of the late Robert Doud, she is admired as a low-key, effective leader who has done a great deal to build confidence in the island's future.

Mackinac Island State Park

Maintenance and upkeep of buildings on the island is a difficult and ongoing process. The island has many underground springs, a great deal of rain, heavy winter snows, and nearly everything here is built of wood, which is adversely affected by the moist conditions. Then of course every nail, paintbrush, and brick has to be transported to the island by boat, which makes it difficult and expensive to undertake many tasks. For the most part, the Fort Mackinac buildings had been receiving only minor alterations and repairs in the years since it had closed as a military post. The structures were very old and needed massive reconstruction and repair.

The metamorphosis began in 1956. By then the Mackinac Bridge was almost complete, and the straits area expected an influx of tourists. Governor G. Mennen Williams felt that Woodfill had the right vision for the park's future, and would be able to help find the funds to finance the needed improvements. He appointed him chairman of the Mackinac Island State Park Commission. It didn't take long for Woodfill to ignite a new dynamism on the commission—not always winning any popularity contests in the process. But his job was to get things done, and he did. His first step was to focus on transforming Fort Mackinac. At that point, the building foundations had rotted, the interiors were basically empty, and the museum was a tiny room with displays that often had little to do with the fort or Mackinac Island.

His idea was to finance the improvements with revenue bonds. It was the same concept that built the bridge—let future admission fees repay the loans. His critics scoffed at the possibility. They felt that people were much more likely to pay to cross a bridge than to see an historic landmark. They believed that there would be a great deal of resistance from visitors who had previously visited the fort for free. Few people could have managed to raise the money, but Woodfill did. He offered the first fifteen year bond for $50,000. There was only one bidder, a Chicago company that had personal connections with Woodfill. Their transaction was virtually risk-free because Woodfill prepared a formal agreement that personally guaranteed the bond's repayment.

The first steps were to repaint the interiors of the fort buildings and to set up a museum in the old barracks that depicted the history of Mackinac Island. These changes were completed by mid-June of 1958, and the fort began selling admission tickets for the first time. Fees were 50¢ for adults and 25¢ for children. The spruced-up fort proved to be a great attraction, and by the end of the first season they had received $54,119 in revenues. That fall, another $75,000 in bonds were sold and major plans for reconstruction, restoration, and exhibits were made. Those first two bond issues were repaid in less than three years.

It wasn't easy to restore a fort that had been actively used by troops from two different countries for over one-hundred years. They studied sketches, drawings, and photos of the buildings to see how they originally looked and how they were changed. Military records were carefully examined to determine how the buildings were used. They stripped away modern additions and studied the arrangement of fireplaces and wear patterns on the original floor boards. This helped to explain a great deal about the primary uses of each room. The final determination of how to complete the restoration was extremely difficult, because most of the buildings had been built during different time periods and used for different purposes over the years. They began with the three blockhouses, and slowly rebuilt foundations, replaced rotting wood, and reconstructed the buildings. Then by relying on letters and diaries from people who had been at the fort, sketches, military records, and their general knowledge of the era, they furnished the rooms as authentically as possible.

The Mackinac Island State Park had also acquired other historic sites during those years. By 1960, they had obtained Mission Church, the Beaumont Memorial, and Biddle House. A few years later they converted the old Coast Guard building into a visitor's center, and made extensive landscaping changes at Marquette Park across the street. By 1970, the crumbling, rotting timbers that had been a reconstruction of old Fort Holmes had been torn down for safety reasons, and they had bought and begun restoration on the old Indian Dormitory. More recently, they purchased McGulpin House in the 1980's and moved it from behind St. Anne's church to its present location.

From 1958 to 1966, the Mackinac Island State Park Commission issued $1,775,000 in revenue bonds, and all were repaid ahead of schedule. By then, they had also begun reconstruction of old Fort Michilimackinac in Mackinaw City. A few years later the Old Mill Creek historic site was discovered, and its reconstruction fell under the commission's care. Today, all three parks are extremely interesting reflections of both the history of the area and of our country. That history is brought to life by costumed staff interpreters who reenact routines from those eras throughout the parks. The number of visitors to all of the historic sites continues to grow, as more and more people appreciate the history and beauty of these unique attractions.

Contemporary Mackinac

During the 1960's, a new crusade was started to allow motor vehicles on the island. Woodfill, Doyle, and other vocal opponents sought to convince supporters that the change would destroy the island's natural charm. Their arguments were so effective that not only was the proposal defeated, but the existing laws were strengthened. In 1964, the island children had a new school to attend, built at a beautiful location on Lake Shore Boulevard. In that same year a 3,500 foot run-

The Murray Hotel on Main Street was one of the many island businesses that underwent extensive remodeling.

Credit: Thomas M. Piljac

way was paved at the Mackinac Island Airport, and five years later a terminal building was completed.

The park wasn't the only part of the island undergoing changes. Many businessmen and residents had also begun to improve their properties. Woodfill encouraged many of the business owners, insisting that they needed more flair and showmanship in their operations. In one instance, he pushed hard to have the Mackinac Island Carriage Tours' drivers wear uniforms, follow the same route, and standardize their talks about the island. Although the changes were eventually adopted, his interference was deeply resented by many at the time.

But the greatest alterations were needed in many hotel buildings. Some were over one-hundred years old, and even with continual maintenance they sustained damage from moisture and wear. In remodeling their structures the owners had to simultaneously preserve the skilled workmanship of the past, modernize the interior, and retain the old-fashioned appearance of the exterior framework.

Renovation programs began in earnest during the 1970's. Most businesses and nearly every large hotel underwent extensive modifications. The transformation was mandated by a new generation of visitors with drastically different expectations than those of their grandparents. They expect a private bath in their hotel room—something that wasn't an automatic amenity in nineteenth century Victorian hotels. They assume that the decor will be tasteful and attractive—again not necessarily true in many places. Most importantly, they expect to walk through buildings that are structurally sound—many of them had crumbling foundations.

In the early 1970's, Harry Ryba bought the Island House Hotel across from the harbor. He began to remodel the building's interior, but it soon became evident that massive repairs to the entire structure were desperately needed. Ground-water springs behind the old hotel had rotted much of the wooden foundation. Part of the old west wing had to be completely torn down—in many places twenty-four inch beams were the consistency of putty and unable to support even their own weight. Much of the hotel's foundation was rebuilt and the interior was renovated. The upgrading and redecoration project has continued through the 1980's, and the island's oldest operating hotel is now a splendid showplace with all the modern conveniences.

Although small alterations had been under way at the Grand Hotel since World War II, it had become a bit run down and the interior decor didn't seem to match the stately exterior. When Woodfill finally agreed to the redecorations in 1976, the Mussers hired New York interior designer Carleton Varney. Varney worked with them to design an elegant summery theme that used contrasts and blendings of color to give the rooms a breezy effect. The Grand's interior was transformed from gaudy to one that fits the majestic image of the building. It now looks exactly as a Grand Hotel should. During the project engineers also found some structural decay in the old building, as well as a forward tilt in the east side of the hotel. The foundation and many supporting walls were refurbished and the tilt was corrected. It added a great deal to the cost of the project, but the building is now in condition to last another century.

One other major change occured at the Grand Hotel in 1983. So many tourists were teeming through the hotel and its grounds that the crowds were disrupting the visits of paying guests. In order to restore its trademark exclusiveness, Musser established an admission fee for all non-hotel guests who wish to visit during the day. The fee doesn't apply after 6 p.m., but all visitors must then comply with the hotel's evening dress code—dresses for women, jackets and ties for men.

In town, the Lake View Hotel was totally redone in a project that began in 1983. When it was finished, the entire structure had been renovated, there were twice as many guest rooms, and the entire hotel had been redecorated. In addition, a new heated indoor pool, and a conference center were added. Most other hotels—the Iroquois, Windermere, Chippewa, Murray, and Mission Point Resort—made changes and renovations by the mid-1980's. In just one decade, many hotel rooms that were old, tiny, and shabby were now nicely decorated with period furnishings and up-to-date conveniences.

Before all of these projects were completed, an important era of Mackinac's history came to an end. W. Stewart Woodfill decided to move to Arizona because of his respiratory ailments. In his book *Grand Hotel*, John McCabe describes the day Woodfill left the island for the last time:

> *"In the Fall of 1978, Woodfill called for a carriage to take him to the ferry dock. Dan Musser, alone, went with his uncle across the lake...Woodfill was leaving Mackinac forever. As he sat in the ferry cabin, chatting with his nephew during the forty minute journey to Mackinaw City, Woodfill never once turned to look at Mackinac Island. W. Stewart Woodfill never looked back."*

Woodfill sold the Grand Hotel to R. Daniel and Amelia Musser in 1979. W. Stewart Woodfill died in 1984.

The wooden boardwalk stretches west from town along the island's lake shore. The west bluff is in the background.

Credit: Thomas M. Piljac

Island Visitors

By 1986, many hotels had extended their seasons. The traditional eight weeks of summer now stretched from May to November. The families that once arrived with piles of luggage to spend a month or two at one of the hotels were no longer the mainstay of the resort business. In fact, the majority of visitors now came for a one day trip and left on the last ferry. Those who spent the night on the island—families, couples, businessmen, conventioneers, and tour groups—would typically stay for just a few days. That pattern hasn't changed. And almost every day a large group of visitors will step onto the island for the very first time.

Let's envision a typical family visit during the 1980's. A man, his wife, and their ten year-old-daughter board the ferry for their first trip to Mackinac Island. They select seats on the observation deck in order to watch the passing parade of boats, and to capture the splendor of the Mackinac Bridge on film. The ferry seems to float over the deep turquoise lake leaving a trail of whitecapped waves spouting behind it. Looking toward the island, they see tall trees rising quickly from the shore to the heights in craggy green outlines against the clear blue sky. As they draw closer his wife points out a few houses nestled in the woods at the top of the island. Soon they recognize the majestic Grand Hotel on a distant hill. They see stately Victorian homes lining the high bluffs and scattered along the boardwalk. The town is a picturesque cluster of old-fashioned buildings huddled together and extending back from the shore. A white, gleaming fort overlooks the village and harbor from a broad-faced hill. The ferry pulls up to a long wooden dock and they follow the crush of passengers down the steps.

They walk toward a young man who is calling out the name of their hotel. He asks them to point out their luggage, then offers directions to their lodgings. To their surprise, he stacks their cases in a tall pile on his bicycle basket and easily pedals away. They stroll along Main Street and glance at the shop windows and restaurants. Several horse-drawn carriages are stopped along the road, and bicyclists wheel around them. The unforgettable smell of horse droppings surprises them, but it is soon masked by the sweet smell of fudge drifting over the sidewalk. They find their hotel and check in, then decide to take a carriage tour for an introduction to the island's attractions. The ride in a horse-drawn buggy is highlighted by the driver's descriptive commentary of the sights. They are impressed by their first glimpse of the Grand Hotel: the flags whipping along the facade, cheerful flowers on the long columned porch, men in top hats and bright red jackets hurrying up and down the stairs. Farther up the road they stop at Surrey Hills to transfer to a larger carriage for the State Park portion of the tour.

While they wait, they look at an exhibit of old photographs, and their daughter is fascinated with a Clydesdale horse quartered nearby. The second part of the tour ambles along serene wooded trails with the shadows of leaves sweeping over the top of the carriage. The driver points out the sights and answers questions as they view the island cemetaries, Skull Cave with its macabre history, and the rugged stone of Arch Rock framed against Lake Huron below. On the way back they decide to end the tour behind Fort Mackinac and walk down to the town.

They rent bicycles, buy a picnic supper, and ride east along Main Street past the park, the yacht-filled harbor, the Island House Hotel, tree-lined residential areas, and beyond the huge Mackinac Hotel (Mission Point Resort) complex. They are alone with the cool waters of Lake Huron on one side and cliffs, flowers, trees, and scattered knolls on the other. When travelers pass in either direction, almost all of them smile and say hello. One hiker volunteers: "Someone told me I could walk around the island in thirty-five minutes, I think they were pulling my leg!" They examine the curve of Arch Rock above and try to find the Fairy Arch. Somewhere on the eastern side of the island they stop to picnic at a pretty cove. They watch the restless blue water while waves dance and leap against the rocky shore. A seagull hovers nearby. When their daughter tosses a scrap of bread toward it they are immediately surrounded by a demanding flock. They quickly gather up their things amid the diving seagulls and hurry on their way. The ride continues at a comfortable pace until they stop for a break at British Landing. As they gaze across the straits from that historic point, their daughter observes that the bridge looks blue from here, although they remember it as green when they crossed.

Early the next day they stroll to Marquette Park in the chilly morning air. They see a carpenter pedal by with a ladder balanced across his handlebars, and crowds pouring off the early ferries. Their daughter dashes off to the playground in the northeast corner of the park, while they take a bench seat and enjoy the scenery. Then they pose the child in front of Father Marquette's monument for a picture. A stubborn seagull is perched on the statue's head and refuses to move no matter how much they shout or clap their hands. Later they buy tickets and walk up the long ramp to Fort Mackinac.

The three join a group in a small wooden building to view a short movie about the island. Following a guide dressed as a soldier, they tour the buildings and watch costumed men and women go about their duties. They are enthralled by many of the exhibits, and he is especially fascinated by a musket firing demonstration. They order lunch at the Fort Tea Room and admire the view from their table. Below are the distant glittering waters of the straits; the long, graceful bridge; Round Island and its historic lighthouse; boats slipping into the harbor; the resplendent grounds of the Grand Hotel golf course; the park filled with brilliantly colored flowers; and a steady stream of people, horses, and bicycles bustling through town. Later they walk down and visit some of the other historic sights that are included on their ticket. Each offers an additional dimension to the history of the island. They also stop at Stuart House museum and see intriguing exhibits from the era of John Jacob Astor's fur company.

They climb the steep slanting hill to the Grand Hotel, pay to enter the grounds, then hurry inside to explore the elegant public rooms. He especially likes the plush parlor and she the luxurious dining room. When the three visitors step onto the long front porch they are awed by its size. They visualize women in ruffled gowns and men in suits and bowler hats, promenading past the columns on sunny afternoons. He mentions that a person could sit in one of the wicker rocking chairs for hours and admire the stunning view. Then it's down the staircase to the massive flower gardens below. Later they follow the road in front of the hotel to the west bluff and

stroll past the stately Victorian homes with beautifully
landscaped grounds.

At a livery stable a few blocks south of the hotel they
rent horses and ride back up the terraced hills through a
wooded trail of soft damp earth sided by towering oak
trees. They follow the twisting, turning roads until they
arrive at Fort Holmes. The old fort is an empty palisade
overlooking an unforgettable panoramic scene. Brilliant
blue water stretches to the horizon while nearby islands
float in the distance, shimmering softly in the late afternoon sunlight. They slowly ride away and return their
mounts. On their way back to the hotel she visits a few
shops in town and can't resist buying some delicious
fudge.

After dinner they walk along the boardwalk to the
quiet rhythm of the lake rolling against the shore. They
sit together on a wooden bench built onto the walkway,
and watch the late ferries head away from the island. As
the sun slowly sinks, the sky turns a rich gold with pale
lavender hues, then a fiery orange-red. The water below
is a rippling reflection of its path. The gray twilight quickly
passes into deep black night. Across the straits, the bridge
lights twinkle on, an arc of color floating above the water.
On either side there are bright glowing dots as towns light
up the distant coastlines. The deep, black sky is now a
blaze of white, shimmering stars, more than they had ever
seen before.

They slowly walk back to the old-fashioned town
with bikes parked along the street. A small group of
people stand before a restaurant in animated conversa-
tion, while three young men still in their waiter's uniforms pedal by and call out a party invitation to some
passing friends. Couples and families stroll along the sidewalks while an occasional taxi rattles along the road.
They buy ice cream cones at an open stand, then pass a
bar with cheerful, energetic music pouring out the open
door. Marquette Park seems especially quiet after the
buoyant atmosphere of the town. While they sit and gaze

at the brightly lit boats docked in the marina, the clear notes of taps roll down from the high limestone walls above. It seems a perfect ending for the day.

The next morning they check out of the hotel and turn their bags over to the bellman who promises to deliver them to the one o'clock ferry. After a nice lunch in town, they make some purchases (including a supply of fudge), then hurry to the ferry dock. He claims their luggage while his wife and daughter settle into seats on the top deck. The boat pulls away and the buildings slowly begin to fade in the distance. Soon the island is once again just a cluster of distant trees with a few houses perched along the wooded heights.

Capturing The Charm

Mackinac Island's natural beauty and rock formations made it a spiritual home for ancient tribes. Its high, humped center caught Patrick Sinclair's eye as a natural fortress for his troops. Set in the perfect location on an ancient watery highway, it became a center for the multi-million dollar fur trade. British and American troops fought to keep it in their hands, and Americans died trying to reclaim it. Later, a consortium of railroad and steamship companies would select it as an ideal place for a resort hotel. The wealthy would spend their summers here with their servants and other visitors. Today it is a timeless wonderland, accessible to all who make the effort to attain it.

What makes this island so special? Why has it endured through so many years of change without losing its unique charm? How has this one spot managed to lure thousands of visitors each summer, from fifteenth century Indians to twentieth century tourists? The island has many wonderful attractions, but when examined individually they do not explain its captivating enchantment on all who visit. It offers natural splendors of dense woods, rambling cliffs, unique rock formations, and surrounding lakes—yet there are many other beautiful places in our country. It is one of the most historic spots in America, but few of us return year after year on pilgrimages to examine our history. The Grand Hotel is a magnificent vacation resort, yet many repeat visitors never enter its grounds. The fact that it is an island—where a visitor's everyday concerns are distanced by miles of water—helps to make it seem a special world of its own. But we wouldn't feel that Mackinac was an extraordinary place if the island were crawling with cars, trucks, fast food outlets, neon-signed motels, phony tourist attractions, motorcycles, and carnival rides.

Mackinac's unique appeal is a special combination of all these factors, along with the feeling that it really is the *place of the great dancing spirits,* the *fairy isle,* and a *land of enchantment.* The perception transforms everyone who experiences the island enough to understand it. Somehow, tired minds are soothed, insurmountable problems seem workable, and worn-out spirits are regenerated after a visit here. Maybe the magic was always a part of the island, or perhaps so many visitors have been happy here that each leaves a bit of themselves on the fairy island, and travels home with the peace of the island in their heart.

CHAPTER 10

Visiting
Mackinac Island

Tourist Season

The warm winds of spring sweep away the last of the frigid ice from the channel. Lush, green grass emerges, and the earliest flowers display their brilliant colors. The ferries begin crossing to the island, and the calm seclusion of winter ends for the five-hundred and fifty year round inhabitants. In mid-May, the first of the 3,500 summer employees, cottage residents, and business owners arrive. In a bustle of activity, homes and shops are cleaned, repaired, and stocked with provisions.

From early June, when thousands of white, purple, and lavender lilacs burst into bloom, traffic to the island steadily builds. Large crowds arrive to celebrate Independence Day, and huge throngs of visitors await the sailboats during the two yacht races. The lively season reaches its climax during the first two weeks of August, with the second Tuesday of the month traditionally being the busiest day of the year. The intensity of the crowds begins to decline after Labor Day, and the soft, sunny days of September become a time of tranquility. When gold and scarlet leaves contrast the deep green of the pines, the end is near. Businesses shorten their hours or close their doors. The season officially concludes when the Grand Hotel closes in early November. The chill of winter returns, and once again the permanent residents settle in for a quiet winter. In six months, they hosted more than 800,000 visitors, sometimes as many as 10,000 in one day.

Destination: Mackinac Island

Mackinac has been blessed with the great natural beauty of thick, dense woods with a variety of trees and plants, fascinating rock formations, meadows of flowers, landscaped parks, gentle springs, and rambling trails. There are also many sites of historical importance including: two forts, several museums and exhibits, and reconstructed homes—all enhanced by costumed men and women portraying their counterparts of another era. You may participate in many appealing activities. In addition to festivals, races, and competitions, you can enjoy golf, tennis, fishing, boating, hiking, bicycling, horseback riding, and carriage drives. A wide variety of quality restaurants and pubs provide evening entertainment. You may prefer a quiet, leisurely meal among friends, or a large social gathering accompanied by music and dancing.

The way to best enjoy your stay on Mackinac is to have a general idea of what you would like to see and do here, while allowing yourself ample time to relax and appreciate the island's pleasures. The first step in arranging for a visit is to select your mode of travel. To reach the island you can ferry over from Mackinaw City or St. Ignace; fly in by private plane or charter flight; or arrive by private boat and dock at the marina.

Automobile   The straits area is easily accessible by Interstate 75 from both the upper and lower peninsulas. Traveling time and mileage will vary among drivers, depending on the route, and number of stops. Here are approximate mileage distances from the following cities:

> Detroit to Mackinaw City   281 miles
> Chicago to Mackinaw City   428 miles
> Sault Ste. Marie to St. Ignace   52 miles

Those driving on the lower peninsula have the option of following a more scenic path by exiting I-75 onto Old Route 27. The road winds through lakes, rivers, and forests, then joins U.S. 23 at Cheboygan for a fifteen minute drive along the shoreline to Mackinaw City.

Horse drawn carriages for Mackinac Island Carriage Tours move along Main Street.

Credit: Thomas M. Piljac

Ferries You can travel to the island from either Mackinaw City or St. Ignace on one of three ferry companies: the Arnold, Shepler, or Star Lines. Ferries between Mackinaw City and the island begin operating from mid-May and cease running between mid-October and early November, depending upon the individual company. Those crossing from St. Ignace run from mid-April until late December. Whether you make the eight mile journey from Mackinaw City, or the five mile voyage from St. Ignace, your passage time will depend upon the vessel and weather conditions. In general, it will take from eighteen to thirty minutes.

Each company has its own timetable of arrivals and departures, which change throughout the season. You may obtain their schedules by calling the ferry companies, or writing the Chamber of Commerce for any of the three cities. The schedules are also readily available at many businesses and information centers in the straits area. Generally, they run every half-hour to hour during the busiest tourist months, from early morning until late evening. During early spring and late fall, they average five crossings a day in each direction.

When you arrive at either of the two cities, you will have no trouble finding the ferry docks or the ticket booths. They are well-marked by signs and advertisements. All three companies provide daily and overnight parking facilities. Since many overnight lots are located a few blocks away from the docks, the companies offer the option of valet parking for those who do not wish to walk. There is a small additional fee for this service.

The ferry crossings are quite safe. In more than one-hundred and ten years of regular service there have been no fatalities. The vessels are inspected yearly by the U.S. Coast Guard to ensure stability, seaworthiness, and the availability of safety equipment. They also perform a complete out of the water examination every five years. Boat operators are tested for their knowledge of the vessel, safety equipment, and first aid, as well as navigational procedures and their ability to pilot in grave weather. To qualify as a captain, the applicant must pass a variety of tests, physical examinations, and have 365 days of experience with a certified operator. The U.S. Coast Guard issues all licenses, and will revoke them if the holder does not follow procedures.

There are two points to remember when traveling by ferry:

1. When you board a ferry for Mackinac Island, watch to make sure that your luggage is put onto the boat. They seldom err, but during busy seasons mistakes can happen.
2. When you leave the island, your hotel porter will not load your luggage onto the vessel until you personally claim it. Make sure that you do so before you depart, or you'll reach the mainland without your baggage.

Private Boat   Through mid-September a State-owned marina in the island's harbor is open daily until 10 p.m. While some yachters hold seasonal berths among the seventy-seven available mooring slips, the rest are assigned spots on a first-come, first-served basis. An average of one-hundred boats arrive every day from June until the end of August, and vessels are often lined up and waiting for the harbor master each morning. They are notified by radio as space becomes available. A maximum visit of seven consecutive days is allowed, after which they must leave the harbor for forty-eight hours before being permitted to return and dock again. For overnight stays, there is a minimum charge for craft up to twenty feet in length, which graduates upward for larger vessels. Payment includes the use of electricity, water, and restrooms. Shower facilities are available for a small fee at the yacht club across the street.

During the yacht races the marina is cleared to make way for the sailboats, and only seasonal slip holders may remain. The Chicago Yacht Club rents both sides of the harbor for three days during the Chi-Mac race, and only a few outer slips are available to transient vessels. After the completion of the big races, the piers are so jammed that the boats 'raft' by mooring two to three craft to a single piling, then allowing late arrivals to hook up to those nearer the wharf. Soon you can almost walk across the harbor without getting your feet wet.

Airport   Mackinac Island Airport is located on the western heights, and has a 3,500 foot paved runway with a clear approach (no wires) from the water. There is a small landing fee, based on the size of the plane. Parking space is available, but no fuel is sold here. Trained personnel are on hand to co-ordinate daytime landings. Be sure to offer your full co-operation so that their excellent safety record can be maintained. For night landings, you can activate the airport lights on a UNICOM frequency. Taxi service is available from the airport.

Charter flights are available to the island from:
Detroit Metropolitan Airport, Detroit, Michigan
Mackinac County Airport, St. Ignace, Michigan
You can contact those airports for details. There is also regularly scheduled airline service from Detroit and Chicago to:
Emmett County Airport, Pellston, Michigan
A limousine service (Wolverine Stages) meets all scheduled flights, and transports passengers from Pellston to Mackinaw City. You can catch a ferry to the island from there.

The Windermere (top) and Iroquois Hotels are just a few of the Victorian-style hotels on Mackinac Island.

Credit: Thomas M. Piljac

Wolverine Stages does not require reservations, but they are appreciated.

Accomodations

A variety of sleeping accommodations are available on the island, and most are within a one to two mile area of the town. Your selection will be based upon availability, budget, and the type of atmosphere you prefer. Small tourist homes and bed and breakfast inns offer a quieter, more intimate place to stay. Mid-sized hotels offer sleeping rooms, a sitting room/lobby area for socializing, a restaurant, and a front porch to watch the passers-by. The big resort hotels have convention centers, pools, several restaurants, bars, and other entertainment facilities. Some private parties also offer their homes or condominiums for rent during the summer season. Contact the Chamber of Commerce for a list of available rentals.

Restaurants

Depending upon your budget, personal preference, and the time of year, a wide selection of dining experiences awaits you. Small diners, family-style restaurants, and quaint pubs offer everything from sandwiches and pizza to full menus. Spend part of a sunny afternoon at one of the outdoor cafes, or picnic along an isolated stretch of shoreline. A number of elegant dining rooms offer pleasant views, a special atmosphere, and fine cuisine. Ice cream, fudge, soft drinks, and snacks are available throughout the day at many locations around the island.

Island Business

The majority of island businesses are concentrated in the two block area bounded by Main & Market Streets. You can explore a number of attractive shops offering gifts, books, souvenirs, photographic supplies, handiwork, clothing, paintings, prints, carvings, pottery, scrimshaw, jewelry, and antiques. Five different shops feature world famous Mackinac Island fudge. Each offers a variety of interesting flavors, while the heavy competition keeps the quality up and prices down. The

Interior of the Astor Street Cafe, one of many dining spots on the island.

Credit: Thomas M. Piljac

bank and post office can be found on Market Street. A laundromat is located on the west end of Main Street, and a drug store and small grocery are on the east end. There is also a marine supply outlet just east of the harbor. Most businesses open in mid-May, but closing dates vary between September and November.

Island Transportation

Although the absence of motor vehicles is an essential part of the island's charm—it is also the most surprising adjustment many visitors face. Everything here is moved by foot, bicycle, or horse. Almost at once, life assumes a more relaxed and leisurely pace. You'll soon discover how pleasant it is to make the transition from the fast moving world of today, to the relaxed world of yesteryear.

Walking   The simplest and least expensive way to travel about the island is by foot. Since the town, Grand Hotel, and

A sign warns bicyclists to the danger of this hill.

Credit: Thomas M. Piljac

State Park historic sites are within a two mile radius they are an attainable goal for most walkers. Although the interior has many hills, none are extremely difficult unless you are in very poor physical condition. There are three very important points to bear in mind as you amble along the roads and trails:

1. Despite the lack of motor vehicles, you must take care when crossing roads. Bicyclists and horse-drawn carriages can accidentally crash into you and cause serious injuries.
2. Watch your feet, especially on roads heavily traveled by horses. There is no car exhaust on the island—but horses have their own exhaust systems.
3. Wear sensible shoes—especially the ladies. If you are not dressed for hiking, carry your fancy shoes in a bag. If you refuse to do that, bring plenty of band-aids and blister cream.

Bicycling   Bicycle rentals are available by the hour or the day at many shops in town, or at most hotels. If you bring your own, you must obtain a license from the police department. Otherwise, you run the risk of having your bicycle impounded. To have it released, you will have to register the vehicle and pay a fine. This regulation is not designed to hassle visitors, but to help them. With the huge number of bicycles on the island, there is no way to prove ownership unless the vehicle has been registered. In any case, the licenses are a status symbol here, when you've collected several years worth you are seen more as an *islander* and less as a *fudgie*.

Although few crimes are committed on the island, bicycle theft is one of the most common. This is considered a serious offense here, because bicycles are the main form of transportation. Most thefts are of privately owned vehicles for 'joy rides'. A good quality lock will deter all but the most persistent thieves.

You probably haven't been in a bicycle-related accident since you were a child. Because of that, and the lack of motor vehicles, too many riders have a false sense of security and aren't cautious enough. There have been serious crashes with debilitating personal injuries, and some riders have been killed. However, if you use common sense and follow the rules of the road, it is a safe method of travel. The most common causes of mishaps are:

1. Two people riding a one-man bike.
2. Traveling too fast downhill.
3. Intoxicated bicyclists.
4. Not following the rules of the road.

In addition to the obvious violations mentioned above, the rules that you should remember are:

1. Horses always have the right-of-way.
2. Stay on the right side of the road.
3. Watch for pedestrians.

4. No bicycles are allowed on the sidewalks or docks.
5. Use a headlight if you bicycle after dark.
6. Be careful when traveling downhill.

Many bicyclists have lost control traveling down some of the steeper hills. The worst of them have signs posted warning you to proceed sensibly, or to walk your vehicle down. Obey the signs, they have been placed there to help you avoid injuries. You should always walk your bicycle to the bottom of the following roads:

Truscott Street: Extends from the top of the east bluff to Huron Street along the lake shore.

Turkey Hill: Stretches between Huron Road on the heights and Fort Street.

Fort Street: Runs next to Fort Mackinac from the heights to Main Street.

In addition, *Cadotte Avenue*, which sweeps along the east side of the Grand Hotel is steep enough to require caution. It is heavily traveled, so if you lose control you run the risk of slamming into one of the many horses, carriages, bicycles, or the median strip—all which can result in serious injuries. Use common sense when riding in the island's interior, especially if you aren't a skilled rider, or if it's very wet and rainy.

Saddle Horses
You can rent saddle horses by the hour at Cindy's Riding Stable or Chamber's Riding Stable on Market Street, or at Jack's Livery Stable on Mahoney Avenue. They will question your riding experience before assigning you a horse, but you must still exercise caution and common sense. Saddle horses are not allowed on Main Street, Huron Street, or Lake Shore Road because of the heavy traffic, but you are free to roam the rest of the island's roads and trails.

Carriages

Official Sightseeing Tour   Regularly scheduled sightseeing tours are offered by Mackinac Island Carriage Tours, Inc. The

Many island summer residents enjoy their private carriages, as this couple demonstrates during an antique carriage parade.

Credit: Thomas M. Piljac

circuit lasts about two hours, and offers a good, overall perspective of the island's attractions. Tickets are available at their booth on Main Street, near the Chamber of Commerce. The ride begins in town, and passengers are transferred to larger, thirty-five passenger vehicles at Surrey Hills. The company offers special rates for students, scouts, or groups, but you must make arrangements with the office in advance. There are two points to remember when participating in the official tour:

1. If you decide to leave the carriage at the Grand Hotel, you terminate your tour and cannot reboard to continue it later.
2. If you disembark behind Fort Mackinac, you can reboard tour carriages when they pass again, but only if there is sufficient space available.

Private Tours A more personalized tour of the island can be obtained by hiring one of the livery carriages lined up at the base of Marquette Park. These liveries are operated by Arrowhead Carriages and Mackinac Island Carriage Tours. You can make arrangements on the spot, or call one of the companies ahead of time and order a pick-up. State your preferences to the driver, or allow them to give you their own tour of the island's sights.

Drive-Yourself Carriage If you prefer to take the reins and drive yourself, you can have a fun-filled excursion guiding your own horse and buggy around the island. They are available at Jack's Livery Stable on Mahoney Avenue. Rentals are by the hour, and several sizes of carriages are available. The vehicles are allowed to travel along Lake Shore Road or the interior of the island, but not on Main and Market Streets in town. In addition, a few interior side roads leading to private residences are off limits, signs are posted in advance.

Taxis Horse drawn taxis are available through Mackinac Island Carriage Tours. You can call for a pickup, or hail one along the busier streets. Taxi fares are determined by distance traveled, with a minimum charge for all passengers. When using a taxi there are several points to remember:

1. If you know you will need a taxi at a particular time, call well ahead to arrange a pick-up to ensure prompt service.
2. Island taxis collect as many passengers as possible while they traverse their routes. Because the horse-drawn vehicles move slowly, it takes time for them to travel any distance on the island. Keep this in mind when you call to arrange for service. For example: Don't wait until fifteen minutes before your ferry departure to call a taxi to Stonecliffe.
3. Consider the weather when calling for service. If it is raining heavily, there will be huge demands on the taxi system.

The Chamber of Commerce information booth is located at the center of Main Street.

Credit: Thomas M. Piljac

4. If you are part of a large group, make your arrangements ahead of time. A last minute call to transport a large group can throw the whole organization into disarray.
5. If you visit the island during the winter, bear in mind that there is only one taxi available in the off-season.

Having Fun On Mackinac

Every visit to the island can be an exciting experience, but your activities will be limited by time, budget, weather, and individual preference. In Chapter Twelve you will find descriptions and information about many island sights and landmarks. In this section you will be introduced to annual events and festivities, as well as a few popular pastimes.

Annual Events   Small entrance fees are charged at some events. Check with the Mackinac Island Chamber of Commerce for details.

EARLY JUNE   Lilac Festival

One of the oldest island festivals, it is held to celebrate the annual blooming of the lilacs. Some of the shrubs date back to the early French settlers, and the thousands of plants represent a myriad of varieties. A parade, complete with marching bands, decorated floats, buggies, prancing horses, and antique carriages highlights the festivities. The events may vary from year to year, but there is usually a Ten Kilometer foot race, a golf tournament at the Grand Hotel, Casino Night, Taste of Mackinac (an opportunity to sample dishes from the island's best restaurants), fireworks, hayrides, guided walking tours, and a Coronation Ball.

LATE JUNE   Music Festival

Classical musicians and singers gather to perform selections that sound especially beautiful amid the atmosphere of bygone days. It is an opportunity to hear compositions as they must have sounded when first written, without the background noises of motor vehicles and machinery.

JULY   Chicago to Mackinac Yacht Race
      Port Huron to Mackinac Yacht Race

Thousands of visitors flock to the island each year to enjoy the boisterous fun of the race weeks, and the hundreds of different boats sailing into the harbor. These popular annual competitions are described in more detail later in this chapter.

EARLY JULY   July Fourth-Independence Day

A day to picnic, hike, and bicycle around the island. After sunset, settle in to watch Mackinac Island's fireworks display over Lake Huron, while simultaneously viewing those presented on the shores of St. Ignace and Mackinaw City.

LATE JULY   Mackinac Bicycle Race

Participants navigate an obstacle course while trying not to accumulate points by making such errors as stopping, falling, or touching the ground with their toes.

LATE JULY   Commanding Officer's Ball

This event is traditionally held on the last Saturday in July. The celebration was an annual occasion while Fort Mackinac was an active military post. The gala was revived in 1981 to raise funds for the island's historic sites. The ball usually has a costume theme (such as Victorian), although it is not required that you dress in clothing of that particular era. The event is open to the public, but all tickets are pre-sold. Call the administrative offices at Fort Mackinac for ticket information and additional details.

EARLY AUGUST   Bicycle Relay Race

Bicyclists race on five man relay teams, with only one racer from each team on the course at a time. Each team has a sponsor who pays the entry fee, provides matching shirts, two spotters, and a timer.

EARLY SEPTEMBER   Mackinac Island Road Race

Runners, joggers, and nature lovers in good physical condition gather to race the 8.2 miles around the island's perimeter. The race is open to people of all ages, with the field divided into a number of classifications.

Weddings   The unique atmosphere of Mackinac Island makes it a popular location for weddings because couples want their celebration to take place at a location that is special and romantic. Some meet and fall and love here every summer, others have grown up or vacationed on the island. You can

A portion of the Grand Hotel golf course as viewed from Fort Mackinac.

Credit: Thomas M. Piljac

arrange to be married at one of the island's churches, the city hall, in one of the hotel lobbies, on the golf courses, at special sights such as Arch Rock, or on a yacht floating offshore.

Golf   The island has two excellent nine-hole courses, both of which are open to the public. The Grand Hotel Golf Course is located just north of town, while the Wawashkamo Golf Links are in the center of the island, adjacent to British Landing Road.

The Grand Hotel Course (the Jewel) was built on the old public cow pasture just east of the hotel in 1911. Today it is beautifully landscaped, and wanders amid trees, flowers, ponds, and pools. It was completely renovated in 1987— several holes were redesigned, the greens were enlarged, and the fairways shortened. The course has been described as small, but not easy.

Wawashkamo Golf Links are located on a portion of the 1814 Battlefield. It is the State's oldest continuously operating course still at its original location, and is registered as a Michigan Historic Site. The links were laid out by Alex B. Smith of Carnoustie, Scotland, who later made golfing history and was named to the PGA Hall of Fame in 1940. He used the topography of the land in his design, sculpting the layout and traps from the existing terrain, rather than artificially adding hills or ponds. Surrounded by trees and nestled among gentle hills on the island's interior, this is one of the few existing links in the United States. Today's golfers can enjoy the same course as their nineteenth century counterparts, and even experiment by replacing their wooden tees with a pinch of sand if they wish. The turf, nineteenth century clubhouse, and the outbuildings were refurbished in the 1980's.

Lake Sports

Fishing the straits has always been a popular pastime. Charter boats are available from Mackinac Island Charters, or from one of several companies on the mainland.

At Quest Water Sports, just east of the marina, you can rent a small sailboat, or charter an eighty-six foot yacht. There is also scuba-diving, board sailing, and water-skiing equipment available for rental.

Night Life

In the evenings, musical entertainment is provided at many island restaurants, hotels, and pubs. The Grand Hotel has dancing every night, and several other establishments feature dance bands throughout the season. During the summer, some ferry lines offer evening dinner cruises.

Yacht Races

Two yacht races draw huge crowds to the island each year to enjoy the beauty and variety of the vessels, and the excitement of the competition. They have been a popular annual tradition since the early years of the twentieth century, and are acclaimed by yachters around the world.

Chicago To Mackinac Race   The first contest was held between several island cottagers who were Chicago natives, and wanted to compete in a long-distance challenge on their yachts. In August, 1898, five vessels raced the 333 miles to the island on a straight course, with no allowances made for differences between the vessels. The yacht *Vannena*, owned by W.R. Crawford, was the first to arrive, fifty-one hours after the small fleet left Chicago. The fourth boat finished three days later, and the fifth dropped out. The yachters held sporadic races over the next decade until it became an annual event in 1907.

The early sailboats were made of wood, and owned by very wealthy men who hired crews to pilot the vessels. Today's boats are constructed of plastic, aluminum, or fiberglass, and are often guided by the owners and their families, who are less likely to be among the very rich. Some are designed very simply, others have multi-million dollar designs with sophisticated on-board computers.

Over three-hundred vessels participated in the 1987 competition. Because of the variety of sizes and styles, the boats are *handicapped* to even the odds. Each craft is placed in one of twelve sections among other vessels of similar size. After making various measurements of the yacht's shape and weight, the race committee of the Chicago Yacht Club assigns each vessel with an ideal finishing time. The real contest is among these sectional participants, and the winner of each class is the craft whose corrected time (the number of hours it takes to run the course after assigned handicaps have been subtracted from the yacht's actual elapsed time) is the shortest. The system is so complicated that the final results are determined by computer. However, it offers a fair balance among the boats and allows all kinds of yachtsmen to compete.

The contest is heavily influenced by weather conditions, which change often on Lake Michigan. On average, it takes thirty-six to forty-eight hours to complete the race. However, in 1975, there was no wind to help the sailboats and the competition took four days. Two of the fastest races were in 1911 and 1987, when the fleet was assisted by 80 mph winds. In the 1911 struggle, the four-sail schooner *Amorita* finished the course in 31 hours and 14½ minutes, the fastest time on record. That record held until 1987, when the *Pied Piper* reached the island in 25 hours, 50 minutes and 44 seconds. The 1987 course was so fast that nine other vessels were also able to top the seventy-six year record. However, neither the *Amorita* nor the *Pied Piper* were victors in their record-breaking years. When the corrected time from the handicapping system was computed, both vessels placed farther down in their class.

Port Huron To Mackinac   In 1925, the Bayview Yacht Club of Detroit started its own competition to Mackinac Island. It usually takes place a few weeks after the Chi-Mac race, when a fleet of yachts dash from Port Huron to Mackinac, a 259 mile contest on Lake Huron. The vessels are placed in section classes, and their finishing time is corrected by a handicapping system similar to the one used in the Chi-Mac. Perhaps one of the most memorable races occured in 1985. Strong winds of more than thirty knots and eight foot waves battered the fleet, knocking ninety-three boats out of the struggle. Fortunately, only one vessel sank. Several boats took on water, and not surprisingly, many of the crews were seasick.

In both events, yachts arrive at the island day and night and are clocked by sophisticated equipment as they cross the finish line. Special high-power spotlights and a star-scope which magnifies starlight are used to locate nocturnal finishers. When the sailors arrive, they dock their craft and gather to share their experiences and exchange race stories, particularly at the Pink Pony Lounge at the Chippewa Hotel. Some find accommodations on the island, others sleep on their vessels. It is one of the most hectic periods of the season for island businesses. Many yachtsmen spend several days shopping, touring, and enjoying the nightlife. Like all visitors, they try to discover as much as they can about the attractions here, and perhaps some are curious about the island's geological history. Before we describe the interesting sites on the island, let's explore that topic in more detail.

The Island

Geology of Mackinac

As you begin your tour of Mackinac you may find its origins quite interesting. The island was formed in four stages. First the crown appeared around fifteen-thousand years ago as the great glaciers began retreating to the north. Waves steadily washed away most of the topsoil, leaving an erosion-proof bedrock surface. Much of the rock was very old, its composition began three-hundred and fifty million years ago when the straits region had a thick layer of rock salt below the limestone surface. When underground water dissolved the rock salt, large caverns formed amid the stone. Eventually they would collapse into stacks of broken rock. Years of continuously circulating water sealed the shattered fragments together into hard, resilient formations called brecciated (broken and cemented) rock. Softer materials were washed away, leaving the stone in various recognizable shapes. The first brecciated formations stood on the steep limestone cliffs of the ancient island, above the remaining meltwater of Lake Algonquin. Today we call them Sugar Loaf, Skull Cave, and Cave of the Woods. About eight-thousand years ago, Lake Algonquin slowly receded to a level one-hundred and twenty feet below that of Lake Huron. The disappearing waters uncovered a land mass which joined Mackinac, Round, and Bois Blanc Islands and stretched to the mainland below. The straits were

Sugar Loaf is one of the oldest rock formations on the island. It was shaped by the steady waves of ancient Lake Algonquin.

Courtesy of Mackinac Island State Park Commission

reduced to a narrow, shallow river that flowed to the north. The water steadily rose over the next 4,000 years, to a point where the top of the limestone cliffs, east and west bluffs, and the site of Fort Mackinac marked the water's edge of Lake Nipissing. The lapping waves beat against the rock, more caverns collapsed, and the brecciated formations of Arch Rock, Chimney Rock, Lover's Leap, Devil's Kitchen, Friendship Altar, Scott's Cave, and Eagle Point Cave were slowly formed. Once again the lake began to recede. Over several thousand years the waters drained from much of the land, and three separate lakes (Superior, Michigan, and Huron) are all that remain of the giant Lake Nipissing. For the last 2,500 years the water level of those lakes has remained fairly constant, but the earth's crust continues to ascend, still rebounding from the weight of the glacier. Mackinac Island is rising nine inches every century.

Nature's Beauty

As you walk along the island paths, you'll notice the beauty of nature with thick stands of trees, patches of colorful flowers, birds flitting from bushes and leafy branches, and animals scampering along the side of the trail. In order to provide a general idea of what you are seeing, we have listed the plants and animals you may encounter while exploring Mackinac.

Trees The island forests have both softwood and hardwood trees. In many areas they date only from the nineteenth century. Prior to that period, most of the forests were chopped down for firewood and building materials. Softwoods such as the White Pine (very tall, limbless for the first ten feet), Cedar (tall, thin, and straight with clusters of flat needles) and Spruce (which looks just like a Christmas tree) are joined by Balsam and Tamarack (Larch) trees. They are heavily concentrated in the wetter lowlands. Hardwoods such as the Sugar Maple are joined by Beech (smooth grey bark), Red Oak, and Black Locust trees, and are found most often in the higher areas.

Plants   Many varieties of beautiful flowers abound on Mackinac. Most residents have lovely gardens, the parks are adorned with beautiful plantings, and Victorian buildings are surrounded by exciting floral displays. The island itself is located in the transition zone between northern and southern plants. Fortunately, species from both climates co-exist in these pleasant conditions. Some wildflowers on the island include:
       Bastard Toadflax, Beach Pea, Bead Lily, Bearberry, Bishop's Cap, Calypso Orchid, Campions, Cattails, Cow Parsnip, Daisies, Goldenrod, Gaywing, Indian Paintbrush, Marsh Marigolds, Marsh Blue Violets, Mayflower, Northern Bedstraw, Primrose, Silverweed, Striped Coral Root, Trillium, Trout Lily, Twinflower, Violets, Wild Strawberries, and Wrinkled Rose. Here are some of the places you will find them:

Beach Area:	Beach Pea, Lady Slippers, Pyrola, Silverweed, Wrinkled Rose
Bogs:	Blueberries, Bog Rosemary, St. John's Wort, Wild Orchids
Evergreen Forests:	Bead Lily, Calypso Orchid, Corn Lily, Twinflower, Wood Nymph
Marshes & Swamps:	Cattails, Marsh Marigolds, Marsh Blue Violets, Mints
Open Meadows:	Campions, Daisies, Wild Strawberries
Woods:	Mayflower, Trillium, Trout Lily

Wildlife   There aren't many animals on the island, and you won't find any deer or bear in the woods. The small land area and large influx of people make it very difficult for large animals to survive here. However, there are an abundance of smaller creatures such as red and grey squirrels, chipmunks, raccoons and Snowshoe Hares.

Birds   The birds seen most often during the summer are the Ring-Billed Gulls and Herring Gulls. Purple Finches, Black-Capped Chickadees, and Red-Breasted Nuthatches make the island their year-round home. During the summer they are joined by Robins, Yellow Warblers, Chimney Swifts, Oven

The rising lake level has eroded much of the island's shoreline.

Credit: Thomas M. Piljac

Birds, American Redstarts, and Swallows. You will also find
Mallard Ducks, Canadian Geese, and Broadwing Hawks, especially during migration periods.

Lake Huron

The island is located in the Straits of Mackinac, a narrow passage that covers the fifty mile neck connecting Lakes
Michigan and Huron. It was carved by the shallow river that
once ran north, until steadily washing waves and continually
abrading ice eroded the surrounding soil, creating an artery
several hundred feet deep and five miles wide.

Mackinac is just barely on the Lake Huron side of the
straits. The lake is 578 feet above sea level, and covers a surface area of 23,000 square miles. It has a maximum width of

101 miles and a maximum length of 257 miles. On average, it has a depth of 195 feet, although in some areas it is as much as 750 feet deep.

If history repeats itself, the lake may rise an additional five feet over the next century. However, it is possible that man-caused changes in the atmosphere (such as the greenhouse effect) can disrupt the natural process. Some believe that a climatic change of more rain, cooler temperatures, and less evaporation is already taking place. Others insist that the record low levels reached in 1964 were unusual, and the rising water is merely returning to its normal height. In any case, in 1986 the water was at its highest level in one-hundred and twenty years. At times, the docks at the marina were completely underwater, and by November of that year the lake was sixty-eight inches above its 1964 level. Thanks to a mild winter with little snow in 1986-87, the lake has receded to a more manageable level. In addition, the shoreline has since been reinforced with boulders, as have the two breakwaters. The docks were rebuilt and raised twelve inches in order to avoid future problems. However, scientists believe that the lake will continue to rise over the long term.

During the summer, Lake Huron is too cold for most swimmers—August temperatures average only sixty degrees. In winter, it never entirely freezes over. However, ice does form along the shores, and sometimes stretches as much as twenty miles into the center. Fields of floating ice are often found in the middle of the lake, where winter gales drive them back and forth. Often piles of these ice floes are driven shoreward and crash in giant stacks along the beach.

Island residents look forward to the winter ice. The narrow band of water between British Landing and St. Ignace freezes over and forms what is called the *Ice Bridge*, a short route of about three and one-half miles. To determine if the ice is sturdy enough for travel, it is probed with six foot steel poles until a uniform thickness (usually four to six inches) is confirmed. When the bridge is declared ready, the islanders dig small holes about one-hundred and fifty feet apart along the route. They use discarded Christmas trees (some decorated with reflecting tape) to mark the route. Residents call it I-75 as a joke, and many bet on the date that the bridge will be thick enough for the crossings to begin.

Islander's make the trip on foot, cross country skis, and snowmobiles. The snowmobile trip can take fifteen to thirty minutes depending on weather conditions. The journey can be dangerous, as cracks can form in the ice making the route uneven and bumpy. A traveler can be caught in a blinding blizzard and have difficulty sticking to the path. But the most hazardous situations can occur when the ice begins to melt. Drivers have been known to break through the ice, and although most jump clear of their machine just in time, every five years or so someone is killed in the attempt. The bridge usually lasts from January to March, although some years (such as the winter of 1986-87) it never forms at all.

Weather
The old joke about Mackinac Island weather is that "if you don't like it, wait a few hours and it will change." The island receives a substantial amount of rainfall every year, but fortunately most showers are brief. The weather during spring and fall varies greatly with more rain and changing temperatures. In general, you can assume that the days will be cool (55-60 degrees) and the nights crisp (40-50 degrees). The summer temperatures average 70-80 degrees during the day with low humidity. The thermometer drops at night, and it can become quite cool. Winters here are actually milder than on the mainland because of the surrounding water. The average temperature is 25-30 degrees, but it can drop to 25 degrees below zero on occasion. Snowfall is also lighter than on the mainland because many storms lose their force as they cross the lake.

Storms   Fall and winter storms periodically do a great deal of damage to the island's shoreline. The northern side of the island is often hit especially hard with portions of the road and trees being washed away. The pavement that circles the island (M-185 or Lake Shore Road) suffers the brunt of the storms' battering waves. Gravel is pushed onto the road by the heavy winds, at times so deeply that the road is completely impassable, and the State Park snowplow must be used to clear it away. Some years are worse than others, and 1985 was a bad one. It may not be typical of area weather, but such years have happened before—and certainly will again.

On September 23, a storm ravaged the newly completed water filtration plant. The surging lake broached the shoreline and crushed concrete treatment tanks. Damages approximated one-half million dollars.

Two months later, a storm did more than $500,000 damage to the M-185 highway. The wind velocity soared to 78 mph, and uprooted huge trees, sent shutters and shingles flying, ripped siding from homes, bashed waves over the boardwalk, knocked St. Anne's cross to one side, and destroyed boats moored on the beach.

Another winter storm brought 50 to 60 mph winds, blowing snow, drifts of ten to twenty feet, and fourteen foot waves to batter the shore. Heavy turmoil under the two foot thick ice broke it into huge blocks, destroying the ice bridge. The wind tossed the chunks high into the air before dashing them against the shoreline.

Timeless Wonderland

Timeless Wonderland

Touring The Island

Mackinac Island's charm is a combination of its natural beauty, exciting history, elegant buildings, and interesting people. Explore the serene wooded paths, and enjoy the grassy knolls, springs, bogs, marshes and wildflowers. Examine the interesting rock formations, and delight in the legends surrounding them. See where the British landed in 1812, and relive the Battle of 1814 at Wawashkamo. Enjoy the scenic views from Fort Holmes, Arch Rock, and the natural overlooks atop the high limestone cliffs. Watch the boats in the harbor; explore the historic buildings, museums, and shops in town; journey back in time at Fort Mackinac and the Grand Hotel.

In this chapter we describe the island's sights, offer a bit of history about each one, and look at some of the myths and legends attached to them. Although you can tour the island by following the descriptions on these pages, our purpose is primarily to provide you with background information. It is impossible for us to create the perfect route, as personal interests and the amount of time you have available will influence your agenda. Once you have read about all of the sites, you can create your own island tour. A general map is included in the front of the book, or you may pick one up at several locations in town. For simplicity, we've divided the island into three sections.

Area One travels the road around the exterior and discusses the features you encounter along the way. *Area Two* describes points of interest in the interior. We do not follow a particular route because the island is criss-crossed by dozens of intersecting paths, trails, and roads. Instead we list attractions and their general location. *Area Three* covers the heavily populated southern zone, and includes the Grand Hotel, the town, Fort Mackinac, and historic buildings of interest.

Area One
Exterior Tour From
Marquette Park To The Boardwalk

The road that extends around the island's exterior is called M-185 or Lake Shore Road where it runs through the State Park; in the heart of town it's referred to as Main Street; and from Marquette Park to Mission House it is called Huron Street. It is an easy road to travel because it is paved and flat, and a popular one because you can enjoy the beauty of Lake Huron on one side of the road, and many points of interest on the other. The distance around the island's outer edge is 8.2 miles from start to finish.

Your trip can take as little as forty minutes or as long as three hours, depending upon your mode of travel and the number of stops you make. There are several places to rest along the route, and you will find picnic tables and trash barrels at some of them. The section of road west of town is the busiest—between Main Street and British Landing. Many travelers start out from the city in that direction, then turn inland at British Landing. We will begin our descriptions in the opposite direction, starting just east of the town's business district.

Marquette Park   This ten acre park below Fort Mackinac was once the sight of the gardens and stables for the military post. In 1906 it was converted to a park, and was dedicated along with the statue of Father Jacques Marquette in 1909. The sloping lawn is a popular picnic spot, and is landscaped with beau-

A replica of a seventeenth century chapel stands in the northwest corner of Marquette Park.

Credit: Thomas M. Piljac

tiful flowers, bushes and trees. In June, thousands of lilacs burst into white, lavender, and purple bloom.

In the northeast corner (behind Indian Dormitory) is a children's playground that includes swings, a slide, and a climbing tower. In the southwest corner are two Victorian-style kiosks that offer information and tickets to State Park attractions (one ticket provides entrance for all State Park attractions on the island). The northwest corner features a Bark Chapel that is a replica of a typical seventeenth century mission chapel. Inside are displays and exhibits that portray Father Dablon ministering to the Indians on the island.

There is an Indian legend about the northernmost point of the park:

The Indian Dormitory served as a lodging house for visiting chiefs and their families from 1838 to 1846.

Credit: Thomas M. Piljac

Many spirits had a subterranean home under the island. They entered near the base of a broad hill above the island's bay (just below the southern gate of the fort). Once an old Indian spiritualist was camped on the heights above, and during his dreams in the night he was awakened by the spirits and led to their haunt. He saw it as a large and very beautiful wigwam inside the hill, filled with assembled spirits. He learned that they left their abode at twilight to engage in mystical dances on the land below the hill (Marquette Park). Although he learned much more, that is all he would ever tell of his experience.

State Park Visitor Center   On the shore directly across from Marquette Park is the Mackinac Island State Park Visitor Center with its informative displays, books, exhibits, and rest rooms. All State Park Historic Sites are open from June 15th to Labor Day, except for Fort Mackinac which is open from May 15th until mid-October.

Indian Dormitory   Admission through State Park ticket.
Built to comply with the Treaty of Washington, the dormitory opened in 1838 as a lodging house for Indian visitors. It closed in1846, and stood empty until 1867, when it reopened as the island schoolhouse. Resident children attended the Thomas W. Ferry School here until 1964, when the new public school was built just west of town.

The Mackinac Island State Park Commission purchased the building in the late 1960's and restored it to the 1840 era. The ground floor has exhibits and displays with a costumed guide on hand to interpret the historical information. Also on view are the living quarters, kitchen, and a reproduction* of Henry Schoolcraft's office as Indian Agent. Indian lodgers slept upstairs in the nineteenth century. Today that area is an Indian museum with displays of clothing, weapons, and artifacts. On the walls are a diorama of Indian drawings arranged to follow the theme of Longfellow's famous poem *Hiawatha*.

Yacht Club   Once a private home, this building across from the State docks was purchased by a small group of Chicago yachtsmen in 1935, who then formed the Mackinac Island Yacht Club. Membership is limited to 225, and the club serves as a social center for its members (about 25% are island summer residents). Showers behind the clubhouse are open to all boaters for a small fee.

Island House   Constructed in 1852, it is the oldest hotel still in operation on the island, and is listed as a Michigan Historic Site. Its combined Victorian-Southern Plantation charm has kept it a popular family hotel, and the long front porch offers a sweeping view of the harbor. The structure has been completely renovated over the last twenty years.

---

*The Indian Agent's office and residence were actually just east of the dormitory on a spacious grounds surrounded by palisades. The buildings were destroyed by a fire in the winter of 1873-74.

Ste. Anne's Catholic Church is one of the oldest parishes in the northern territory. The current building was constructed in the 1870's.

Credit: Thomas M. Piljac

Harbor Haldimand Bay stretches along the town's lake shore. Ferries regularly shuttle in and out transporting freight and island visitors. In early July the harbor is jammed with boats having just completed the Chicago to Mackinac Yacht Race.

Stairway To The East Bluff Two side streets to your left, Bogan Lane and Church Street, abruptly end at the island's cliffs. Each has a well-built wooden stairway (complete with rest platforms) leading to the east bluff.

LaFramboise House   This is a private home, not open to the public. Located just west of Ste. Anne's Church, it was once the home of Magdalaine LaFramboise. One of the interesting women of Mackinac's history, her life is described in Chapter Six.

Ste. Anne's Church   The building is open to visitors as long as services are not in progress. Originally called the Mission of St. Ignace, the parish began in 1670 as Father Dablon's birchbark chapel. It was first moved north to St. Ignace, then south across the straits when the French built Fort Michilimackinac. In 1742, many of the Indian parishioners decided to relocate further south. The parish records were copied, and the Indians took the originals as well as the parish name with them. The church at the fort was renamed *Ste. Anne de Michilimackinac*.

In 1780, it was one of the first buildings Major Patrick Sinclair transferred to Mackinac Island. It was placed at the corner of Market and Hoban Streets, where the Michigan Bell Telephone building is located today. Around 1825, the church cemetary was overcrowded and Magdalaine LaFramboise donated the lots east of her home to the parish. The structure was moved to the new location by 1827, and most of the graves were transferred to a new cemetary in the interior. By 1872, the old church was in terrible condition. It was torn down, and the parishioners attended Mass at the old Mission Church and at the Courthouse Building until the new one was completed. When the new church opened in 1878, the only remainders from the original building were the pews and a painting of Ste. Anne. In the 1890's a choir loft, steeple, and front steps were added to the structure. It is an old-fashioned church with many beautiful carvings, paintings, statues, and stained glass windows.

A museum located in the church basement displays books, records, and religious articles dating back to 1695, as well as paintings and stained glass windows from the original structure.

The shrine gardens just east of Ste. Anne's were laid out in 1962. You can follow the Stations of the Cross along flower-

The interior of Ste. Anne's is rich in the fine details of nineteenth century carvings and paintings.

Courtesy of Mackinac Island State Park Commission

bordered walkways; and view the graves of Magdalaine LaFramboise and her daughter, Josette LaFramboise Pierce.

Mission Church   This Protestant church was built under the direction of Reverend Ferry in 1829-30 through a combination of donated money and labor. The congregation had a varied membership that included teachers, school pupils, village residents, officers and clerks of the American Fur Company, Government Agents, Indian converts, and soldiers and officers from the fort. At its largest it had eighty members, including distinguished islanders such as Henry Schoolcraft and Robert Stuart. When they gathered in the tiny church on Sundays, the members from the fort would march to the door, stack their muskets outside, and file into the pews—leaving one man outside to stand guard over their arms.

The Ferrys left the island in 1834. Although they never had a large number of converts, their work did a great deal to educate the children of the island. By then the fur trade was dying, and fewer Indians were coming to Mackinac (many had been relocated to reservations in the west). The Protestant Mission had closed by 1838, and the land and buildings were sold to a private party. In the 1870's, the Catholics of Ste. Anne's Parish used the building to hold services while their new church was being built. The Mission Church reopened briefly in 1895, as the "Union Chapel of Mackinac Island" under the sponsorship of two summer residents, Milton Tootle Jr. and Frank F. Dinsmore. It soon closed, and was eventually purchased by the Mackinac Island State Park Commission and restored as a historic site.

Mission House   Not open to the public.

Built to house Indian children and teach them reading, writing, math, and practical work such as farming, blacksmithing, sewing, and cooking. The school was constructed in 1825 by the Reverend William Ferry and his wife Amanda, early Protestant missionaries on the island. Over five-hundred pupils attended the school over the years, many being day students who resided with their families on the island. Students ages ranged from four to eighteen years. Most children spoke only French or Indian dialects when they first came to the classroom. At first the Ferrys hired an interpreter, but when that proved too difficult for teaching efficiently, the children learned English.

The Ferry family lived in the west wing, the center comprised the dining room and offices, and the east wing held the schoolrooms. Church services were conducted in the upper room of the east wing of the building until the Mission Church was built several years later.

In the early 1850's, Mission House was turned into a hotel that rivaled the Island House. It closed after World War II, and is now owned by the Mackinac Island State Park Commission. It is used as a dormitory for summer employees.

Mission Point Resort   Most of these buildings were originally constructed by Moral Re-Armament, the organization described in Chapter Nine that owned many island properties after World War II. The buildings later became Mackinac College, then were sold and turned into a resort hotel complex. Since the early 1970's, it has had a number of different owners and names, most recently the Mackinac Hotel. Quite a few renovations have been completed, and the new conference center was built near the lake shore in the 1980's. As of this writing it is being renovated under new management, and is known as Mission Point Resort.

Robinson's Folly   This scenic overlook stretching 127 feet above the beach is at the center of a number of island legends. The site is named after Captain Daniel Robertson, Commander of Fort Mackinac from 1782-87. Over the years his name was corrupted to *Robinson*, and the bluff was named *Robinson's Folly*. No one knows how the legends began, but several of the more well-known versions are:

1. He built a private summer home at the edge of the cliff to get away from the fort. It was the sight of a good deal of revelry, and Robertson could be found here smoking and drinking with his brother officers every night. But either heavy winds or a crumbling cliff caused the house to fall to the shore. An 1882 guidebook claimed that debris could still be seen on the beach below.

2. Walking near this spot, Robertson thought he saw a beautiful maiden. He tried to approach her, but she kept backing up toward the edge of the cliff. As he rushed forward to rescue her, the girl dissolved into thin air and Robertson fell to his death on the rocks below.

3. Robertson had been part of the garrison at Michilimackinac in the 1763 massacre. An Indian maiden saved his life, and they became very attached to one another. Robertson also had a white wife, and when he took command of the

Fort all three came to Mackinac to live. He built a house here for his Indian girlfriend, but pressure from his wife forced him to break off their relationship. The Indian girl lured him to the house for one last meeting, then she enticed him to join her at the edge of the cliff. When he did, she grabbed his arm and jumped, killing them both.

4. Robertson built a house near the cliff for his future wife, an Indian girl. A warrior had wanted to marry her and was extremely jealous and angry that she had chosen the white man instead. Their wedding banquet was celebrated at the house, and during the party an army sergeant spotted the jealous Indian hiding in the bushes with a gun. He jumped in to stop the shot and was killed. Robertson struggled with the Indian until they were at the edge of the cliff. The Indian slipped, reached out, and grabbed onto a root...and hung there above the rocks below. When the girl sprang forward to help pull him to safety, he grabbed her arm and yanked her over the cliff, and both fell to their death.

5. A beautiful young Indian girl was betrothed to a loathsome brave, but she loved Robertson and he loved her. He built a house for her on the cliff that overhangs the shore. The rejected brave found the house and killed the woman while Robertson was out. Robertson came home as the Indian was leaving, they fought and struggled near the edge of the cliff and both fell to the rocks below.

Most of the legends can be traced back to the 1840's, and probably say more about attitudes and prejudices of the time than they do about reality. It is also interesting that they sprang up at the beginning of the tourist era, which would seem to indicate that they were created for the entertainment of visitors. But most legends have some basis of truth to them, and no doubt Robertson committed some kind of 'folly' here and had his name attached to the spot. We do know that Captain Daniel Robertson did not die on Mackinac Island, he left the island after giving up command of the fort in 1787.

On the rocky cliffs above Lake Huron, Robinson's Folly is both a scenic overlook and the site of several island legends.

Courtesy of Mackinac Island State Park Commission

Water Pumping Station   This modern facility (completed in 1987) pumps water from Lake Huron, chlorinates and flouridates it, then sends it up to a reservoir near Fort Holmes. Distribution throughout the island is accomplished with gravitational assistance.

Giant's Stairway, Fairy Arch, Fairy's Kitchen, Echo Grotto Because so much of the island has been preserved, it's a bit shocking when you come across evidence of other sites that were deliberately destroyed. Along this route were four points of interest that are discussed in nineteenth century guidebooks, but no longer exist today. We mention them both to point out features that visitors once would have enjoyed, and to illustrate the disappointing loss of irreplacable objects for future generations.

As you travel along the road past Robinson's Folly (but before you reach Dwightwood Springs), there were several beautiful rock formations that were formed over thousands of years. No one is sure why they were eradicated, but it is commonly believed they were demolished to make gravel for the road around the island.

Another arched rock was located just past Robinson's Folly, and was called the *Fairy Arch*. Natural limestone stairs known as *The Giant's Stairway* led up to it. A nearby cave filled with tiny rock formations was called the *Fairy's Kitchen*. There are many legends and romances connected to these sites.

The most common tale was that the fairy spirits guarded the Giant's Stairway to keep the giant Unk-ta-hee from reaching the cliffs. If Unk-ta-hee ever reaches the top, he will claim the island as his kingdom, and pull it below the waters.

Fortunately, a road crew made sure that Unk-ta-hee would never make it to the top by blowing up the stairway.

Farther down the road a recession in the bluff formed a grotto, which multiplied captured voices with an echo effect.

Dwightwood Springs   Edwin O. Wood, an east bluff cottager, donated funds to create a resting place for visitors to refresh and enjoy themselves at this tiny spring. It was a memorial to his son Dwight, who died in 1905 while trying to save his brother's life. Edwin also wrote the famous history of the island, *Historic Mackinac*, which appeared in the early years of the twentieth century.

Arch Rock   Above the road, one of Mackinac's most famous sights is clearly visible between the cliffs. The limestone arch of brecciated rock stands almost 150 feet above the water, and is fifty feet wide at its broadest point. A staircase and trail climb the hill. At the top you will find a viewing platform and public restrooms.

A wooded shelter stands in front of Dwightwood Springs along the island's eastern shore.

Credit: Thomas M. Piljac

The Indians believed that this rock was *Manitous Landing Place*—where the Great Spirit entered the island each morning with the rising sun. It was also the bridge over which departed souls could find their resting place on the island. Here is the legend of its creation:

A Chippewa band lived on the shores of Lake Huron. She-Who-Walks-Like-The-Mist was the very beautiful daughter of the chief, and many braves wanted her for their wife. She was also a hard worker and her father was very proud of her. At first she was friendly to many of the braves, but suddenly she changed and would sit silently with downcast eyes instead of welcoming them. Finally her father grew very angry and told her: "You must take a husband and produce many sons. I have never beaten you, but I will now unless you tell me why you are acting this way." She replied: "Two months ago, I paddled to the eastern shore to collect wild rice. It was late and the stars

The graceful imposing Arch Rock towers high above Lake Huron.

were in the sky when I was returning. Suddenly, a handsome Indian brave appeared to me. He wore clothing of white deer-skin covered with beautiful designs. Even more wonderful was his robe of shining light. I have never seen anything like it." Then he spoke to me.

"Oh my beautiful one," he said, "I have watched you in your village for a very long time. I am the son of Chief Evening Star and I live high above you. Although I am a Sky Person, I want you to be mine for all time. When I told my father of your beauty, he allowed me to descend to earth and ask you to join me in my home in the sky."

"What did you say to him?" the Chief asked.

"Father, I told him that I would marry him."

Her father became very angry. "You shall marry no one at all!" he cried. He grabbed her, tied her hands and feet, and shoved her into their canoe, then quickly paddled to the island of Great Dancing Spirits. There he dragged her up to the huge rock which towered above the beach and tied her to it.

"Here you shall lie," he said, "until you decide to be a proper daughter and obey me."

She stayed there many days, suffering from the hot sun and pouring rain, shivering in the heavy winds that blew up from the lake. As she wept, her tears flowed upon the rock. Slowly, they began to melt the stone—until at last an arch appeared beneath her and she was left on a high bridge. That night, the rays of the evening star appeared through the arch, and her handsome brave walked down the rays from the sky. He unloosed her bonds, gathered her into his arms, and carried her up the beams to the land of the Sky People, where they lived together forever.

There is another mini-arch half way up the cliff to Arch Rock. It can only be seen from below. Old guidebooks refer to this as *Sannillac Arch*. Today it is called *Fairy Arch*. Legend proclaims this smaller arch as the gate through which fairy children entered. The adult fairy spirits came through Arch Rock.

Old Power Plant/Generating Station   Oil fueled generators located in this building once provided electricity for the island before underwater cables were extended from St. Ignace. It also served as the water intake station for the island.

Lone Lake   Secluded in a wooded glen, this small mirrored pond is visible on the north side of the road. Particularly attractive in the early morning hours, this quiet pool is the spring nesting area of wild ducks and geese.

Wildflower Trail   Just off the road is a short, three-hundred yard wildflower trail that offers the three major habitats (forest, beach, and swamp) on the island. Along the trail are exhibit plaques explaining the plants and type of land that you are seeing.

Pointe Aux Pins   Translated from French, "point of pines" marks the northernmost tip of the island. It is also the half-way point on your trip around the island. You can see the mainland of the upper peninsula to the north and west. To the east are the St. Martin Islands and the mainland beyond.

British Landing   This is the spot where British soldiers and their Indian allies came ashore during their 1812 invasion. Later, American forces landed in the same location in their 1814 attempt to retake Mackinac. It is also the place where the ice bridge forms each year for winter travel to the mainland. St. Ignace and the Mackinac Bridge can be very clearly seen from this point. A snack shop, picnic area, nature center, and restrooms are available for public use during daylight hours.

A nearby one mile nature trail travels from the shoreline to a wooden observation platform overlooking the north end of the island and the marshes of Croghan's Water. The path moves from the cool, wet conditions of the shore where evergreens flourish to the shady hardwood trees. Small patches of stones along the trail are remnants of ancient shorelines. Displays describe plants and animals common to the area.

There is an Indian legend about the ice bridge. It is said that centuries ago a peaceful tribe called Mishinemackinawgo lived on the island. One winter, Seneca Indians from New York crossed the ice and annihilated the tribe except for two young lovers. The pair hid in caves, and when they thought it was safe they fled across the frozen water on snowshoes made of fir branches. To confuse any Senecas that might discover their tracks, they turned their shoes around so that it looked as if the steps were approaching (instead of leaving) the island, and made it across safely.

Brown's Brook   This little brook along the side of the road is fed by underground springs. Rainwater that has seeped through the loose limestone rock into underground caverns and channels is the source.

Chimney Rock   A chimney-shaped, brecciated limestone formation on the bluff above the road. It once stood on the shore of ancient Lake Nipissing, and was formed by its lapping waves.

Ski Area   On the bluff below Stonecliffe is a large cleared area with no brush or trees on the side of the cliff. This is the site of a failed 1960's attempt to introduce a ski program to Mackinac Island.

Lover's Leap   Shortly before Devil's Kitchen is a limestone formation that rises 145 feet above the shore. Its name originates from an Indian legend.

Lo-tah, a Chippewa woman, sat high above the waters on a lonely rock, watching for the return of the warrior canoes. Her young brave had gone to fight the enemy in the east, to prove his worth to her father so they could marry. One day she saw tiny specks on the horizon, and to her joy they slowly turned into canoes. But as they neared, she heard the warriors chanting the death song. She searched among the faces for her beloved, but then her spirit told her that he had died. She remained atop the great rock for seven sleeps. Each night her lover would appear to her in a dream as a beautiful bird. On the eighth day, she knew it was time to join her beloved. That morning her father found her crumpled body at the base of the rock.

Devil's Kitchen   This cavern was gouged out of the rock years ago when lake levels were much higher. Nineteenth century guidebooks mention that the water of Lake Huron often rose so high that the entrance was covered and the cave inaccessible. Here is an interesting legend attached to the spot:

An Indian tribe had been summering on the island. When it was time to move to their winter hunting grounds on the mainland, an old blind man was left behind. His beautiful young granddaughter, Willow Wand, insisted on staying to care for him. She loved a brave warrior who was away on a journey, and her grandfather was concerned that he would never find her because she had not gone with the rest of the tribe.

"I have placed a white deerskin with vermillion markings high on the cliff," she told him. "That way my beloved will know to find me here, and he will rescue us both."

Devil's Kitchen.

Courtesy of Mackinac Island State Park Commission

The old man was worried because they were surrounded by danger. At nearby Devil's Cave lived a group of cannibal giants who would destroy them if they were found. The old man prayed to the Great Spirit to protect them. Willow Wand found a cave on the cliffs that was out of sight of the cannibal's cave. She led her grandfather there and they settled on the ledge, but soon discovered that a she-bear lived in the back of the cave. The girl wanted to try and kill it, but her grandfather said: "No, let all here live in peace." The bear seemed to understand his words, and returned to the back of the cave.

In time, their food and water ran so low that Willow Wand would cry in her sleep for water. As he listened to her, it reminded the old man of the time of his daughter's death. She had told him then that Willow Wand had inherited a gift of magic from her father, a gift that if properly used would give her great powers as a medicine woman. One of her powers was the ability to bring forth springs of pure water from the earth. But she could not be told of this power until she had undergone seven days of fasting, which would mark her entrance into womanhood. On the seventh night, Willow Wand leapt from her sleep and struck the rock wall with her hand, crying "Water!" A tiny stream burst forth from the rocks at once, and as they drank her grandfather told her of her gifts. Now he could rest at last, so he lay down and slept.

Later that night Willow Wand could hear screams of terror coming from the Devil's Kitchen. She looked down to see her young lover being bound and dragged into the cave. When she screamed, the chief of the cannibals (Red Gee-bis) looked up and saw her. He immediately perceived that she held great powers, so he stopped the ceremony. He used his own magic and suddenly appeared on the ledge next to Willow Wand, demanding that she give him her hand so that he could steal her powers. She laughed mockingly, then struck the wall and sent a mighty gush of water that flung the chief into a hole and quenched the torture fires. Then Willow Wand sent a bridge of rainbow mist for her young man to climb to her side. She cut his bonds, gave him a pipe to share with her grandfather, then brought out more water to drown the demons and put out their fires forever.

When the rest of the tribe returned the following spring, the people found Willow Wand, her husband, and her grandfather living comfortably in their cave. The terrors of the horrible Wen-di-goes were forever ended, and their abode, the Devil's Cave where they roasted and ate men was quiet at last.

Fenwick's Cache   On the cliff above Devil's Kitchen is a small cave opening. Legend says that the fairies hid there while the devil cooked his food. In *Historic Mackinac*, Edwin Wood mentions that a grown person can crawl in, stand up, and have a good view from a lookout hole. He says the spot is named for Bishop Edward Fenwick, who did a great deal of work for the missionaries. But no one knows why this spot is called his cache.

Old Distillery   A distillery was once located at the bottom of the west bluff. When the British invaded in 1812, the villagers sought refuge behind its thick walls. It is believed to have been built atop an Indian burial ground.

Island School   The Mackinac Island school has an average enrollment of one-hundred students. Constructed in 1964, it offers a complete educational program from kindergarten through the twelfth grade.

Boardwalk   The original wooden walkway was constructed in the 1930's. The one-half mile long deck hugs the southwest shore of the island, and extends from the beach below the Grand Hotel grounds to the city. It was completely rebuilt in 1986, at which time the end ramp, hand rails, benches, and scenic viewing points were added.

Area Two
Interior Tour, Arch Rock, Sugar Loaf,
Skull Cave, Fort Holmes, 1814 Battlefield
As we mentioned earlier, the island has many interior roads, paths, and trails but our descriptions won't follow a particular route. We begin with the east side of the island, and move to the west.

Scout Barracks   The barracks and parade ground located behind Fort Mackinac are the destination of over five-hundred Michigan Boy Scouts and Girl Scouts each year. They assist the historical interpreters at Mackinac Island State Park Commission exhibits, and help with trail maintenance and litter removal projects.

Rifle Range   Behind the fort parade grounds and south of Skull Cave is a clearing that leads to the heights behind Fort Holmes. Troops stationed on the island regularly used this area for target practice, and you can still see the bare hillside where brush and trees were blown away. It is accessible from Rifle Range Road.

Crow's Nest Trail Running along the bluff east of Fort Mackinac is the Crow's Nest Trail. From a point just west of the east bluff cottages you may hike this quiet path, or descend a walkway to Marquette Park.

East Bluff/Cottages Many of these stately homes were constructed in the late nineteenth century, as described in Chapter Seven. Overlooking the Straits of Mackinac, these lovely summer houses occupy a peaceful, less traveled portion of the island. Additional information about island cottages can be found in the description of the west bluff homes in *Area Three*.

Cass Cliff A memorial bronze tablet on the east bluff marks the cliff. Located near the woods and Crow's Nest Trail, it honors Lewis Cass, who visited the island in 1820 as Governor of the Michigan Territory. He was a teacher, lawyer, explorer, soldier, diplomat, and statesman. The monument was dedicated in 1915.

Anne's Tablet In the woods to the east of the fort lies a small hidden knoll just off of Crow's Nest Trail. There you'll find a one acre memorial to Constance Fenimore Woolson, who wrote the popular novel *Anne* which was set on Mackinac Island. Woolson was the great-niece of James Fenimore Cooper *(Last of the Mohicans)*. She died in Italy in 1894.

There are benches circling the site with all of Woolson's published works engraved in granite. The memorial was a gift to the people of Michigan from Woolson's family in 1917. A magnificent view of the harbor awaits visitors to this lovely, secluded spot.

Arch Rock Arch Rock is a powerful limestone formation towering above Lake Huron. A nearby staircase leads to the Nicolet Watch Tower, and a commanding view of the surrounding region. A bronze memorial tablet honors Jean Nicolet as the first white man to enter the Straits of Mackinac. Accessible from Arch Rock Road (east from Huron Road) or by a stairway leading up from Lake Shore Road (M-185).

Arch Rock, as seen from a viewing area atop the heights.

Courtesy of Mackinac Island State Park Commission

Lime Kiln Lime Kiln Trail is in the deep woods, between Sugar Loaf Road and the Rifle Range. It leads past the ruins of the old lime kiln used by early soldiers. In its original state, it was a furnace six feet deep and fifteen feet across. Here they burned limestone to make the mortar, whitewash, and plaster that was used in the construction of many island buildings and the walls of Fort Mackinac.

Sugar Loaf This cone-shaped rock of brecciated limestone was originally part of the nearby cliffs, but years of erosion have worn away the weaker soil and left the formation standing alone. It is situated on the most ancient part of the island, and was once surrounded by the waters of Lake Algonquin.

Sugar Loaf as seen from Point Lookout.

Courtesy of Mackinac Island State Park Commission

A small cave about halfway up on the north side marks the level of the highest shoreline. It is the largest limestone stack on the island, seventy-five feet above the ground and 284 feet above the water.

Some Indian legends say that it was the wigwam for the Great Spirit (Gitchi-Manitou) when he came to the island. Another legend says that it was made by Man-a-boz-ho, messenger of the Great Spirit. He was capable of super-human feats, but in his old age he came to live where the first humans were born, the island of the Great Dancing Spirits.

Ten braves who lived in a tribe to the south decided to venture to the island and find Man-a-boz-ho so that he would grant each of them the special wish they held deep in their hearts. They traveled to the Straits of Mackinac and carefully sprinkled tobacco on the face of the calm water. They were a bit fearful as they drew close to the great island, for this was a sacred place. Summoning their courage they beached their canoes, and filed up the cliffs to the rocks and forests at the top.

They came upon Man-a-boz-ho as he sat on a white deer hide below a great cliff. His long white hair was decorated with many fine eagle plumes that moved slowly in the lake breeze. He sat silently with a pipe in his hand and watched the young men. The first brave stepped forward, and placed his gifts of tobacco and wampum on the deer hide. "Grandfather, we have come to ask that you grant our wishes," he told him. Man-a-boz-ho sucked his pipe and nodded. Then he spoke, and his voice was like that of the great Thunderbird. "I shall see," he said.

The first youth asked to be a great war chief, so that he could always drive away the enemies of his people. Man-a-boz-ho granted his wish. The second wished to be a great hunter, so that his people would never go hungry. Again, Man-a-boz-ho granted his desire. The third asked to be a powerful medicine man, the fourth a strong dancer, the fifth an orator who spoke wise words, the sixth a great teller of legends, the seventh a maker of swift canoes, the eighth the handsomest of braves, the ninth a fast runner and the strongest in games. Man-a-boz-ho granted them all their wishes.

When it came time for the tenth to speak his greatest desire, all waited wondering what it could be. The young brave stepped forward and placed his gifts on the deerskin. "I wish that I may never die, but that I shall live for all time," he said.

Man-a-boz-ho's wrinkled face became clouded with anger. He raised his hand and pointed the stem of his pipe at the youth. "You have asked the one gift that no mortal can have," he thundered. "But I have given my word that all requests shall be granted, you will have your wish of eternal life."

While the others watched, their friend began growing, twisting, spreading, until he became a tall rock. He stands there today, living forever on the heights of the island of the Great Dancing Spirits.

Fort Holmes   Fort Holmes can be reached by traveling Fort Holmes Road, or by a stairway leading up the bluff from Rifle Range Road.

The area is the highest point on the island, 168 feet above Fort Mackinac, 325 feet above the lake, and 896 feet higher than the Atlantic Ocean. Five-thousand years ago this spot would have been a small island, with water lapping seventy-five feet down the hill.

At the start of the War of 1812, the British used this high ground to force the surrender of Fort Mackinac. The British garrison later reinforced the heights, built a block-house and storage buildings for ammunition and powder, and named it Fort George. When the Americans regained the island after the war, they added to the fortifications (see Chapter Five), and renamed it Fort Holmes in honor of the brave major who died during the American attack of 1814. It was used primarily as an observation post. Soldiers were never permanently stationed there because of the lack of a water supply.

All accounts of activity at Fort Holmes cease in December of 1817, and it is believed that it was destroyed during target practice later in the nineteenth century. The buildings were reconstructed in 1936, but they fell into disrepair and were torn down during the 1960's. Today it is just a grassy wall with a thick wooden entrance, but you can see the fortifications of the original stronghold and walk the ramparts.

This promontory provides a magnificent view of Lake Huron, the surrounding islands, and the mainland. Between 1852 and 1908, various wooden observation towers were built, but they were removed for safety reasons after numerous accidents. There was a curio shop here from 1898 until after World War I.

Point Lookout   Along the trail to Fort Holmes is Point Lookout. A wooded shelter offers a stunning view of forests, Lake Huron, and Sugar Loaf.

Skull Cave   Located near the intersection of Rifle Range and Garrison Roads, the cave is at the base of a thirty-foot high limestone stack that was part of the ancient island over eleven-thousand years ago. Wave action from the ancient lakes cut

Skull Cave.

Courtesy of Mackinac Island State Park Commission

away the softer material surrounding it, as well as weaker rock on the west side of the stack where the cave eventually formed.

It is believed that this was the bone-filled cave where Alexander Henry slept shortly after surviving the Indian uprising at Fort Michilimackinac. The source of the bones could have been Indian burials, a massacre by a warring tribe, a band of Indians trying to escape a flood and drowning, or a receptacle for the bones of prisoners devoured at war feasts.

Cemetaries   The three island cemetaries are grouped together off Garrison Road.

The Catholic cemetary has been used since the late 1820's, when the church was moved from its original location at Market and Hoban Streets. Many of the graves from the old churchyard were relocated here.

The Protestant cemetary is the northernmost of the three, and has been used since the 1830's, when the first mission was established on the island.

The Post or Military cemetary holds graves of military personnel and their families who died while on duty at Fort Mackinac. There are about 142 graves, but not all have been identified. It is believed that the unidentified plots include the graves of six British soldiers who died in the War of 1812.

Center Of The Island When you reach the intersection of the following roads you are at the center of Mackinac Island. They are: British Landing, Annex, Crooked Tree, and Garrison Road.

Great Turtle Park A park, complete with playground, baseball diamond, basketball court, horse-riding ring, picnic area, and restrooms is located adjacent to Garrison Road. It was once a gravel pit, but the dedicated efforts of the members of Mackinac Island Recreation and Development have turned it into a community asset. Long hours of hard work and a host of fund-raising activities have provided a much-needed play area and athletic arena. Eventually the facilities will include a recreation center and an indoor pool.

Surrey Hills Mackinac Island Carriage Tours maintains this complex north of the Grand Hotel off of Hoban & Garrison Roads. Here, tour groups transfer from small carriages to larger thirty-five passenger buggies for the State Park portion of their journey. Visitors may inspect a carriage museum, antique surrey, livery equipment, a Clydesdale horse, and a working blacksmith shop. Food and gift shops are also available.

Harrisonville This residential area is north of Surrey Hills. The homes of many year-round island inhabitants share the area with several employee housing complexes as well as the condominiums and apartments of summer residents. The

Harrisonville General Store, an old-fashioned corner grocery, is the center of the community. Once called the Indian Village, residents today still refer to it as the *Village*.

Airport   Although a grass landing strip was cleared on the island before World War II, the airport did not have a paved runway or terminal building until the 1960's. Today, it is a modern facility with up-to-date equipment. (See Chapter Ten for more details). If you visit the airport, please do not wander along the runways or in the plane parking areas without first obtaining the approval of the airport manager.

Wawashkamo Golf Links   An Indian Chief provided the name Wawashkamo (which translates into *Crooked Trail* or *Walks a Crooked Path*) after watching an early round of golf. Established in 1898, this is the oldest unchanged golf links in the State, and is now a Michigan Historic Site. It is open to the public. (See Chapter Ten for more details).

Cave In The Woods   A marked trail leading southwest from State Road brings you to a long, low, limestone cave located one-hundred and forty feet above Lake Huron. It is one of the oldest rock formations on the island. The opening is small, you must bend down to enter. When Lake Algonquin surrounded the island this would have been a beach.

Crack In The Island   By continuing on the same winding footpath that leads past Cave in the Woods, you will arrive at a long, shallow fissure on the western heights just north of the airport. It was once much longer and deeper than it is today, but during the nineteenth century it was used as a garbage dump. It is said that years ago one could drop a stone into the crack without being able to hear it land. Horses were said to have fallen into the fissure and disappeared. Some geologists believe that it was formed by an ancient earthquake. Others are convinced that underground waters eroded the softer rock that once filled the crevice.

There is an Indian legend about this spot:

One of the island's many tree-lined paths.

Courtesy of Mackinac Island State Park Commission

The crack was created by Git-chi Man-i-tou, the Great Spirit, before he fled to the Northern Lights. He stamped his foot and created this giant crevice, and gave it magic powers. This land of the Great Dancing Spirits was once inhabited by giants. Git-chi Man-i-tou decided that they must leave the earth, so he turned some into 'waiting spirits' and others into 'wandering demons'. The waiting spirits became rocks, pinnacles, and boulders. The demons became cruel and heartless men. One giant refused to become a rock or a man, but tried to go to the 'Under Land' (where the spirits of the dead dwell) through the crack in the island. This crack lay in a place of deep shadows and there were no footholds. When the giant tried to descend he found that his fingers froze to the mouth of the opening as punishment. He was sentenced by Git-chi Man-i-tou to hang there forever, dangling above the terrible dark cavern. It is said that his hands can still be seen today beneath the scaling limestone. Although the giant cannot move, he has cruel powers that he likes to use. Should anyone step on those giant stone fingers, they will instantly be struck with misfortune.

On the day that the Great Spirit completes his spells, the crack will split and fall apart. The island will sink once more, and the red man will prevail.

Battlefield   Originally this land was part of the grant Michael Dousman received from the British after the 1812 invasion. Dousman used the land to grow grain to produce rum, a lucrative commodity at the time.

The Battle of 1814 took place on both sides of British Landing Road. The Americans came across Croghan's Marsh, the British forces were waiting where Wawashkamo now stands. Their lines were near the present clubhouse, and their artillery positioned on a rise to the north. Indian allies were hidden to the east and west in the surrounding woods. The American lines were across from the present first and fifth fairways, and they were unable to see the Indians from the clearing. An empty field stood between them.

On the northern side of British Landing Road, across from Wawashkamo, is a display that shows the lines of march and a diagram of the battle of 1814. Further down the road a little path on the northern side leads to a small mound of rocks with a historical plaque dedicated to the soldiers who died in the battle.

Around 1819, Dousman sold the farm. It was eventually purchased by Michael Early, who farmed hay and vegetables. When he died, his sons Peter and John received the property and divided it. Peter leased part of his land for a race track in 1894. In 1898, the founders of Wawashkamo leased the land for their golf links. Peter died in 1923, and his heirs sold the proprty to the State for $18,750. John sold most of his larger portion to the State around the same time for $50,000. John's grandson now owns a parcel of land on British Landing Road, and operates the nearby Cannonball Snack Shop.

Eagle Point Cave   Located off of Scott's Road, it is a tiny cave set in a small cliff, surrounded by trees and brush. There were once stone stairs leading up to it, but they have decayed. It was called Eagle Point by the Indians who worshiped these birds as divinity because of their fearlessness. They believed it was a popular resting spot for eagles.

Scott's Cave   Some older maps of the island list Scott's Cave Road. It is now called Scott's Road because the cave isn't there any more. It was once east of Croghan's Water, toward the lake shore, and was blown up some time in the last century, probably for road gravel. The name "Scott" most likely came from former post commandant Martin Scott.

An 1882 guidebook said that it had a low entrance, but once inside a very tall person could stand up. It also had a very dark hidden chamber.

Croghan's Water   Located between British Landing and the 1814 Battlefield, this marsh is a drainage area for rain and melt water from the surrounding woods and fields. It is not fed by streams or underground springs, and goes through wet and dry cycles. Usually it is very wet in the spring, and dry in the fall. The area is named after Colonel George Croghan, who commanded the American forces in the August, 1814 invasion. It is also believed that Peter Early operated a distillery in a cave near here, but it has never been found.

Friendship Altar   Located at the end of the nature trail from British Landing. The altar is an isolated limestone stack with a large tree growing in the crown of its formation. Nearby is Lake Nipissing Bluff, the former shoreline of that lake. Beyond the bluff is a trail that leads to Croghan's Water.

The Indian legend of Friendship Altar is as follows:

A teacher came among the Indians and each day he stood at the altar and taught them. They learned to till the soil, to perform the arts of the land and the sea, to hunt, dress skins, build canoes, and fish. But as men progressed they began to kill each other. The teacher was sad. He told them, "I taught you to work and live. Don't waste time fighting. Live as friends." They ignored him, rejected his advice, and quit coming to his lessons. Soon only the birds came. He decided to leave, but before he left he taught them to sing, so that they could cheer plodding men. They could tell men in their song that the teacher would come again and help all men to be friends. Then the teacher ascended to the top of the altar, stepped on a magic vine, climbed up, and disappeared into the sky.

Area Three
Historic Buildings, Business District,
Grand Hotel, Cottages, Stonecliffe

Doud's Grocery Store   On the east end of town, across from Marquette Park, stands one of the oldest businesses on the island. It was started in the late nineteenth century by James Doud, an Irish immigrant. The general store was originally located at the head of the Arnold Dock, but was destroyed by a large fire in 1941. It was then relocated to its present site, and is one of the few island businesses open year round.

McGulpin House   Located near the corner of Fort and Market Streets—behind Doud's. Admission through the State Park ticket.

This is believed to be the oldest house on Mackinac Island, built in the 1770's or 1780's. It may have been one of the buildings that was dragged across the ice from old Fort Michilimackinac. Originally located behind Ste. Anne's Church on Huron Street, it was moved here and restored by the Mackinac Island State Park Commission in the early 1980's. Historians believe it to be the former home of William McGulpin, a baker for the American Fur Company, who bought the house in 1817. Restored to the era when McGulpin owned it, this building is a good example of French-Canadian architecture, with its distinctive style, sharply pitched roof, and complex connections between logs. Early sketches of the island showed that these homes were traditionally enclosed with a five-foot stockade fence to establish property borders. As with many early buildings, the roof was covered with cedar bark shingles, which were held in place by thin wooden poles nailed

McGulpin House may be the oldest home on Mackinac Island.

Credit: Thomas M. Piljac

to the roof boards. Clapboard siding, a room addition connected by a doorway on the south side, and enlarged windows
were added in the 1820's.

Inside is a model display of how the house originally
looked, and drawings and a wall exhibit show how it was
changed over the years (layers of wallpaper, wood, plaster).
The original first floor walls were constructed with hand-hewn
logs laid horizontally, one on top of the other. They are connected at corners with dovetail joints. Clay mortar was used
in the cracks between the logs to weatherize the building. The
house would have been whitewashed inside and out.

Trinty Episcopal Church   In 1842, the first Episcopal services were held in the upper room of Fort Mackinac by the
Fort Chaplain, Reverend John O'Brien. Soldiers from the fort
built the altar and Bishop's chair, which are still used in the
church today. In 1873, a congregation was formed, and members met at the old courthouse (now City Hall) for services
until the present building west of Marquette Park was completed in 1882. The Rt. Reverend Thomas F. Davies, D.D., was

Episcopal Bishop of the diocese of Michigan, and a summer resident on the island during the late nineteenth century. He frequently officiated at the services. The church is still an active congregation, and is open to visitors when services are not in progress.

Fort Mackinac   This beautifully restored military post evokes a strong sense of preserved history, and is superior to most similar locations across the country. It was originally built by the British, who were concerned about American attack on the less defensible Fort Michilimackinac during the Revolutionary War. For more than one-hundred and ten years it served as an active military post, changing hands three times between British and American forces. It was a visible sign of each nation's military presence in the region as they struggled for control of the lucrative fur trade. Additional details about life at the fort for the average soldier can be found in Chapter Five.

Since this fortress was constructed to repel southern (American) attackers, it was built atop a broad-faced hill overlooking the harbor. Although the southern walls were three-feet thick to shield it from naval bombardment, the remainder of the compound was weakly protected with a combined barrier of limestone and wood picket fence. This thick, white enclosure dotted with musket loopholes, and guarded by towering blockhouses offers the appearance of a mountain citadel.

Two entrances provide access to the compound today. The northern gate (back) is located off of Huron Road on the Avenue of Flags. The southern portal (visible from Marquette Park) can be entered by ascending a ramp that gently climbs one-hundred and fifty feet to the top of the cliff. Begin your tour with a fine orientation to the fort and island by viewing the twelve minute slide show: *The Heritage of Mackinac.* It is presented many times each day at the old commissary building near the southern entrance.

You are free to examine the buildings and exhibits on your own, or under the tutelage of a costumed interpreter. You

The interior of the Post Hospital at Fort Mackinac.

Courtesy of Mackinac Island State Park Commission

can view the Blockhouses, Quartermaster's Storehouse, Post Headquarters, Bath House, Soldier's Barracks, Schoolhouse, Hospital, Officer's Quarters, Canteen, Post Commandant's House, Guardhouse, and more. Each location is arrayed to reveal its most interesting period, and present the functions conducted in that building. Informative displays at each point of interest will help to enhance your comprehension of life at Fort Mackinac. There are additional live demonstrations of military life including: cannon and musket firings, fife and drum musical concerts, and re-enactments of court martials.

If you wish to dine at the Tea Room, it is located on the south side of the Officer's Stone Quarters (just west of the guardhouse). It offers patio dining with a lovely view of the park, lake, and town below.

Old Post Hospital High on the bluff east of the fort sits a small cluster of buildings that were once medical facilities.

The large structure served as a hospital, while the adjacent building housed the staff. A small shed at the rear was the fort morgue. These buildings presently house employees of the Mackinac Island State Park Commission, and are not open to the general public.

Major's and Captain's Quarters   Buildings are not open to the public.

Located slightly northwest of the fort, these houses were officer's quarters built in the late nineteenth century. When a second company was added to the post after the island became a national park, additional housing was required. The cottage located on the summit (next to the Governor's Mansion and across Fort Street) is used by State officials and visiting dignitaries. The second cottage was the original officer's quarters, and was later used as the Michigan Governor's summer residence until 1945.

Governor's Summer Residence   Patrick Doud originally constructed this house (west of the Major's and Captain's Quarters) in 1902, at a cost of $15,000. The exterior is native Michigan white pine, while the interior is yellow pine from Georgia. There are twenty-five rooms, including eleven bedrooms and eight bathrooms. The Mackinac Island State Park Commission purchased the private residence in 1945, and refurbished it with the help of prisoners from Jackson prison. It then became the summer residence of the Governor of Michigan.

The mansion is opened for limited public tours during the summer months. Tickets are available at the State Park Visitor Center. The tour includes the living room, with its dark wood panels and large windows that offer a view of the straits; the dining room with its elegant wooden ceiling of octagonal design; and the sun room which includes photos and other memorabilia of John F. Kennedy, who visited the island in 1960 while still a United States Senator.

Market Street   Market Street, one of the richest centers of history in America, is located one block north of the docks.

The Beaumont Memorial honors Dr. William Beaumont, who made several important medical discoveries while stationed at Fort Mackinac.

Courtesy of Mackinac Island State Park Commission

John Jacob Astor's American Fur Company was headquartered here in 1816. Other points of interest include the Beaumont Memorial, Matthew Geary House, Stuart House Museum, Biddle House, and the Benjamin Blacksmith Shop. Scattered among these historic sites are city hall, the police and fire departments, a library, post office, and bank, as well as numerous shops, businesses, and private residences.

Beaumont Memorial   Located on the corner of Fort and Market Streets, admission is by State Park ticket. Originally the site of the American Fur Company's retail store, this building was reconstructed in 1954 by the Michigan Medical Society. It is a memorial commemorating Dr. William Beaumont, whose experiments on Alexis St. Martin's stomach led to many important discoveries about the human digestive system (see Chapter Six). Displays include a number of Beaumont's possessions, as well as dioramas depicting Beaumont and St. Martin during their times together.

Once the home of a manager for the American Fur Company, today Stuart House is a city-owned museum.

Courtesy of Mackinac Island State Park Commission

Matthew Geary House Not open to the public. Located west of the Beaumont Memorial, this home was built before 1848. It is considered an excellent example of island architecture of the mid-nineteenth century.

Post Office The Mackinac Island branch of the United States Post Office is open twelve months of the year to supply the needs of island residents. This site was the original location of the American Fur Company's clerks quarters. Approximately five-hundred clerks labored here during the summer months.

Stuart House Museum Operated by the City of Mackinac Island. Admission through a small entrance fee.
        This three-story building was erected in 1817. It is a good example of the New England/Colonial architecture which was brought to the frontier by eastern settlers. The building is

named for Robert Stuart, who was a manager for the northern department of the American Fur Company. Here, he and his wife Elizabeth entertained important visitors and the people of Mackinac society. In addition, the many spare rooms were used to house company men visiting the island. The Stuart's lived here for twenty years, from 1817 to 1837.

In the 1840's it was purchased by Ronald McLeod who turned it into a hotel. It was the first hotel on the island and could accomodate seventy guests, many of whom were ship captains and traders.

During the 1870's, new owners remodeled the building and named it the John Jacob Astor House Hotel. To enlarge the structure they added a three-tiered porch that connected it to the clerk's quarters on one side, and the warehouse building on the other. It served as a popular island hotel until the early twentieth century. After the hotel went out of business, the buildings and the porch fell into disrepair. The porch sections were torn down in the 1930's.

The building was revived as a city museum in 1941. Today it has many interesting rooms filled with antique furniture. You'll find a canopy bed that was once Patrick Sinclair's; an 1824 A.J. Keough piano with seventy-six ivory keys, instead of the usual eighty-eight; two settees that were owned by the Stuarts; and items from the American Fur Company warehouse such as original ledgers, scales, desks, and a safe. There are also interesting displays including old photos and sketches of the island, and samples of the many kinds of furs that were bought and sold by the company. Upstairs is a large open hall area and many additional sleeping rooms. Don't miss these interesting exhibits of life on the American frontier.

American Fur Company Warehouse The building was constructed in 1810 with hand-hewn beams, and was once the heart of the company's operations on the island. Here the thousands of pounds of fur pelts were sorted, cleaned, and baled, then hoisted by pulley to the upper levels for storage. That pulley is still on the top floor of the building. Today this struc-

Biddle House is one of the many State Park historic sites open to the public.

Courtesy of Mackinac Island State Park Commission

ture is used as the island's community center, and is operated by the Lion's Club.

City Hall/County Courthouse Constructed in 1834, this building is the second oldest city hall in Michigan. Until 1882, it housed the Mackinac County Courthouse—at that time the County Seat was relocated to St. Ignace. Over the years, Protestant, Catholic, and Episcopalian congregations held their services here while waiting for their various churches to be built. Today the city hall and police department are housed here.

Biddle House Admission by State Park ticket.
A portion of the original house may have been built as early as 1780, utilizing an architectural style typical of rural Quebec. Over the years, additions were completed as the needs and finances of the tenants allowed. The most prominent resident was Edward Biddle of the well-known Philadelphia family. He was a prosperous independent fur trader, who held several important posts on the island including surveyor and sheriff. His home was a typical dwelling for an upper-middle

class family of that era. Construction methods of the period can be inspected, and the house is authentically furnished Interpretive guides offer demonstrations of the many tasks the lady of the house would have performed, including cleaning, spinning wool, and baking. The building was restored through the donations and assistance of the Michigan Society of Architects in 1959.

Benjamin Blacksmith Shop   Admission by State Park ticket.

Located behind Biddle House, the shop is a working museum. A blacksmith using nineteenth century equipment hammers the red-hot iron into nails, hinges, brackets, candleholders, fireplace tools, and kitchen utensils (they no longer make horseshoes). The smith uses a mild, low-carbon steel which can be shaped by hammering, when heated to 1400 degrees Fahrenheit. The museum is the original blacksmith shop that served the island for many years, and includes a bellows, drill press, horseshoes, carriage parts, machinery, and other equipment.

It is named for Robert H. Benjamin, who came to the island in 1874 and purchased the 'Star Blacksmith Shop' from a former Fort Mackinac soldier. He placed his new business adjacent to a log home he had built for his family, located further west along the road just past the intersection with Cadotte Avenue. The shop stood on posts facing Market Street. That area is called *Benjamin Hill*, and the Benjamin family still maintains a home there.

Prior to the construction of the Grand Hotel and the summer cottages there wasn't enough work for a year-round blacksmith, so Benjamin spent several winters working in Cheboygan. By the time the Grand Hotel opened he was a permanent resident, and in 1897 he became the island's postmaster. His fourteen year old son Herbert took over the blacksmith shop and operated it throughout his life, while his father alternated between Postmaster (when the Republicans were in office) and Sheriff of Mackinac County (when they were not). Robert also served as the island's Mayor from 1903 to 1907, and in 1916.

When Herbert died in 1967, his son Robert E. Benjamin (who owns several businesses in town) donated the Blacksmith Shop to the Mackinac Island State Park Commission, with the stipulation that the building be moved to another location. The current museum is partially constructed from the wood of the original structure.

Original Site of Ste. Anne's Church and Cemetary First located at the intersection of Market & Hoban Streets—the present Michigan Bell Telephone building.

When Major Patrick Sinclair decided to relocate his fort to Mackinac Island, one of the first structures transferred was Ste. Anne's Catholic Church. In this manner Sinclair hoped to entice civilians to follow the garrison to the island. The church stood here from 1781 to 1826. At that time the graveyard (where the Village Inn stands today) was filled to capacity, so Magdalaine LaFramboise gave some of her Huron Street land to the parish. The church building was then moved to its current location, and the graves were re-located to a cemetary in the interior.

Main Street Many island businesses, including gift and souvenir shops, fudge shops, bicycle rental shops, the island book store, restaurants, and several hotels line this street. A small City Park in the center of town is equipped with public restrooms, benches, and a small rest area across the road. The Chamber of Commerce is located here, as well as the docks and Mackinac Island Carriage Tours ticket booth.

Little Stone Church If you turn north from Market Street onto Cadotte Avenue you will travel to the Grand Hotel. On your way you will pass the scenic First Congregational Church, a pretty building of grey stone and stained glass windows that depict scenes from Mackinac's history. The congregation began holding services in private homes in 1896, before the church was completed. It is still active today throughout the summer season. The church is open to visitors when services are not in progress.

The Grand Hotel is one of the largest summer hotels in the world.

Credit: Thomas M. Piljac

Grand Hotel Golf Course/The Jewel   The golf course covers the area that was once the town's public cow pasture. It is open to the public, and described in more detail in Chapter Ten.

Woodfill Memorial   Midway up Cadotte Avenue on the west side of the road is a small, horseshoe-shaped marble memorial surrounded by floral plantings. It is a lovely spot to enjoy the view of the lake, or to study the passing parade of people and horses. It is dedicated to W. Stewart Woodfill, who did so much for the Grand Hotel and Mackinac Island.

Grand Hotel   At the top of the Cadotte Avenue hill stands a magnificent white building of Michigan pine, built in Greek Revival style. Its huge porch is supported by forty three-story pillars and decorated with flowers and flags. The hotel has 286 rooms and can accommodate six-hundred guests. There are three bars, several dining areas, a theatre, convention center, ballroom, and many shops to explore. Non-hotel guests pay a small admission charge to enter the hotel and grounds during the day. The fee is refunded if you purchase lunch in the Main Dining Room. Each day *High Tea* is held between 4 and 5 p.m. in the parlor. This is open to the public. You can dine on pastries, finger sandwiches, and sherry in an elegant atmosphere while a musician entertains in the background. The sweeping lawns below the hotel include beautiful flower gardens, walkways, benches, a small woods with an exercise path, a fountain, an in-ground swimming pool, and a beautiful view of the straits.

West Bluff/Cottages   Just west of the Grand Hotel a number of majestic summer cottages have been built on leased State Park land (described in Chapter Seven). These magnificent old homes are well-kept, beautifully landscaped, and offer one of the best views on the island.

Most are Victorian or Queen Anne style structures of balloon construction. They were built to accommodate large families and their servants, and contain ten to twenty rooms. Each home has interesting features such as widow's walks, cupolas, turrets, or leaded glass windows; and some have extraordinary interior decor including pressed tin walls, and embossed linoleum walls (Lincrusta) made from rolling heavy patterned steel rollers in wood pulp. Many cottages still have their original antique furnishings, and all have large porches facing the straits.

The cottages on the east bluff contain many of the same features, and were generally constructed by the same builders. Cottages on both bluffs are popular tourist attractions. The residents are accustomed to people staring at their homes from the road, but do not appreciate strangers in their yards or peeking through the windows. Respect their privacy and allow them to enjoy their homes.

Pontiac's Trail   As you travel up West Bluff Road, you can stop to rest at a viewing area near the edge of the cliff that overlooks the lake, Mackinac Bridge, and other island sites. To the west, is a quiet, secluded trail. It is open to the public as long as you do not leave the path, and offers additional perspectives of the surrounding scenery.

Annex   Extending back from the bluff are the Annex cottages, the area developed by Gurdon S. Hubbard in 1882, and described in Chapter Seven. The area has many small roads lined with residences. You can stroll along the roads and view the homes, but remember that the cottages are on private property.

Stonecliffe   To the west of Annex Road is the Stonecliffe resort (on Stonecliffe Road), originally a private home built by Michael Cudahy in the early 1900's. The estate is now operated as a quality hotel with large landscaped grounds and a nine-hole golf course. The hotel is the only one that is open during the winter season (from Christmas to New Years) for visitors who arrive by plane or ferry (if the straits are still open). Stonecliffe is a small, old-fashioned hotel and restaurant in an area set off from the commotion in town. Condominiums have been constructed on the grounds, and are available for purchase or rental. A subdivision *(Wood Bluff)* is nearby.

CHAPTER 13

Islanders

Mackinac Island is more than a unique blend of natural beauty and old-fashioned charm. It is a delicately balanced community of two governments (city and state park), and five diverse groups of people (year-round inhabitants, summer residents, business owners, summer workers, and tourists). This unusual combination, as well as the island's isolation, has continued to intrigue visitors over the years. In this chapter we will try to provide general information about the city and state park, as well as the people who live and work here.

Mackinac Island State Park

The state park is the largest landowner on the island, with holdings of 1,700 acres. It is run by a small staff and a governor-appointed commission that was created in 1895. They are responsible for all park sites on Mackinac Island, as well as Colonial Michilimackinac and Old Mill Creek on the mainland. It is the second largest operation of historic sites in the nation, only Williamsburg, Virginia is more extensive.

As part of their administration of Mackinac Island, they supervise the maintenance and upkeep of Fort Mackinac and all other historic buildings, as well as the governor's mansion, airport, and roadway and trail systems. Although M-185 is a State highway, the park contracts from the State to do regular maintenance work on the road, such as trash and manure

243

removal. In addition, they plan and create displays and exhibits, and continually expand and develop the living history program at these sites. Other responsibilities include:
coordinating the scouting program, publishing books and
materials, and handling land leases.

Most of the land leases today are renewals of those original grants of the late 1800's and early 1900's. In 1958, the commission ruled that they would no longer authorize new leases.
In addition to renewing existing leases, they review property
improvements and additions to ensure that the original
Victorian atmosphere is being maintained. One recent example was the purchase of large satellite dishes by some lessees.
The commission created regulations that require permits for
such displays, and suggested that they be concealed behind
shrubs or fences.

Operations are handled by a small number of people. In
addition to the Park Commission, the hired staff of the three
parks totals approximately one-hundred and twenty employees during peak summer season. During the winter,
the reduced staff plans and co-ordinates for the upcoming
year, and brings out new publications. In addition to the
winter staff, the park will contract out maintenance and
improvements on the sites such as carpentry, masonry, and
restoration work.

The park operations are funded by State appropriations.
Historic operations are self-funded through bond sales which
are repaid through admission fees. During peak season, 3,500
people a day visit Fort Mackinac alone.

City of Mackinac Island
The city, formed on March 20, 1900, has its headquarters
in the historic courthouse building on Market Street. This is
still an old-fashioned small town, where the fire siren blares
every day at noon. Its operations are controlled by a mayor,
city council, clerk, and a number of boards and commissions.
They are responsible for police and fire departments; the

upkeep and maintenance of property, including the Stuart House Museum and island cemeteries; overseeing the management of the Department of Public Works for water, sewage, and landfill; maintenance of city streets and lights; and collecting and distributing revenues. The overseers must also perform a complicated juggling act between the normal problems of every small city, the yearly influx of tourists, the needs of the State Park and businessmen, and the necessity to preserve the island from over-development.

The city receives most of its income from property taxes, business licenses, motor vehicle permits, and franchise fees. The franchise fees are from the three ferry lines, which pay 1½% of their gross receipts from all fares transported to the island. In 1985, they contributed $68,670. In 1987, they hauled an estimated 800,000 passengers to Mackinac.

Major projects, such as the new water and sewage plants, require outside financial assistance. This city of five-hundred and fifty permanent residents does not have a tax base large enough to fund the improvements necessary to host nearly one-million visitors every year. Because so many of the island's services are used by non-residents, these projects are financed by a combination of grants and bond issues. For example, it took seven years to co-ordinate the planning and funding for the recent thirteen-million dollar water and sewage projects. The city hired a firm in Lansing to arrange a combination of financial assistance from: the city budget, State appropriations, city revenue bonds backed by the Federal Housing Authority, two Small Cities Economic Development Grants, an Urban Development Action Grant, grants from the Michigan Department of Transportation, the Economic Development Agency, the Environmental Protection Agency, and the Department of Natural Resources.

Police Department

The department has four officers and one dispatcher during the winter. In that season the police concentrate on checking properties, answering complaints, watching for snowmobile and hunting violations, and planning for the upcoming tourist season. When summer arrives seven more officers and two dispatchers are added to the force, and two Michigan State Troopers are assigned to work on the island. The additional manpower is made necessary by the dramatic increase in population as winter ends. For example: From January to May 11, 1985 there were nine arrests on the island. From May 12, to November, 1985 there were 172 arrests. In 1987, the one month jump was equally impressive. There were eleven arrests in the month of May, and forty-seven arrests in June.

Most offenders are in the 17 to 24 age group, and many are summer employees away from home for the first time. The most common charges are alcohol related: minors in possession, altered identification, and disorderly conduct. The second most frequent crime is bicycle theft. The police have an excellent recovery record for registered vehicles, and even occasionally dive into the harbor to retrieve them. When it becomes necessary to incarcerate a perpetrator, they are placed in one of two cells at the station. They remain there until they post bond, or are transported to the St. Ignace jail. In 1984, thirty-five people were held, out of 750,000 visitors.

Each summer the largest influx of people arrives during the two yacht races in July. The police force is increased considerably during that period, as Mackinac Island officers are joined by those from the Michigan State Police, Mackinac County Sheriff's Department, city police from the mainland, and conservation officers from the Department of Natural Resources.

The department is also responsible for issuing and enforcing bicycle (see Chapter Ten) and vehicle permits. The Chief of Police processes motor vehicle applications for the city in co-operation with the Mackinac Island State Park Commission. They are then presented to the city council for a vote. All are issued on a case by case basis, and applicants are expected to apply well in advance. These permits are primarily issued for construction and utility vehicles. Restrictions are eased substantially from November to May.

Many officers who have served on Mackinac Island have described it as a pleasant experience. Unlike their mainland counterparts, they have more contact with people due to their patrol methods—walking and bicycling among them. In addition, most of their encounters are positive ones with happy people on vacation. However, the department does have a motor vehicle on the island for emergency situations.

Fire Department
The danger of fire is always present. When you consider the minimal spacing between hundred-year-old wooden buildings which make up the Mackinac Island business district, you have an idea of the potential problems facing the fifteen man volunteer fire department. Because of their isolated location, they are well-trained. Each has completed at least one sixty hour course of basic fire-fighting, and the department holds a minimum of sixteen drills a year.

They have a motorized fire truck that carries 750 gallons of water, and additional equipment including an emergency generator, various types of hoses, a smoke ejector, ladders, breathing apparatus, and fire extinguishers. In addition, the Mackinac Island State Park Commission has two fire trucks available for use on the island. Five emergency phones are handy to take fire reports, one for each officer of the department and one at the police station. The fire-fighters on the island have done a great job of containing fires in the past. However, when an October of 1987 fire in town threatened the entire business district, they requested outside assistance for the first time. To give you an idea of what can and did happen, here is the story

The three-story John W. Davis building, erected in 1898, was the only brick structure on Main Street. It housed "The Big Store" on the first floor, and a number of apartments on the second. On October 15, 1987, the department received a call at 9 p.m. reporting that the building was on fire. They responded at once, but the fire was spreading rapidly and threatening the surrounding wooden structures. While they desperately fought to contain the blaze, fourteen firemen arrived from St. Ignace on the Mackinac Express catamaran. A pumper truck was transported from St. Ignace on the Mackinac Island State Park Commission's LCN landing craft. Ten firemen from Mackinaw City came aboard Shepler's ferry and helped to fight the flames. They brought their water cannon 'deluge gun' and two portable pumps. Also assisting were seven members of the U. S. Coast Guard arriving on their boat, and two police officers each from the St. Ignace, Mackinaw City, Michigan State Police, and Mackinac County Sheriff's departments. Members of other fire departments were on standby at St. Ignace and Mackinaw City including those from: Cheboygan, Pellston, Brevort, Moran, and Carp Lake.

Ty's Restaurant stayed open all night offering coffee and food, and the Grand Hotel and Horn's Gaslight Bar also provided food and refreshment to the fire-fighters. The blaze was brought under control by 1:30 a.m. Damage: The John W. Davis building interior was completely gutted. Betty's Gifts, Memory Lane Mall, Ryba's Fudge, nearby apartments, as well as the roofs of some adjacent buildings suffered smoke and water damage. Fortunately, when the building was remodeled several years ago, block fire walls had been constructed between each of the neighboring structures.

As of this writing, the cause of the fire has not been determined. The State Fire Marshall has concluded that the blaze began in the northeast corner of the basement, and that it was not caused by arson. The assistance from outside departments is part of a mutual aid pact among police and fire departments in the straits area. Had the fire occured after the ferry lines stopped operations at the end of December, the movement of additional manpower and equipment to the island would have been hampered. Hopefully, the dedicated volunteers, professional training, and constant surveillance will continue to keep this danger under control.

Ambulance Service
The island has a volunteer ambulance corps of fifteen Emergency Medical Technicians. Their equipment includes a new ambulance purchased in 1987, and like all emergency

vehicles on the island, it is motorized. Patients are evacuated to a mainland hospital by air when their condition has been stabilized, or by ambulance via the state park landing craft if necessary.

Municipal Services

Since 1986, the functions normally supervised by the Department of Public Works, such as the waterworks, pumping stations, sanitary landfill, and waste treatment plant have been managed by Williams and Works Company of Grand Rapids, Michigan. The city decided to have a private contractor handle the personnel, project management, record keeping, reporting, and laboratory work in order to have the advantage of corporate resources such as training, support personnel, and trouble shooting. A company superintendent lives on the island to manage the operations.

Fresh Water Treatment Plant Construction on the new water treatment plant on the eastern side of the island began in May, 1985. In 1986, a severe winter storm damaged the facilities so badly that they had to be rebuilt. The completed project went into service in January of 1987, replacing the antiquated system of wooden pipes that had been constructed in the early 1900's. The plant pumps water from Lake Huron and treats an average of 600,000 gallons a day. The water is then sent to a reservoir near Fort Holmes, and is distributed by a pipe system that takes advantage of the gravitational forces of the island.

Waste Water Treatment Plant This plant is located on the western heights of the island, not far from the intersections of Annex and Stonecliffe Roads. The old system was unable to handle the heavy summer volume, and the island was ordered to cease polluting the straits with sewage by the Water Resources Commission. A new, modern plant was constructed as part of the thirteen million dollar project completed in 1987.

Landfill   The obvious problem on a small island with a large number of visitors is what to do with all the trash generated each year. In 1980, the city enacted a new policy to extend the life of the landfill and limit the risk of polluting local ground and surface water. The program mandated the division of all trash, separating biodegradable wastes—such as paper products, food scraps, leaves, and grass trimmings—which break down and decompose. These are placed in bags labeled 'compost', which are then sent through a shredder, mixed with horse manure, and watered. When the material breaks down it is used as fertilizer. Non-biodegradable wastes are placed in bags labeled 'landfill'. They include items made of plastic, metal, glass, clothing, string, and twine. These bags are then buried.

While the need for such separation to preserve the life of the landfill is clear, the actual practice isn't easy and it is taking time for the city to obtain the necessary co-operation and compliance. We try separating our trash when we visit, and it definitely takes an extra effort. Simple items such as an envelope with a plastic window must be taken apart, the paper belongs in the 'compost' bag, the plastic in the 'landfill'. If you multiply that out hundreds of times every day, you can understand why it takes time for it to become second nature.

To further enforce the regulations, the city is requiring the name of the resident or business on each bag so that violaters can be located. Screen systems to filter the compost bags have been installed, although they are not totally reliable. Ultimately, compliance will improve and the waste disposal problem should lessen. The only other alternative will be to remove trash from the island by barge.

Electricity

The Edison Sault Electric Company provides electric service to the island. Power generated on the mainland is transported by large underwater cables. Three Edison employees living here keep the system running smoothly. The majority of maintenance work is performed during the off season, so as not to disturb the town's peaceful ambience with the intrusion of modern boom trucks and digging equipment. In 1986, as part of the utilities' reconstruction, overhead electric lines were buried underground in the main part of town.

Mackinac Island Airport

Built with a combination of City, State, and Federal funding in the 1960's, it is now administered by the Mackinac Island State Park Commission with help from the Department of Transportation. Landing fees alone do not cover operational costs, so airport funds are supplemented by Federal and State appropriations. Plans for continued improvements include: repaving the existing runway, fencing the airport grounds, paving a parallel taxiway, and the construction of a parking pad with tie-down facilities.

The airport is operated by a manager and two assistants during the summer season, and by the manager and one assistant during the winter. The State Park handles snow removal, and a fire truck is available at the airport for emergencies. As an official weather observation station for the National Weather Service, it is equipped with monitoring devices to measure visibility, temperatures, dew point, weight of air, cloud cover (distance between ground and clouds), and altimeters to measure the height at which planes are flying.

Island residents have one plane available for flights on and off the island throughout the winter. Passengers pay a transportation fee, as well as the cost of any freight transported (such as groceries). Freight charges are determined by the pound. There are more details about using the airport in Chapter Ten.

Mackinac Island Medical Center

If you require medical attention while visiting the island, the Mackinac Island Medical Center is located on Market Street. The facilities include examination rooms, an x-ray machine, laboratory, EKG machines, and an emergency room. During the summer the center is staffed with a doctor, two resident physicians, a nurse, and an x-ray technician. It is open

year-round and is funded through patient billing, private donations, as well as State and local contributions. After mid-
September the center reduces its hours and staff to a doctor
and a nurse until the following spring.

Mackinac Island Public School

The public school was built in 1964, and is located below
the Grand Hotel on Lake Shore Road. Average attendance for
the twelve grades and kindergarten is approximately one-
hundred students, with a staff of ten teachers. Some instruc-
tors handle double grades, but the small class sizes still offer
a great deal of individualized attention. The students are
offered a well-rounded course of study, including music, art,
and physical education. Extra-curricular activities feature
basketball, volleyball, and golf teams; but the small size of
the school prohibits larger team sports. A number of educational and cultural field trips are also undertaken each year.

The largest expense for most school districts is transportation—that's one thing the island school can cut from its budget. It owns one bus, which is kept on the mainland, for school
trips and athletic events. Although there are no cars on the
island, the school tries to prepare the students by offering a
driver's education course at the high-school level. The students commute to the mainland to participate in the program.

Mackinac Island Library

The Mackinac Island Library is presently located on
Market Street, but plans have been made to relocate to the
old public works building on Windermere Point (Lake Shore
Road and Boardwalk). The new site will be much larger, but
funds for renovations of the old building could run between
$100,000 and $200,000, and that goal has not yet been reached.

The library has over six-thousand books, and is a part of
the Hiawathaland Co-op for inter-library loans of books and
videos. A microfiche machine and access to microfiche col-
lections are among its other services. Membership fees are a
non-returnable $5 per person and $10 per family, and video
rentals are $2 per night.

The library is open on a limited schedule, with hours varying from season to season. They are posted on the door, or you can check with the Chamber of Commerce.

U.S. Post Office
The Mackinac Island branch is located on Market Street. During the winter it is one of the smallest post offices in the Upper Peninsula region. From January 1 to April 1, mail is delivered to the island by air. With the large volume of visitors every summer, it becomes one of the larger postal centers, with increased staff to handle the heavier load.

Newspaper
The *Town Crier* has been the island's newspaper for more than thirty years. It is published every Saturday during the summer, and once during the Christmas season. The paper offers many interesting insights of the island and its attractions, as well as features and gossip about the people of Mackinac, and helpful information for visiting tourists.

The staff includes several columnists who live or summer on the island, and three newspaper interns from the University of Michigan who handle story writing, advertising, production, sales, and distribution. Their work on the paper offers them overall experience in the business, and gives the Town Crier a fresh slant every season as the interns discover intriguing details about Mackinac.

You can purchase a paper in one of the many counter boxes in town, or stay in touch with island events by subscribing for a modest yearly fee.

Most Valuable Resource
One of the biggest problems that every resident and business owner faces is the limited availability of land. The island is approximately 2,200 acres in area, with 1,700 of them belonging to the State Park. Of the remaining five-hundred acres, Stonecliffe retains 25%, and the Grand Hotel holds another large portion. City owned property is primarily the land in the business district of Main and Market Streets. There

are only a few hundred remaining acres for other hotels, restaurants, shops, summer cottagers, and year-round residents to share. Those limitations are reflected in high taxes and skyrocketing land prices.

Rentals for business properties in town can run $13,000 to $15,000 a year for smaller establishments and $30,000 to $35,000 a year for larger ones. Employers then have the additional expense of obtaining housing for their summer workers. Larger business owners maintain their own dormitories or apartment complexes that offer employee housing for a nominal rent. Yet, the available accommodations are always inadequate for the demand. For one thing, although college students are more willing to accept cramped lodgings than most, the youngsters of today are not willing to sleep six to a room, whereas their counterparts thirty years ago would. Secondly, most employee housing is located in town or along Lake Shore Road, on valuable real estate that could be turned into profitable bed and breakfast inns, restaurants, or shops.

Several island business owners have tried to resolve the problem by building apartment complexes in Harrisonville to house their employees. As previously mentioned, "The Village" is a small interior community composed primarily of permanent residents. The property owners here have not been thrilled at the prospect of having hundreds of college-age students deposited in their neighborhood. They are concerned that as transients, they will have little respect for the area. In addition, most summer employees are in an age group where noise and high jinks are an important part of their after work activities. While the new apartments will undoubtedly provide housing that is superior to their present cramped Victorian quarters, it's going to be a difficult balancing act to keep the students and year-round residents on pleasant terms.

Smaller businessmen have a more difficult problem. In order to keep good employees, the owners must find them a place to live and supplement their rent. Even the city has difficulty housing the additional members of the police force each summer, and is considering plans for constructing employee housing. Perhaps island schoolteachers have the most difficult time of all. While some rent permanently or own their own homes, others must vacate their winter quarters for the summer owners, which means moving all of their possessions twice a year. If they wish to stay on the island through the summer, they have to struggle to find housing while demand is at its peak. Some resolve the problem by working for a room, perhaps by caring for the grounds and buildings of a summer cottager. Others leave.

Year-round island residents, such as those in Harrisonville, face another major concern. Their home values have soared, but that would only be beneficial to them if they sell their property—which would mean leaving the island. Their children are finding it impossible to buy homes in the neighborhood they grew up in, and many are leaving the island.

There are new homes and living quarters being built on private property in Harrisonville. *Surrey Ridge* has two and three bedroom condominiums with Victorian exteriors that were selling in the $100,000 area in 1987. In 1983, George Staffan (owner of the Stonecliffe estate), formed a private association to create *Wood Bluff Subdivision* on his lands near the hotel. Thirty-five lots were made available, and regulations set out for their construction. They include: Houses must be Victorian style, house designs must be approved by the association, and phone and electric lines must be placed underground. New homes in this subdivision were selling for more than $145,000 in 1987.

Many older homes, especially those built in the late 1800's and early 1900's, are valuable properties. Some have waiting lists of prospective buyers. These houses sell for $200,000 or more, depending on location and condition.

Social Structure

In your home community there is a social structure that you are perhaps only vaguely aware of. A few businessmen or professionals who are considered the well-to-do; a large middle class that manages to maintain a decent home and lifestyle; and the poor who barely eek out a living and sometimes require financial assistance. The average ages of most of the residents are probably thirty to fifty years, with smaller numbers of retirees, children, and college-age students.

Now imagine if this delicately balanced structure was thrown into confusion for six months of every year, with a new influx of the affluent—some there for pleasure, others for business. In addition, a whole new work force made up not primarily of families, but of single, college-age students enters your area. And throughout that period about 800,000 other people pass through. And this happens every year, year after year, for generations.

It wouldn't be hard to recognize the benefits of additional jobs and services, and the ties of home, friends, and family might encourage you to accept the changes. However, it would be only natural for you to hold yourselves a little apart from these newcomers—after all, it is your home community for twelve months of the year.

If you were one of the newcomers, you would probably socialize with those who share your interests. Those summering for pleasure with their counterparts, those operating businesses with theirs. And young summer workers would stick together, although sub-groups might form between management and hourly workers; and employees who are here for the first time and those who have been returning for several years.

Yet members of all these groups have two things in common to bind them together in this community. They care about it so much that they work to improve it—raising money for better services, recreational facilities, and the preservation of landmarks and historic sites. They also have shared activities, with those musically inclined forming a group, or those who enjoy horseback riding or card-playing banding together. And through such experiences, newcomers and year-round inhabitants can rub elbows. Summer employees, business owners, cottage residents, and community leaders find a common ground to meet.

On Mackinac Island, these inter-actions are further influenced by over-lapping histories. Many families of permanent residents have deep roots on the island, with histories going back for eighty, one-hundred, and two-hundred years.

Main Street on Mackinac Island.

Credit: Thomas M. Piljac

The same is true for some summer cottagers and business owners. In addition, cottage owners might own businesses; summer employees can be children of cottagers—or dating members of their families, and so on.

Administrators and Business Owners

Whether they own large island enterprises such as R. Daniel Musser and Harry Ryba, maintain medium-sized operations, or are small shopkeepers renting space on the island, all business people face the task of trying to balance their desire to maintain a profitable operation with the need to preserve the island's old-fashioned charm. Many sit on boards, councils, committees, and commissions to resolve the inevitable conflicts, work to bring about improvements, and use their knowledge and influence to benefit the island.

In an era where most business owners give only lip service to their concerns about the community, islanders

generally do all they can to improve it. They come from varied
backgrounds: those that operate family-owned enterprises that
have been passed down through the generations; those who
came to the island for a summer's work only to find that they
enjoyed it so much that they found a way to stay and make
a living; and those who recognized its potential years ago and
laid their groundwork before the large tourist boom.

You might find it a bit difficult to identify them on your
island visit. We are used to corporate heads traveling in fancy
cars with an entourage. Here, that gentleman that just passed
you on his bicycle might well be Mr. Ryba or Mr. Musser going
to the office. The lady who rang up your dinner may own the
restaurant, but be filling in this evening for a summer worker
recently returned to college.

Summer Workers

The island's main industry is tourism. As a seasonal
business in an isolated location, most of the summer work
force has to be imported. Since there are very few year-round
jobs with most companies, business operators must draw on
a work force that is willing to work six months of the year,
relocate for that period, and tolerate cramped housing. Obviously, the ideal source for most such jobs are college students
on summer break.

Many come for the first time because they learned of
available positions through school, friends who had worked
here, or of the general need for workers at a popular summer
resort. They come from all types of backgrounds and educational levels, and for most it's a chance to make money, gain
work experience, and enjoy the pleasant surroundings. For
some, it's not an easy adjustment. It might be their first time
away from home with too many new-found freedoms. They
may have difficulty adjusting to the distances—separated by
water from large stores and convenience shopping. But every
year a portion of them will become so enamored with the
island that they will return year after year. Some will continue
after they have completed their schooling, juggling winter and
summer jobs. Others, such as the Jamaican waiters at the

A dock porter transports luggage to the ferry on his bicycle.

Credit: Thomas M. Piljac

Grand Hotel, return each year for a chance to make more money here in six months than they can in a full year at home.

Most of the positions available are fairly obvious: managers, waiters, waitresses, hostesses, busboys, chefs, hotel clerks, chambermaids, bellboys, dock porters, taxi and carriage drivers, and shop workers. There are a few additional jobs that require special talents, such as musicians at the Grand Hotel or costumed historical interpreters at the State Park. Perhaps the most unusual position—the one that attracts the most attention in our modern motorized world—is that of street sweeper. Basically, they sweep and scrape horse droppings from the road with wide-mouthed shovels and hard bristle brooms, and place them in their wheelbarrows. Each sweeper is responsible for his own section of the road, and when the wheelbarrow is full he dumps the contents into a dray kept for that purpose behind city hall. They work during the day, while street flushers work during the early morning hours, hosing away excess refuse on Main and Market Streets to give them a fresh, clean start in the morning. Some sweepers are employed by the city, others by the Grand Hotel. Workers from Mackinac Island Carriage Tours, Arrowhead Carriages, Jack's Riding Stables and Cindy's Riding Stables also have specific areas of the island that they keep clear.

Wages for all workers are based upon their experience, skill level, responsibilities, and number of hours. Some pay a nominal rent and have the rest subsidized by their employer. A few island businesses offer discounts to summer workers on their purchases. The Grand Hotel has an employee cafeteria that serves three meals a day for a minimal charge. Other large establishments that own restaurants might offer discounts on food. For higher level employees at some businesses the 'perks' might include free meals and housing.

Employees work long hours during peak season, often ten to twelve hours a day, six or seven days a week. This causes a bit of a problem toward the end of summer. Most employers ask for a commitment from their workers to stay on the job until a certain date—usually in September or October. Yet after a few months of working long, hard days with few breaks, many employees suddenly decide they want a rest period before they return to school. So they quit early. This leaves the businesses short-staffed in the fall, and the owners must try to find, hire, and train new personnel to finish out the season. Those workers that haven't left often pad their incomes by working two or three jobs. Employers are trying to limit the annual exodus by offering end of season bonuses, usually a percentage of the worker's total earnings.

Business owners also hire year-round residents in the summer. They don't have to find housing for them, or worry about their leaving the island in September. However, business owners do have to pay into the State unemployment fund, and when workers file, this payment is drawn from the company's account. Applicants must work for at least twenty weeks to qualify, and non-residents need not apply.

Summer Cottagers

Summer cottagers make the island their home for part of every year. Some stay the entire summer, others open up their homes and come and go throughout the season. In 1985, there were approximately fifty-five summer residences on the west and east bluffs, in the Annex, and scattered around the shore. In that same year, only three cottages on the island still belonged to the original families that constructed them. They are: The Annex cottage built by Ernst Puttkammer (Helen Puttkammer); the Annex cottage built by William Dunning (John & Mary Gilpin); and a cottage at British Landing built by George Packard (John & Jane Manikoff). Many of today's residents first came to the island as visitors and eventually purchased summer homes; or had family members that worked on the island who purchased property and passed it down through the generations. Others have old family ties to the island, although they no longer live in the original homes built by their ancestors.

During the summer season these residents enjoy many activities, including bridge, horseback riding, carriage driving, golfing, tennis, boating, and participating in charitable and community activities. Their children and grandchildren enjoy the same delights that children here always have—bicycling, swimming, horseback riding, exploring, and participating in various sports.

The cottagers take a great deal of pride in their homes. Not only because they are a legacy for themselves and their children, but because they feel a deep responsibility for maintaining these historical properties and contributing to the beauty of the island.

Some properties are in such demand that potential buyers wait in line to purchase them. Other cottages are snapped up virtually sight unseen by people eager to own an island summer home. It is not an inexpensive investment. Property holders on State Park land still pay lease rental to the State, in addition to the purchase price of the home. They also pay property taxes to the City of Mackinac Island. The upkeep and improvements are still subject to review by the Mackinac Island State Park Commission, which monitors purchases to ensure that the dwellings will be used only as single-

Two stately Victorian cottages along Lake Shore Road.

family units; and reviews all proposed construction to ensure that it will be architecturally compatible with surrounding homes.

These old houses often require a great deal of maintenance. The wet conditions on the island easily rot wood and destroy paint. Some years the owners find that they must undertake major projects in revamping the construction of the old buildings, other years minor work is sufficient. They face problems such as shifting—the houses are of balloon construction, built on pilings with a skirt around them. The exquisite craftsmanship (carved moldings; unusual floor, wall, and ceiling coverings) in these old homes is irreplaceable, and continued maintenance is required in order to keep the situation manageable. To replace simpler items (such as a broken doorknob) they rely on suppliers from the *"Old House Journal"* and *"Renovators Supply Book"*. There are also several local craftsman who specialize in the restoration and care of island homes.

The owners today have tried to maintain the Victorian decor suitable for such homes, and many have furnishings, heirlooms, and antiques from the same era. Some had to do a great deal of restoration work when they purchased the homes, because previous owners made changes that detracted from the original decor.

Modern cottagers don't arrive with the large staff of servants that their predecessors once did. They have been replaced by modern conveniences, and part-time help who work on the property in return for a room.

The cottages are closed during the winter months, and are prepared for the cold weather by draining the pipes and having antifreeze placed in them. Shutters are installed to seal the windows and protect them from battering winds. Despite some of the heavy winter storms that hit the island, most survive with very little damage, except perhaps a few trees knocked down or loose shingles on the roof. Some residents hire caretakers who watch the house during the winter, and have everything cleaned and ready for them when they arrive in the spring.

This elegant summer home on the island's west bluff is typical of the Queen Anne style of architecture popular in the late nineteenth century.

Credit: Thomas M. Piljac

Year Round Residents

The heart of the island's population is its five-hundred and fifty year-round residents. Many are descended from early settlers, and claim French-Indian ancestry. Most of the remainder have fathers, grandfathers, or great-grandfathers who came here to find work, whether as a carriage driver, park staffer, teacher, or independent businessman. Families have deep roots here, and like many small communities it takes time for newcomers to be accepted. The residents have strong ties to their families, neighbors, churches, and the island itself. They help each other, provide support, and pitch in whenever there is a need. Friendships run deep, built on a foundation of caring and a sense of unity.

Islanders today aren't as isolated as past generations were. With modern transportation, a trip off the island is a short ferry, airplane, or snowmobile ride. The twenty to thirty minute journey is about the same as most suburbanites face when

This gracious summer cottage on the west bluff was built in the 1890's in the Queen Anne style of architecture.

Credit: Thomas M. Piljac

they want to shop at larger stores, dine in nice restaurants, or attend cultural events. Any isolation today is primarily self-imposed. Some prefer the relaxed pace of life here, and remain on the island as much as possible.

The residents face their share of problems. Divorce, juvenile delinquency, drug use, and alcoholism are present, just as they are in every community. The neighborly atmosphere of a small town can be smothering at times, everyone knows each other's business, and if you do something community members disapprove of, those judgements or characterizations can last a lifetime. Perhaps the most difficult problem for most residents is that there are only enough jobs to go around for six months of the year.

In 1985, three-hundred and twenty-five of the island's residents were laid off and filed for unemployment. At most, they receive fifty to fifty-five percent of their regular wages, based on the number of dependents. Because the entire area (including St. Ignace and Mackinaw City) relies on tourism as an economic base, and the high cost and difficulty of continually traveling to the mainland in search for work, island residents need only file once at the beginning of the collection period. After that checks are sent by mail, with a card they must return. These checks, and whatever monies were saved from summer work are the only winter income most islanders have, with no hope of obtaining more. They must carefully juggle their budgets, and deal with the unexpected expenses that every family faces.

A Perfect Place To Grow Up

Few children today have the good fortune to grow up in a community as friendly as Mackinac Island. Here they can roam safely, and spend their days bicycling, fishing, walking, exploring, horseback riding, golfing, boating, playing tennis, and skating. In the winter ice skating, cross-country skiing, and snowmobiling (if over the age of twelve) are common forms of entertainment. Children have a great sense of security from extended family relationships, and the opportunity to grow up in a location that is rich both in beauty and history. In the summer, they meet visitors from all over the world, an enriching experience that sometimes gives them the feeling that their home *is* the center of the world. One of the disadvantages of growing up on an isolated and peaceful island is trying to learn how to live and compete in an aggressive, fast-paced world. Parents here try to prepare their children for this change by occasionally taking them off the island to shop, visit families, and attend cultural and sporting events as well as other other social activities. Older children usually search out summer jobs on the island to gain experience and additional income.

Mackinac In Winter

After Labor Day, children return to school, businesses shorten their hours, and the island's hurried pace slackens as tourism declines. Many residents look forward to the opening of hunting season, a time to break away and pursue pleas-

A winter view of the west end of Main Street in the early 1900's. The Lake View Hotel is in the background.

Courtesy of Mackinac Island State Park Commission

urable activities after a long summer of hard work. The inhabitants also eagerly await the winter months, and the peace and seclusion that they offer. They watch expectantly for the first heavy snowfall, so they can roam the quiet trails on cross country skis or snowmobiles.

Few businesses remain open from November to May. Most residents travel to the post office each day, and usually encounter a friend or two along the way. The bank, medical center, and library are also open for limited hours. Doud's Grocery Store, Harrisonville General Store, and Alford's Drug Store (some years) remain open throughout the winter, as does the islander's favorite bar—the Mustang Lounge.

Recreational activities in the winter are similar to those of most small midwestern communities. In addition to enjoying outdoor sports, residents pursue crafts and hobbies, visit each other's homes, watch television and VCR movies, play games such as cards or bingo, gather at the Mustang Lounge, or attend dances and basketball games. They also hold a Christmas Bazaar, with lots of baked and handmade goods, a raffle, auction, and many booths. Profits go to benefit island churches and the medical center. During the first week of February, they hold a winter carnival sponsored by Mackinac

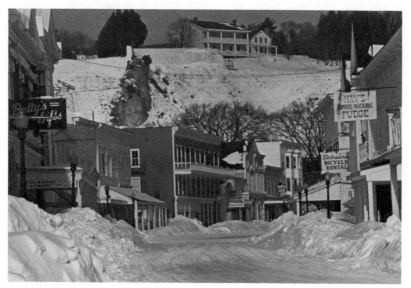

Winter still brings plenty of snow, as this 1980's photograph of the east end of Main Street shows.

Courtesy of Mackinac Island State Park Commission

Island Recreation and Development. They enjoy snowmobile and cross-country skiing contests, a dogsled race, snow soft-ball, square dancing, and musical entertainment.

Island residents live out their daily lives like all American families, yet they don't have to worry about having two cars in the driveway, or dealing with the fast pace most of us live by. They do have to cross the lake to do most of their shop-ping, and be organized enough to keep the cupboards well stocked. If they need a fuse, nail, light bulb, or a certain spice—and its not at the local store—they must travel to the main-land to pick it up, or pay a freight charge to have it delivered. There is no doubt that the islander's love their lifestyle, some have never known any other. To them, it is well worth any inconvenience they might face.

Community Groups

The island brings out something special in everyone who comes here to stay. Summer and year-round residents are especially active in forming groups for the betterment of the island. We have listed some of these non-profit organizations here, to provide an idea of what kind of assistance is needed on the island.

Friends of Mackinac Island Medical Center   Seeks donations to supplement the income of the medical center, so that it can remain open year round.

Mackinac Associates   Raises money through memberships and donations in order to provide additional capital to the Mackinac Island State Park Commission. They sponsor the restoration of historical sights, an educational outreach program for children visiting the island, and other activities of benefit to the park. Members receive unlimited admission to Fort Mackinac, Colonial Michilimackinac, and Old Mill Creek, as well as discounts on guest passes, Mackinac Island State Park Commission publications, and museum gift ship items.

Mackinac Island Historical Society   Formed in 1953 to collect and preserve items that relate to the island's history.

Mackinac Island Horseman's Association   Founded in order to promote equestrian skills, and the humane treatment of horses. The group is responsible for raising the horse ring at Great Turtle Park. Each year island children and adults have an annual horse show, which is their only opportunity to demonstrate their skills. It is too difficult and costly to transport their mounts to the mainland to enjoy outside competitions.

Mackinac Island Music Society   This group of music lovers presents many enjoyable shows year round. During the winter they offer concerts at Christmas, mid-winter, and in spring. In summer, the ranks swell as cottagers and college students return to the island, and performances are much more frequent. They also sing at Trinity Episcopal Church, Ste. Anne's Catholic Church, and a number of weddings and other private functions. The group performs all types of music: modern, a cappella, show tunes, folk songs, and contemporary American music.

Mackinac Island Needlework Guild   This group gathers to do needlework projects for charitable events. They have produced items for the Christmas in July Bazaar, a needlepoint rug on display at Stuart House Museum, and upholstery for kneeling cushions at Trinity Church.

Mackinac Island Recreation & Development   Formed in 1979, this organization promotes the development of recreational activities on the island for children, adults, and summer visitors. Their greatest accomplishment has been the creation of Great Turtle Park. These dedicated islanders labored long hours to transform a donated gravel pit into a safe and healthy environment for their children to play in. Today there is a softball field, basketball court, playground equipment, picnic area, horse ring, and rest rooms. The supporters continue to work very hard to obtain additional funds, with most of their income being derived from the sale of the *Seasons of Mackinac* annual calendar. They also sponsor activities for children, including cultural field trips off the island. Future plans for the park include a running track, and their larger goals are an Olympic size swimming pool and a community center. The pool would encourage more individual sporting activities among schoolchildren, who have no public facility at this time. The community center would replace an ancient building in town. The organization hopes to obtain income for continued park maintenance and expansion by holding dinners, weddings, dances, and other activities at the center.

Wawashkamo Restoration & Preservation Fund   This group raises funds to preserve, restore, and maintain the grounds and buildings at historic Wawashkamo Golf Links. They have a number of fund-raising activities, including an annual Ice Cream Social.

Diverse Groups Joined Together

As we mentioned at the beginning of this chapter, Mackinac is intriguing because of the large number of different groups of people who come and work together here each year. Perhaps it is the island's peaceful, easy atmosphere, or perhaps it is the people that it attracts, but for the most part they all work together in harmony. Each group that lives here for any length of time feels an additional sense of unity—because they are not tourists. Not that they in any way resent tourists, quite the contrary. Each recognizes that without the summer visitors, the island would not have regularly running ferries, a modern airport, jobs for residents, up-to-date municipal services, or even many shops—much less a beautiful park and many historic sights. They all feel that it is their special duty to both preserve the island and encourage its use.

They accept the large crowds, though most deal with the worst crushes in peak season by avoiding the town. Quite possibly their greatest frustration, and one that we've heard and felt throughout the years, is that too many visitors pay no attention to where they are going—they simply step onto roads in front of moving carriages or bicycles without a second thought.

Fudgies, the common term for visitors, really reflects several emotions about the tourists. The name in its strictest definition refers to those who hop off a ferry, spend a few hours in the shops, buy several pounds of fudge and leave—still referring to the island as *Mackinack*. But in practice, it is generally applied to all tourists. The term shows disappointment in the visitors for not taking the time to appreciate their beautiful island. Nearly everyone we spoke to suggested that the most important thing we could tell future visitors was to do just that. It also reflects their pride—a way to differentiate themselves as privileged residents of this exceptional land—from those who may only borrow a few short moments of the special feeling of Mackinac. There is no harm in the term, and perhaps it adds to the island's charm by allowing visitors to have their own special name. Because, no matter who you are, or how long you may stay, the island is a magical place of wonderment. You are indeed a lucky person if you have an opportunity to enjoy it, whether it's for one day—or for twelve months of the year.

CHAPTER 14

Surrounding Area

If you have additional time during your visit to northern Michigan, there are several nearby cities and islands that you may find interesting. We have not been able to list every community here, but primarily the larger towns and better known sites. Contact the Michigan Department of Tourism, or the Chambers of Commerce in these areas for additional information.

Cheboygan

Located southeast of Mackinaw City on Lake Huron, this is one of the larger cities in the area. It was founded in 1845 by Jacob Sammons, who had been a cooper (barrel-maker) on Mackinac Island. The next year a sawmill was built along the Cheboygan River. As settlers continued to arrive, the lumber industry grew, and other mills were soon built. The city thrived with its lumber businesses, and today it has an airport, paper mill, shops and stores, as well as a few light industries. Like many northern Michigan towns, it now enjoys a large number of summer tourists, including those who dock at the harbor marina. It also offers the only ferry access to Bois Blanc Island. There are several parks and a large assortment of recreational facilities available to visitors in town, and Cheboygan State Park and many smaller lakes are nearby. The city is extremely proud of its Opera House, which makes it a cultural center for the region. The historic building was restored in 1984, and offers a wide variety of performances ranging from ballet to bluegrass concerts.

The U.S. Coast Guard Cutter *Mackinaw*, which breaks the massive ice floes that impede ship passages in the area during late fall and early spring, docks at the mouth of the Cheboygan River. It is the largest such ship on the Great Lakes, 290 feet in length, and powered by six, 2,000 horsepower engines. A rocking mechanism and specially designed propellers help it to cut through the ice. Tours are available when the ship is in port.

Old Mill Creek

Hidden three miles south of Mackinaw City, this facility is operated by Mackinac State Historic Parks, which is an umbrella name for the Mackinac Island State Park Commission's operations on the mainland. It is open from mid-May to mid-October, and the purchase of one ticket admits you to Old Mill Creek as well as other historic sites in Mackinaw City.

It is believed that the first industrial complex in Northern Michigan was located here over two hundred years ago. The site was discovered in 1973 by an amateur archeologist, and artifacts were excavated that linked the mill to Fort Michilimackinac.

Historians know that Robert Campbell lived here in 1790, operating a sawmill, gristmill, and farm. The land was probably granted to him by Fort Commandant Patrick Sinclair who recognized the need for such facilities in the area. It may have been given to him as compensation for his loss when the fort was moved to the island. When Robert Campbell died, his son John operated the complex. In 1819, he sold the land to Michael Dousman (the man who played a role in the British invasion of Mackinac Island in 1812).

Today the six-hundred acre park is a reconstruction of that industrial complex. You can view a water-powered sawmill, a British colonial workshop, and watch history come alive with costumed workers performing tasks as they would

Old Mill Creek.

Courtesy of Mackinac Island State Park Commission

have been done two-hundred years ago. A network of nature trails stretches for three miles, some with scenic overlooks and panoramic views of the straits and Mackinac Island. You may picnic, watch the beavers work on their dams in Mill Creek, study interpretive displays describing area plants, animals, and geological features, or stroll through the museum. Throughout most of the summer you may also watch archeologists discover our not too distant past.

Mackinaw City
Located at the northernmost tip of the lower peninsula of Michigan, this is the site where the French constructed Fort Ste. Phillipe de Michilimackinac in 1715. When the British later moved the fort to Mackinac Island, the area was seldom used. It was revived in 1881 when it was reached by the Michigan Central Railroad.

A view of a portion of the water powered mill.

Courtesy of Mackinac Island State Park Commission

Both before and after the village was incorporated in 1881, it was used as a ferry base for travelers to Mackinac Island, as well as a supply depot for the railroad companies shipping materials to and from the mining and logging towns of the upper peninsula.

When more and more tourists began traveling by car in the twentieth century, it became an infamous bottleneck. Cars sat here for hours waiting to cross by ferry to the upper peninsula during the summer season. When the "Mighty Mac" bridge was completed in 1957, automobile traffic increased and more vacation facilities were built. Today it hosts tourists throughout the summer, and is a stopping point for many Mackinac Island visitors.

Like Mackinac Island, its main industry is tourism, and its year-round population is quite small—about eight-hundred persons. There are many shops, stores, restaurants, hotels, motels, campgrounds, and recreational facilities supplying visitors needs.

Several locations in this area are operated by Mackinac State Historic Parks. The purchase of one ticket admits you to Colonial Michilimackinac, the Maritime Museum, the sloop Welcome, and Old Mill Creek.

Colonial Michilimackinac   Once known as Fort Michilimackinac, the name has been changed because of its similarity to Fort Mackinac. Open from mid-May to mid-October, it is a reconstruction of the original fort (1715 to1781) built on this site. We have described the fort's interesting history in earlier chapters of this book. Archeologists have worked to factually reconstruct the era and objects that were once part of the post. There are many interesting interpretive displays that describe how that work was done and how conclusions were reached. An orientation center, traders houses, and a birch bark canoe are located outside the walls. Inside the stockade, you can explore the rowhouses where the men and their families lived, the original Ste. Anne de Michilimackinac Church, the guardhouse, barracks, commanding officer's house, blacksmith shop, priest's house, powder magazine, and storehouse. Each location includes period furnishings and displays to accurately recreate your sense of history. As a part of the living history program, costumed men, women, and children demonstrate the daily life their counterparts experienced several hundred years ago.

Maritime Park   Adjacent to the orientation center at Colonial Michilimackinac, the park is open from Mid-June to Labor Day. You may explore the *Old Mackinac Point Lighthouse*, which was originally built in 1892, and which is now a museum depicting the maritime history of the area.

Welcome   The *Welcome* is a reconstruction of a 1775 trading vessel, and is located at the Mackinaw City Marina. This fifty-five foot wooden-hulled armed sloop is open for tours from June 15th to Labor Day. John Askin, a trader out of Fort

Michilimackinac, owned the vessel, and used it to transport
supplies and materials from the straits area. It traveled with
a crew of eight men, and was armed with two swivel guns and
two blunderbusses. Patrick Sinclair, the Fort Commandant,
purchased it in 1779 and used the sloop to transport troops
and supplies while moving the fort to Mackinac Island. The
ship was lost in a storm in 1781. There is no record of where
it went down.

Restoration was completed in 1980, after seven years of
work and $400,000 in expenses. Today it conducts an annual
summer sailing excursion (contact park for the date). It leaves
Mackinaw City, sails past Mackinac Island, then returns to
the dock. The ship winters on the Cheboygan River, the same
place that the original *Welcome* was moored.

Mackinac Bridge

Also known as *Mighty Mac*, this graceful structure spans
the Straits of Mackinac, and connects Mackinaw City and St.
Ignace. The story of the bridge's construction is described in
detail in Chapter Nine.

It is open year-round to motor vehicle traffic. The small
toll that travelers are required to pay is used to retire the bond
issues that support maintenance and construction costs. The
original fee was $3.75 per car, today it is $1.50. Commuter
coupons for those who cross frequently are available. The
largest volume of traffic ever recorded for one day occurred
on July 1, 1978 when 24,569 vehicles passed over the straits.
That record still stood as of June, 1987.

On one day of every year, pedestrians are allowed to walk
across the bridge. That is during the famous "Labor Day Bridge
Walk" that takes place on—you guessed it—Labor Day. The
tradition began in 1958, and the hikers are always led by the
Governor of Michigan. It is one of the most popular annual
events in the State. In 1986, about fifty-thousand people
walked the bridge.

The walk traverses the entire five mile bridge, beginning
in St. Ignace and ending in Mackinaw City. The Mackinac
Bridge Authority rents more than ninety school buses to trans-

port walkers from Mackinaw City to St. Ignace before the walk, and return them afterward. The buses begin loading at 6 a.m., and a small fare is charged. If you decide to join this event, remember that the bridge is not entirely closed to motor vehicles during the walk. No running, jogging, skating, bicycling, unicycling, climbing on bridge railings, or walking in the driving lanes is allowed. No dogs (except seeing-eye dogs) can walk across, and there aren't any restrooms on the bridge.

St. Ignace

Located on the southern tip of the upper peninsula, this historic city was named after St. Ignatius Loyola by early French missionaries. It is the second oldest community in the State, and much of it sprawls along the waterfront or perches atop green highlands. It was the center of French influence and the fur trade in the Great Lakes area in the seventeenth century. Here, Marquette established the Mission of St. Ignace and the French later built Fort de Buade. In its earliest days, only the Jesuits called it St. Ignace, traders and official French documents referred to it as Michilimackinac.

After the fort closed and the Jesuits left the area in 1706, traders and Indians occasionally camped here. A new settlement wasn't begun until 1801, when a few fishermen built cabins along the shore. By 1834, a thriving town with a Catholic church once again flourished.

Today it is the Mackinac County seat with approximately three-thousand year round residents. Most inhabitants work in the tourism industry, although the second largest employer is the State. There are shops, restaurants, hotels, motels, campgrounds, golf courses, a casino, and other recreational facilities which cater to travelers, as well as an airport. Here are just a few of the interesting things to see and do in St. Ignace:

Father Marquette National Memorial Museum & Park   This fifty-three acre park is situated at the junction of I-75 and US-2. It is an open air memorial that overlooks the straits, and includes a modern museum, picnic area, and walking trails.

This reproduction of an eighteenth century trader's cabin stands outside of Colonial Michilimackinac.

Courtesy of Mackinac Island State Park Commission

The museum known as *Marquette Among the Hurons* is located here, and features displays of the seventeenth century world of missionaries living among the Hurons. It includes the life and travels of Father Jacques Marquette, depictions of Native American life before European contact, and the resulting cultural changes.

Sea Plane Rides   Located near the Star Line Dock is an interesting attraction. . . a seaplane! In 1987, there were two rides available: The Long Ride: ($20 per person-minimum of two passengers) lasts fourteen minutes and flies over Mackinac Island and Mackinac Bridge. The Extra Long Ride: ($25 per person-with a two passenger minimum) lasts eighteen minutes and flies over Mackinac Island, the Mackinac Bridge, Bois Blanc Island, and Round Island. Available during the summer months. Contact the pilot near the dock for details.

Hiawatha National Forest A nearby wilderness retreat complete with trails, streams, lakes, picnic sights, and campgrounds, is available for your enjoyment.

Castle Rock Approximately three miles north of town, it rises 195 feet above the water. It was a traditional lookout spot for the Chippewa Indians, and offers an excellent view of the area. It is open from mid-May to mid-October.

Sault Ste. Marie

Located fifty miles north of St. Ignace on the St. Mary's River, at the Canadian border. The name translates to: "Rapids of St. Mary's," and is pronounced *Soo Saint Marie*. It is the third oldest community in the U. S., and Michigan's oldest city.

One of the early Jesuit missions was located here, and in 1641 the city was named by Fathers Isaac Jogues and Charles Raymbault. Father Marquette served at the mission in 1668. There were several French, then British, trading posts here in the eighteenth and nineteenth centuries. After Lewis Cass, the Governor of the Michigan Territory, negotiated an 1820 Indian treaty, Fort Brady was built here and served the region until it closed around the time of World War II. Henry R. Schoolcraft (author and Indian agent described in Chapter Six) lived here before going to Mackinac Island.

A canal on the river opened in 1855, linking lakes Superior and Huron. The most famous sites today are the *Soo Locks* (national historic site), which replaced a large portion of the rapids. You can watch them in action from the deck of a tour boat or an observation platform. Huge ships lock through the channel, with water levels rising or falling in order to ease the vessels into Lake Superior or Lake Huron. There is also a nearby park, an information center that shows films about the history of the locks, and a train ride that gives a historical tour of the city, including a view of the locks.

You can tour the retired freighter, U.S.S. Valley Camp, and its marine museum depicting the history of Great Lakes ships. There are many other surrounding locations to explore, including historic lighthouses, and nearby Tahquamenon Falls State Park. The Vegas Kewadin Casino is on a nearby Indian Reservation. Open to the public with legal gambling such as bingo, blackjack, and poker.

Today Sault Ste. Marie is a large city, with businesses, shops, cultural facilities, parks, historic homes, a marina, river walkway, and nearby camping, fishing, boating, golfing, and the Hiawatha National Forest.

Surrounding Islands and Lighthouses

Round Island   Located directly south of Mackinac Island, and north of Bois Blanc Island. The Indians called it *Minnisais* (Little Island) and *Nissawinagong* (Middle Place). It is controlled by the U.S. Forest Service, and remains a wilderness area that is protected from commercial and residential development. The only additions to the island are the lighthouse and its outbuildings. Boaters often stop here during the day for a picnic, and hike on this uninhabited little island.

Round Island Lighthouse   Although it appears to be on its own separate island, the old-fashioned lighthouse that is seen so clearly from Mackinac Island's harbor is located on a thin peninsula shooting off from the main part of Round Island. Rising water levels have covered the land link and washed away the trees and shrubs. The piece of land that holds the lighthouse and its outbuildings is sixty feet wide and three hundred feet long.

Built in 1895 with help from Mackinac Island contractor Frank Rounds, the lighthouse is four stories high. Remnants of an old steam electric generator that provided electricity to run the lights, and steam to operate the booming fog horn can still be seen. The first (ground) floor housed equipment and machinery. The second floor had an apartment for the lighthouse keeper and his family. The third floor held the apartment of the assistant lighthouse keeper and his family. Above the third floor was the light tower, which originally used kerosene lamps until they were later replaced by electric beams.

Prior to 1924, it was manned by a crew of three. In that year, the shining beacon was replaced by an automatic light, and a single caretaker remained. When the new automatic beacon (the lighthouse that stands off the breakwater of Mackinac Island) was built in 1948, the caretaker left. A lantern continued to hang outside the old lighthouse at night, until it was de-commissioned in 1957. Today it is part of the Round Island Scenic Area of the Hiawatha National Forest.

The structure was severely damaged by gale force winds in October of 1972. Many island lovers, with the help of the Town Crier newspaper, began a drive to raise funds for repairs. In 1976, the building foundation was reinforced with steel, and some wind damage was repaired. Over the ensuing years more repairs and improvements have been completed. In 1986, more than three-hundred tons of rocks were placed around the buildings to protect the shoreline from rising Lake Huron.

Mackinac Island Beacon   In 1948, an 137 foot automatic beacon was constructed near the breakwater at Haldimand Bay to replace the Round Island Lighthouse. It has a range of four miles, and is controlled from a station on Biddle Point by cables that run along the lake bottom. Banks of sealed lights flash a steady warning, as two fog horns pierce the darkness. Modern radio transmitting equipment sends out a signal beam to show its location in bad weather.

Bois Blanc Island   Located south of Mackinac Island and just five miles north of Cheboygan, the name means 'white wood'. It is pronounced *Bob Low* or *Boys Blank* depending on who you talk to. The island is the largest in the straits, over forty square miles, but it is not well-developed. Much of the land is owned by the State, or by private property holders. There are twenty-four year round residents, small docks, and regular ferry service from Cheboygan.

The land is primarily wooded, with some marshes and a small lake. It is a popular location for fishing and hunting. Soldiers from Fort Mackinac cut a great deal of wood here after the supply on Mackinac Island had been depleted.

Drummond Island   Located off the eastern Upper Peninsula near the Canadian border, it is the largest island in the Great Lakes, with an area of 136 square miles and forty inland lakes. It is surrounded by more than fifty outlying islands and can be reached in all seasons by a fifteen minute ferry ride from De Tour Village. The island was named by the British, who held it from 1814 to 1828, when the border commission declared it part of U.S. territory. It was one of the last British posts in the Northwest. This area is popular as a summer playground—with many cottages and campgrounds, boating, swimming, hunting, fishing, tennis, and golf. There are also marine facilities and an airport.

Les Cheneaux   Fifteen miles northeast of Mackinac Island, and about thirty-five minutes from St. Ignace are thirty-five islands in northern Lake Huron. The name means "The Snows," and they are pronounced *Lay Sheno*. A number of summer cabins and cottages, as well as camping, boat docks, boat rentals, and swimming are available. They are a popular fishing and hunting destination.

CHAPTER 15

Fascinating
Facts

Addresses   Island homes do not have house numbers. When new police officers come to the island, they must learn a home's location by the occupant's name.

Aurora Borealis   A luminous meteoric phenomenon displaying the polar lights of the northern hemisphere. Streamers, bands, curtains, and arcs of light are frequently visible through the island's clear evening skies.

Books   In 1863, E.E. Hale wrote a short story for Atlantic Monthly. The story begins with a narrator saying he was "...Stranded at the Old Mission House in Mackinac, waiting for a Lake Superior steamer which did not choose to come..." The story was titled *"A Man Without A Country,"* and went on to become an American classic. Although many readers take the narrator's words literally, in truth Edward Everett Hale never saw the Old Mission House Hotel nor visited Mackinac Island.

Carriage Tours   Mackinac Island Carriage Tours is the oldest livery in continuous operation in the United States.

Docks In Winter   The only time the ferry companies are able to perform major maintenance projects on the island docks is during the winter, when the ice freezes, and makes a base for the replacement of pilings.

Ferries   In 1878, Arnold's Ferry Line became the first to serve the island. Their first shipment was ten boxes of fresh fish from Mackinac Island to Chicago.

Ferries In Winter   Where are the ferries parked during the winter? Arnold Ferries are anchored at a local dock. Shepler's pulls their boats out of the water by crane, and places them on large brackets at their Mackinaw City dock. Star Line parks their boats in the Cheboygan River, where the flowing water protects their aluminum hulls from ice damage.

Flies   The cool, moist weather and the large number of horses attracts flies during the summer. To help combat the problem, a full-time 'Fly Control Officer' is appointed each year. The officer sets special traps, inspects those at the island stables and landfill, and works to educate residents and businesses in progressive preventive measures.

Horses In Winter   The lack of suitable pasture requires that most horses on the island be shipped to Pickford or Rudyard for the winter. They begin leaving in late August as the season slows down, and most are usually gone by November 6th. The only horses that winter on the island are those that pull the one taxi and the delivery drays. The horses are transported to the farms in groups, accompanied by volunteer riders. They are brought back to the island the same way each spring.

Mackinaw Boat   The Mackinaw Boat was distinctive to the Great Lakes because it was especially suited for inland waters. The vessel handled well in rapids, could be carried across portages, and transported heavy cargoes. It was widely used as late as 1890. The Mackinaw Boat was really an overgrown birchbark canoe. The larger ones were thirty feet or more in length, six or seven feet wide at the middle, and tapered to a point on either end. When there was a breeze, a sail supported by a small mast amidships helped to propel the vessel.

Mackinac Bridge—Suicides   This stately bridge has not suffered from the large numbers of suicides that have plagued the Golden Gate Bridge in San Francisco. Only two situations have occurred in thirty years. In 1974, an abandoned car was found on the bridge with the engine running. However, the driver was never found, so it's not officially classified as a suicide. On September 5th, 1985, a truck driver reported a man standing near his car at 5 a.m. When a patrolman arrived a few minutes later, he found the car, but no driver. They later recovered the body of a man in his early 60's. No one saw him jump, so it's classified as a 'probable suicide'.

Mackinaw Coat   The name refers to a short-style of coat made of thick wool or a blanket-like material. The design is usually a bright colored plaid, or woven bars of color. It is said to have been created when the soldiers at the fort did not receive their supply of winter coats one season. There was an excess in the blanket supply, so the commandant had seamstresses sew coats for the men. The soldiers preferred the mobility of these shorter coats to the heavy long coats that were then standard military issue.

Murder   In 1960, a very bizarre event occured on peaceful Mackinac Island. Someone was murdered. A woman was walking up to Stonecliffe from Lake Shore Road. Her body was found later with her hose wrapped around her neck. Although there are lots of theories about what happened, no one really knows and the murderer was never found. As far as we know, this is the only murder that has taken place on the island in contemporary times.

Post Office   The Mackinac Island Post Office is one of the few profitable centers in the United States. All mail is collected at the office, so there is no expense for delivery.

Presidents Who Have Visited The Island   Although the only President of the United States to visit the island while in office was Gerald R. Ford in 1975, several other U.S. Presidents have come to the island both before and after their terms. They include; Ulysses S. Grant, Theodore Roosevelt, Harry S. Truman, and John F. Kennedy.

Shipwrecks   Off of Mission Point (near Robinson's Folly) there is a red Coast Guard buoy that marks the rock ledge where the steamer *Peshtigo*, which was transporting lumber, went aground in 1908.

Street Signs   The only street sign on Mackinac Island is at the corner of Fort and Market Streets.

Sunrise/Sunset   At the Straits of Mackinac you can watch the sun rise on one Great Lake and set on another.

Swimming The Straits   In July, 1961, Mary Margaret Revell swam from Mackinac Island to Mackinaw City and back. The total trip took 7 hours and 28 minutes.

THE NUMBERS OF MACKINAC ISLAND

805,050   people were transported to Mackinac Island in 1987 by ferry.

306,420   eggs are used in the Grand Hotel kitchens each year.

276,506   meals were served in the Main Dining Room of the Grand Hotel in 1982.

210,726   people visited Fort Mackinac in 1987.

THE NUMBERS OF MACKINAC ISLAND

45,000 gallons of paint were used when the Mackinac Bridge was recently repainted.

39,142 pounds of potatoes were used by the Grand Hotel kitchen in 1982.

15,809 pounds of butter were used by the Grand Hotel kitchen in 1982.

7,392 pounds of dishwasher soap are used in the Grand Hotel kitchen in one season.

3,000 planes land and takeoff at the airport each year.

2,300 privately owned bicycles are on the island in summer.

1,000 rental bicycles are on the island.

904 feet above the lake stands the crown of the ancient island.

700 tons of hay are used on the island every summer.

600 breakfasts are served at the Grand Hotel on an average day.

578 feet is the height of Lake Huron above sea level.

550 horses are on the island during the summer.

450 people are employed by the Grand Hotel, the largest employer on the island.

270 horses work for Carriage Tours during the peak of summer.

250 couples are married on Mackinac Island each year.

198 planes arrived here in the largest single day of airport traffic.

175 people are employed by Mackinac Island Carriage Tours.

142 feet above Lake Huron hangs the famous Arch Rock.

65 different desserts are made at the Grand Hotel each day.

55 public passenger carriage licenses are allowed on the island. Each license represents one share of stock in the privately owned Mackinac Island Carriage Tours.

54 people can be loaded every five minutes by Carriage Tours during the height of summer.

30 tons of hay are brought to the island every week during peak summer season.

29 tons of Prime Rib were served at the Grand Hotel in 1982.

25 years is needed for Lake Huron to turn over its entire volume of water.

15 taxis transport people around the island.

10 street sweepers are employed by the city alone.

Land of Enchantment

History is often made by a handful of people with the vision, determination, and courage to go where none have gone before, and to accomplish what had until then been the impossible. When applied to the story of a particular place, an accident of geography can be as important as the citizens who shape the community. Mackinac Island has been fortunate in both its location and the men and women who have journeyed here.

Beginning in the seventeenth century, its strategic location along the trade routes destined Mackinac to become an important social center. Its high cliffs formed a natural fortress that caught the eye of Patrick Sinclair, who was eager to move his garrison to a more defensible position. Years later, John Jacob Astor's decision to headquarter his American Fur Company here made the island a center of commerce, and aided in attracting other businessmen and settlers to invest in its future. The island's location—isolated, but not far from heavily populated cities such as Detroit and Chicago—made it a popular vacation destination. As the network of steamship and railroad lines spilled into the region, it was easy to increase profits by transporting paying passengers to the straits, in addition to removing ore and lumber from the Upper Peninsula. Mackinac Island became the ideal spot for an elegant resort hotel. The transit companies, with the help of John O. Plank, created one of the most magnificent sum-

mer resorts in the world. When islanders conceived the idea
to preserve the land for future generations, their efforts soon
made Mackinac our second national park—and later Michigan's first State Park.

Fortunately, none of these groups had to fight powerful
conglomerates to protect the resources here. There was no ore,
gold, silver, copper, or timber to attract big business. All it
had to offer, from the beginning of time, was its location in
the straits, quiet beauty, history, and the whisper of Indian
legends. From the days when carriage drivers petitioned to
have motor vehicles banned, to modern debates over the place-
ment of satellite dishes, most islanders have tried to balance
private goals and objectives while simultaneously maintaining and preserving the unique features of Mackinac. We must
recognize our obligation to those many men and women who
realized the treasure they possessed, and toiled to preserve it
for the appreciation of future generations.

Somehow, the fascinating charm of this tiny island
manages to overwhelm travelers who have seen many awe-
some, imposing, and magnificent sites around the world. And
the combined appeal of its people, history, and location will
continue to lure visitors as long as there are those who love
to wander. Yet there are no miraculous transformations when
a visitor first sets foot on Mackinac Island. The ingredients
are here—but it is what each person does with them that will
make their visit either a disappointment, or an unforgetable
experience.

Perhaps it would help if you take a few moments after
you arrive, and immerse yourself in the history and
atmosphere of the island. Take a seat—in Marquette Park, at
the marina, or in a wooded knoll on the heights, and think
about all those who have been here before you. Respectful
Indians paddling by, dropping packets of tobacco as offerings
to the Great Dancing Spirits. . .Father Dablon describing
Christianity in his tiny bark chapel. . . Soldiers hauling water
and timber to the fort, and standing on the lonely ramparts
each day. . . Indians with their teepees lining the beach. . . A
brigade of voyageurs rapidly paddling toward the shore, their
chants echoing over the water. . . Coureurs de bois collecting

a winter's wages at a trader's store, then spending them on a continual celebration...Magdalaine LaFramboise hurrying along the street, her grandchild in tow, headed for her Huron Street home...Elizabeth Mitchell, one day an elegant hostess entertaining at card parties, the next a lonely wife paddling away to visit her husband on Drummond Island...Dr. William Beaumont studying the wound of an unenthusiastic Alexis St. Martin...Henry Schoolcraft, intently listening to Indian tales around the campfire...Reverend William Ferry earnestly building his Mission House to educate the Indian children... Commercial fishermen drying their catches on the docks... Steamships chugging into the harbor...Aristocratic ladies from the Grand Hotel strolling through the shops while their husbands play golf and tennis...Cottagers seated on their verandas enjoying the view, or driving their magnificent carriages along dusty streets...Yachts darting into the harbor during the races, their sweeping sails fluttering in the breeze.

Each time you visit will add to your collection of island memories. Waking up to the steady sound of horses clip-clopping along the quiet streets. Coming upon an unexpected overlook while hiking a lonely trail and being swept away by its beauty. Arch Rock in the early morning sun, gentle waves lapping the shore. Delicate wildflowers along the paths, and the beautiful, colorful gardens around many homes. Sleek yachts gliding into the marina. Stately ore boats passing through the straits. The short blast of the noon fire siren. The sound of the fog and ferry horns in the harbor. Main Street, crowded with carriages and visitors. People strolling along the sidewalk amid the sweet smell of fudge, admiring the displays in the windows. The whir of bicycle wheels. The cry of seagulls constantly circling the shore. The stirring sounds of a fife and drum concert at the fort. Cannons thundering throughout the day. The sun setting behind Mackinac Bridge. The change that comes over the island when the last ferries leave, as the atmosphere loosens and relaxes among those fortunate enough to stay behind. The bugle call of taps every evening.

Mackinac is an enchanted land somewhere in time. Once you experience it, it will always be a part of you. It is for us, and will be for you. See you there!

About The
Authors

Thomas M. and Pamela A. Piljac are married and reside in Portage, Indiana. Their love of travel and affinity for Mackinac Island have inspired them to write this volume, with the hopes that others may better enjoy and appreciate it. The Piljacs have written five other books, and hope to someday reside on the island.

Bibliography

Armour, David A., editor, *Attack At Michilimackinac 1763*, original edition by Alexander Henry, Mackinac Island State Park Commission, Mackinac Island, Mi, 1971

Armour, David A., *David and Elizabeth, The Mitchell Family of the Straits of Mackinac*, Mackinac History vignette, Mackinac Island State Park Commission, Mackinac Island, Mi, 1982, reprinted from Michigan History, Volume 64, No. 4, July/August, 1980

Armour, David A., *Michilimackinac: A Handbook To The Site*, Mackinac Island State Park Commission, Mackinac Island, Mi, 1980

Bjorklund, Karna L., *The Indians of Northeastern America*, Dodd, Mead & Company, New York, 1969

Bowen, Dana T., *Lore Of The Lakes*, Dana Thomas Bowen, Daytona Beach, Fl, 1940

Cantor, George, *The Great Lakes Guide Book*, The University of Michigan Press, Ann Arbor, Mi, 1985

Cobb, Charles E. Jr., *The Great Lakes Troubled Waters"*, National Geographic, Vol. 172, No. 1, July, 1987

Danziger, Edmund J. Jr., *The Chippewas of Lake Superior*, University of Oklahoma Press, Norman OK, 1978

Davis, James S., *Mackinac Island Scout Service Camp*, Mackinac History vignette, Mackinac Island State Park Commission, Mackinac Island, Mi, 1975

Dunbar, Willis F., *Michigan. . .A History of the Wolverine State*, Wm. B. Eerdmans Publishing Co., Grand Rapids, Mi, 1980

Ellis, William Donohue, *Land of the Inland Seas*, American West Publishing Company, Palo Alto, Ca, 1974

Forester, Cecil S., *The Age of Fighting Sail*, Doubleday & Company, Garden City, Ny, 1956

Froncek, Thomas, *Voices From the Wilderness*, McGraw-Hill Book Company, New York, Ny, 1974

Fuller, Iola, *The Loon Feather*, Harcourt Brace Jovanovich, Orlando, Fl, 1940, 1968

Gavrilovich, Peter, *"The Island In Winter,"* Detroit Free Press Magazine, Detroit, Mi, March 13, 1983

Gringhuis, Dirk, *Lore of the Great Turtle*, Mackinac Island State Park Commission, Mackinac Island, Mi, 1970

Gringhuis, Dirk, *Were-Wolves and Will-O-The Wisps*, Mackinac Island State Park Commission, Mackinac Island, Mi, 1974

Havighurst, Walter, *Three Flags At the Straits*, Prentice-Hall Inc., Englewood Cliffs, NJ, 1966

Henry, Alexander, *Attack At Michilimackinac 1763*, edited by Dr. David A. Armour, Mackinac Island State Park Commission, Mackinac Island, Mi, First published: 1809, reissued 1971

Koehler, Aileen Poole, *"Wawashkamo Golf Club,"*, Wawashkamo Golf Club, Mackinac Island, Mi

Kubiak, William J., *Great Lakes Indians*, Baker Book House, Grand Rapids, Mi, 1970

Longfellow, Henry Wadsworth, *Favorite Poems of Henry Wadsworth Longfellow*, *"Song of Hiawatha"*, Doubleday and Company, Garden City, Ny, 1947, 1967

Mackinac Island News, *"No History of Mackinac is Complete Without Story of Island Carriage Operation,"* St. Ignace, Mi, Sunday, August 30, 1936, page 6

Maslowski, Peter, *For the Common Defense: A Military History of the United States of America*, The Free Press, Division of McMillan, Inc., New York, 1984

May, George S., *The Reconstruction of the Church of Ste. Anne de Michilimackinac*, Mackinac Island State Park Commission, Mackinac History vignette, Mackinac Island, Mi, 1964

McCabe, John, *Grand Hotel: Mackinac Island*, The Unicorn Press, Lake Superior State College, Sault Ste. Marie, Mi, 1987

Millett, Allan R., *For the Common Defense: A Military History of the United States of America*, The Free Press, Division of McMillan, Inc., New York, 1984

Nelhiebel, Victor R., *The Wonder of Mackinac*, Mackinac Island State Park Commission, Mackinac Island, Mi, 1984

Page, Lorena M., *The Legendary Lore of Mackinac*, Ann Arbor, Mi 1934

Peterson, Eugene T., *Mackinac Island: Its History In Pictures*, Mackinac Island State Park Commission, Mackinac Island, Mi, 1973

Peterson, Eugene T., *Mackinac In Restoration*, Mackinac Island State Park Commission, Mackinac Island, Mi, 1983

Porter, Phil, *View From The Veranda*, Mackinac Island State Park Commission, Mackinac Island, Mi, 1981

Porter, Phil, *The Wonder of Mackinac*, Mackinac Island State Park Commission, Mackinac Island, Mi, 1984

Quaife, Milo M., *Lake Michigan*, The Bobbs-Merrill Company, New York, 1944

Recktenwald, William, *"Supersail,"* The Chicago Tribune Magazine, Chicago, IL, July 12, 1987

Steinman, David B., *Miracle Bridge at Mackinac*, In collaboration with John T. Nevill, Wm. B. Eerdmans Publishing Co., Grand Rapids, Mi, 1957

Town Crier, various newspaper articles in issues 1985 through 1987, Mackinac Island, Mi

Van Fleet, James A., *Summer Resorts of the Mackinaw Region*, Ann Arbor, Mi, 1870

Widder, Keith R., *Mackinac National Park* 1875-1895, Mackinac Island State Park Commission, Mackinac Island, Mi, 1975

Widder, Keith R., *Reveille Till Taps*, Mackinac Island State Park Commission, Mackinac Island, Mi, 1972

Widder, Keith R., *Michilimackinac: A Handbook To The Site*, Mackinac Island State Park Commission, Mackinac Island, Mi, 1980

Williams, Meade C., *Early Mackinac*, Avery Color Studios, Au Train Mich, First published 1897, Reissued March, 1987.

Wood, Edwin O., *Historic Mackinac*, volumes one and two, The Macmillan Co., New York, 1918

Woodfill, W. Stewart, *Grand Hotel: The Story of An Institution*, The Newcomen Society in North America, New York, 1969

INDEX

More
About
Mackinac

Mackinac Island is a timeless wonderland rich in history and natural beauty. The following quality products provide a fascinating look at the sights, history, and Indian lore of the straits region. Guaranteed to meet your satisfaction.

BOOKS

#MB1 **Mackinac Island: Historic Frontier, Timeless**   **$12.95**
Wonderland, Vacation Resort

A complete guide to the Mackinac of today, and the historical center of yesteryear. Includes tips for vistors, descriptions of island attractions, and 75 fascinating photographs. Softbound. Piljac

#MB2 **Mackinac Island: Its History in Pictures**   **$15.00**

More than 360 historic photographs and sketches are lavishly presented. They depict the fascinating history of Mackinac Island in exciting detail. Hardbound. Peterson

#MB3 **At the Crossroads: Michilimackinac During**   **$15.00**
the American Revolution

British, Americans, and Indians clash for control of the upper Great Lakes. 279 pages, 210 illustrations, expanded edition. Hardbound. Armour/Widder

#MB4 **View From The Veranda**   **$7.00**

Describes the history and architecture of the stately summer cottages. Includes more than 100 photos and illustrations. Softbound. Porter

BOOKS

#MB5   **Lore of the Great Turtle**   **$3.75**

Delightful retelling of the Indian legends of Mackinac Island. Softbound. Gringhuis

#MB6   **Attack at Michilmackinac, 1763**   **$3.75**

Alexander Henry's tale of his travels and adventures on the northern frontier, including his capture during the Indian massacre at Fort Michilimackinac. Softbound. Armour

#MB7   **Reveille Till Taps**   **$1.50**

Detailed description of the daily life of soldiers stationed at Fort Mackinac. Includes illustrations and photographs. Softbound. Widder.

OTHER PRODUCTS

#MB8   **The Magic of Mackinac**   **$19.95**

This delightful video portrait of Mackinac explores the history of the island, its people, and attractions. Your guided tour features the many natural wonders and historic sites, and highlights the island's scenic beauty. Excellent photography and narration allow you to recapture the magic of this enchanted island. VHS only

#MB9   **The Sights and Sounds of Mackinac**   **$6.95**

A souvenir packet that allows you to capture the experience of a Mackinac Island visit using an audio tape and a booklet of thirty-five color photographs. This package also includes one mini-poster (described below). Individual choices of mini-posters not available with packet. You will find this selection a delightful surprise for such a low price.

#MB11 **The Seasons of Mackinac**   **$7.50**

Enjoy island scenes throughout the year with this beautifully photographed annual calendar. Sales help support Mackinac Island Recreation and Development, a non-profit organization that sponsors Great Turtle Park and a number of island activities.

Order form is on the following page

Order Form

Bryce-Waterton Publications
P.O. Box 5512, Dept. M9
Portage, In 46368

NOTE: If this is a library book, please photocopy this page. Do not tear it out.

- -

Please rush me the following products:

Item #	Quantity	Brief Description	Price	Total
MB1	_____	Mackinac Island, Historic Frontier...	$12.95	_____
MB2	_____	Mackinac Island: History in Pictures	$15.00	_____
MB3	_____	At the Crossroads: Michilimackinac...	$15.00	_____
MB4	_____	View From the Veranda	$ 7.00	_____
MB5	_____	Lore of the Great Turtle	$ 3.75	_____
MB6	_____	Attack at Michilimackinac	$ 3.75	_____
MB7	_____	Reveille Till Taps	$ 1.50	_____
MB8	_____	Magic of Mackinac video	$19.95	_____
MB9	_____	Sights and Sounds of Mackinac	$ 6.95	_____
MB11	_____	Seasons of Mackinac calendar	$ 7.50	_____

Sales Tax (Indiana residents only) _____

Shipping (add $1.75 per item) _____

TOTAL _____

☐ My check or money order (U.S. Funds only) for $_____ is enclosed.
☐ Please charge my (check appropriate box) ☐ Visa   ☐ Mastercard.

Account Number _ _ _ _ _ _ _ _ _ _ _ _ _ _ _ (list all numbers on card)

Interbank Number _ _ _ _ (Mastercard only) Expiration Date: _____

Signature _____

Ship my order to (please print clearly):

Name _____

Address _____ Apartment _____

City _____ State _____ Zip _____

Phone _____